Faith at the Frontiers
of Knowledge

Copyright 2018 Kenneth R. Ross

All rights reserved. No part of this publication may be reproduced, stored in a retrieval system, or transmitted in any from or by any means, electronic, mechanical, photocopying, recording or otherwise without prior permission from the publishers.

Published by
Luviri Press
P/Bag 201 Luwinga
Mzuzu 2
Malawi

ISBN   978-99960-98-18-5
eISBN   978-99960-98-19-2

Luviri Reprints no. 2

Luviri Press is represented outside Africa by:
African Books Collective Oxford (order@africanbookscollective.com)

www.mzunipress.blogspot.com
www.africanbookscollective.com

Editorial assistance and cover: Daniel Neumann

First published by Kachere Series, Zomba in 1998.

Faith at the Frontiers of Knowledge

Edited by
Kenneth R. Ross

Luviri Press

Luviri Reprints no. 1
Mzuzu
2018

Luviri Reprints

Many books have been published on or in Malawi that are no longer available. While some of these books simply have run their course, others are still of interest for scholars and the general public. Some of the classics have been reprinted outside Malawi over the decades, and during the last two decades, first the Kachere Series and then other publishers have achieved "never out of stock status" by joining the African Books Collective's Print on Demand approach, but there are still a good number of books that would be of interest but are no longer in print.

The Luviri Reprint Series has taken up the task to make those books on or from Malawi, which are out of print but not out of interest, available again, through Print on Demand and therefore worldwide.

While the Luviri Reprint Series concentrates on Malawi, it is also interested in the neighbouring countries and even in those further afield.

Luviri Reprints publish the books as they originally were. Usually a new Foreword is added, and where appropriate, new information has been added. All such additions, mostly in footnotes, are marked by an asterisk (*).

The Editors

Foreword

Of the many books published in Malawi over the past twenty-five years few have such range as this one in terms both disciplinary approach and subject matter. A book that embraces the natural sciences, social sciences and humanities is certainly not lacking in ambition. It arose out of a very particular context, the scholarly community that was assembled at the University of Malawi's Chancellor College in the 1990s. It was a comparatively small University. As subsequent developments have shown, it was much too small to meet the demand for tertiary education in the country. However, for a period of time it made for a concentration of creative scholars from a variety of disciplines who came to know each other well and who had the shared experience of being an academic community in the midst of a society that was rapidly changing socially and politically.

Many of them were also people of faith and interested in exploring the inter-relation of their faith and their academic inquiry. This meant that for purposes of scholarship this community had certain distinctive advantages. There was a natural interaction between academics working in different disciplines. Since in total they numbered around 120 they knew each other well and were often comparing notes. In contrast to the Western academy where faith is often regarded as a different realm to that of academic inquiry, the African context prompted a more wholistic understanding where the vision of faith informs our understanding across the board.

The trend in academic life has continued to be towards specialization, with rather few scholars showing concern for the unity of knowledge, nor for the inter-relation of faith and knowledge. Even in the Malawi context, colleagues have looked back on the eight years of the Faith and Knowledge Seminar, 1990-97, as a high water mark in inter-disciplinary engagement within the University. While faith continues to play a significant role in Malawi life this was perhaps the most sustained attempt to explore the inter-connection of the life of faith and the cutting edge of academic research. It is therefore much to be welcomed that it can remain available as a Luviri Reprint.

No attempt has been made in this collection to arrive at a systematic or comprehensive conclusion. More modestly it offers a sample of different lines of academic inquiry with each demonstrating the relevance of a faith perspective to its field. It is to be hoped that the continuing availability of this volume will stimulate others to contribute to the unity of knowledge that is so greatly needed in our time.

Kenneth R. Ross

Argyll, Scotland

May 2018

Contents

Introduction: Faith, Science and Society	9
1. Stewardship of the Environment and the Pressures of the Modern World: Is There a Christian Response?	19
2. The New Commandment and the Selfish Gene	30
3. The Role of Creativity in Mathematics	41
4. The Physical Concept of Time and the Christian Concept of Eternity	49
5. Accountability: Living Our Faith? An Information Systems Perspective	58
6 The Rights of the Child in the Christian Context	81
7. The AIDS Crisis: A Challenge to the Integrity of the Church in Malawi	104
8. Singing, Dancing and Believing: Civic Education in Malawi Idiom	123
9. "Not War but Defence of the Oppressed"? Bishop Mackenzie's Skirmishes with the Yao in 1861	142
10. What About Those Difficult Phases in the History of Black People?: A Christian Appraisal of the African Experience	161
11. Paradigm Shift in Scientific Advance: A Model for Christian Conversion in the Modern World?	179
12. Christianity and the Visual Arts in Malawi	196
13. Christianity: Liberative or Oppressive to African Women?	217
14. Christian Missions and Western Colonialism: Soulmates or Antagonists?	239
The Faith and Knowledge Seminars 1990-1997	259
Notes on Contributors	262

Introduction: Faith, Science and Society

Kenneth R. Ross

A legacy of the European Enlightenment is the common assumption, in educated circles, that there is an inevitable conflict between science and faith. Even in Africa, where most societies have a strongly wholistic traditional worldview, the acids of modernity have often dissolved any connection between the pursuit of science and the practice of faith. This book is the product of a sustained process of reflection on the relation of faith and knowledge which occurred at an African University in the 1990s. It seeks to promote a much more positive understanding of the interaction of faith and knowledge than that which commonly prevails in academic circles. This endeavour is rooted, first, in the very nature of Christian faith. A proper understanding of Christianity makes plain that the kind of self-criticism and correction which science demands of faith is not something it finds strange or alien. For built into faith is its own dynamic which drives it towards explanation and definition. This was what was grasped by the early Christian thinkers who described theology as "faith seeking understanding". A Christian believer cannot rest content with a faith which is esoteric and out of touch with the total human intellectual endeavour.

While there always remains an important sense in which the gospel is "foolishness to the Greeks", at the same time a faith which trusts in one who claimed "I am the truth" is driven to explore that truth in relation to the whole of our field of knowledge. As Gerhard Ebeling commented: "Because Christian faith knows itself to be decisively concerned with truth and bound to the truth, confrontation and agreement with the total awareness of truth belongs unalterably to its living character. The inner necessity of theology as a responsible accounting for the truth of the Christian faith is based on this, so that theology as such already implies openness to a comprehensive concern for the truth. Meeting and communicating with all scholarly fields must be affirmed by theology as things that fundamentally belong to its own constitution."[1] Such communication, moreover, is not a matter of interaction between closed and comprehensive systems of knowledge. Our understanding of Christian faith is always provisional - "we see through a glass darkly"[2] - and can always be illumined by fresh historical and critical perspectives. Equally, the frame of knowledge within which we understand ourselves and the universe around us, is constantly changing and developing. Far from being static and settled, the frontiers of knowledge are moving every day. In this movement, faith has a part to play - that is the conviction which has united the authors of this book and which we hope will be demonstrated by the frontiers which we invite our readers to traverse.

This Christian perspective is at odds, in significant respects, with the understanding of the frame of knowledge which has prevailed wherever modernity has cast its spell. For central to post-Enlightenment thought is a dualistic distinction between "public truth" and "private values".[3] The disciplines of science are understood to belong to one side of the divide, the practice of faith to the other. The results of scientific investigation are public truth which all reasonable citizens must accept. Convictions held in the realm of faith, however, have supposedly no empirical basis and everyone is free to follow their own taste and inclination. In this environment, as is well known, many people have become so secularized that religion has ceased to have any meaningful place in their lives. Others continue to practise religion but strictly in the "private" realm of their lives with no reference to the "public square" or professional life. For the academic, this often means that there is a complete disjunction between cherishing faith in the family and community, and pursuing science in the academy. In the African context, where traditionally religion has permeated the whole of life, this is a profoundly alienating arrangement, injurious alike to the faith community and the academic community. For modern people

---

[1] Gerhard Ebeling, *The Study of Theology,* London: Collins, 1979, p. 83.

[2] 1 Corinthians 13:12.

[3] See Lesslie Newbigin, *Foolishness to the Greeks: The Gospel and Western Culture,* London: SPCK, 1986, pp. 35-37.

everywhere it means, in the chilling words of Walter Kasper, that: "Religion became a purely internal affair and lost its connection with reality ... The objectification of reality and the withdrawal of religion into subjectivity leads both to a flattening of reality and an emptying of religion. The world becomes godless; God becomes worldless."[4]

The 20th century has, however, witnessed the gradual disintegration of the dualistic Enlightenment frame of knowledge which once seemed so convincing. The relativity theory and quantum theory advanced by Einstein and other leading physicists, broke down the closed Newtonian understanding of the structure of the universe. The open-structured character of the universe invited a multi-levelled and multi-disciplinary inquiry if science was to be true to the reality with which it was now confronted. At the same time, the philosophical coherence of the Enlightenment began to unravel, especially since the golden age promised by the prophets of reason failed to materialize. The postmodern critique of modernity has achieved a certain levelling of the playing field since the perspective of Christian faith is judged to be no less valid than that of the Enlightenment. The outstanding problem for Christian faith in the context of post-modernity is that it is accommodated on the basis that it offers one perspective of equal validity to many others. To be true to its own identity, however, it must bear witness that *the* clue to human nature and destiny is found in the incarnation and resurrection of Jesus Christ. What is offered in this book are the attempts of a number of scholars, schooled in modern and post-modern frames of thought, to consider the place which this witness may have in relation to their various disciplines. The proposal being put forward is that the Christian vision can, at times, play a critical role in achieving scientific advance at the frontiers of knowledge.

This exercise not only rises out of the very nature of faith, it is also integral to academic inquiry. For there are limits to what can be achieved by any discipline operating in isolation. Finally, there must be an attempt to form a unified field of knowledge. As T.F. Torrance

---

[4] Walter Kasper, *The God of Jesus Christ,* New York: Crossroad, 1984, p. 10.

commented: "If Universities ... are really to be today what they ought to be, namely centres of creative cultural unity and progress in the society which sustains them, they must pursue research in *all* branches of human knowledge, and yet in such a way that they open the way for the development of their basic, natural interconnections in a creative synthesis. In a unitary understanding of the universe, of which the University by its very nature should be an essential correlate, the main specializations which are inevitably pursued must be bridged through inter-disciplinary study, so as to allow for the rise of a creative cultural unity within the University as a spiritual whole."[5] It is this bridge which made the seminars on which this book is based attractive to a wide cross-section of the University community in Zomba. The faith perspective offered a viable meeting point for practitioners of all disciplines and provided one place from which the University could begin to form a creative source of cultural unity. In the contemporary African situation thoughtful people suffer a deep sense of fragmentation as they are pulled in different directions by the often conflicting claims of modernity, indigenous tradition and Christian faith. The recovery of *universitas* is a healing and inspiring process. Hence the enterprise which is exemplified by the essays collected in this book, is one which has a critical role to play in the academy's fulfilment of its vocation in an African society.

The origins of the book lie in late 1989 when the Chancellor College Chaplain, Robin Quinn, was talking with some of members of the academic staff who were bothered about the apparent lack of any meeting point between the faith which they professed as Christians and the scholarship in which they were engaged as academics. Robin threw down the challenge: would some of them be prepared to present a public seminar introducing some aspect of the interface between their scientific research and their Christian faith? Their acceptance of that challenge marked the birth of the Faith and Knowledge Seminar, originally organised within the College Chaplaincy but soon moving its base to the Department of Theology and Religious

---

[5] Thomas F. Torrance, *The Christian Frame of Mind,* Edinburgh: Handsel Press, 1985, p. 59.

Studies. The aim has been to provide a forum in which scholars from every field of study represented at the University can meet together to consider the relevance of Christian belief .to their research. There has been a two-way flow of intellectual traffic. On the one hand, insights thrown up by scientific research have sometimes illumined our understanding of Christian faith. On the other hand, there have been occasions when Christian convictions and values have provided the clue which made possible a breakthrough at the frontiers of knowledge. On some 60 Thursday afternoons at 1600 hours in the Chancellor College Senior Common Room, this two-way exchange has taken place. Contributions have come from the disciplines of biology, classics, computer science, demography, education, English literature, history, home economics, law, mathematics, medicine, philosophy, physics, psychology, political science, public administration, sociology and theology.[6] It was an invidious task to have to make a selection for inclusion in this book. What we are able to offer is a representative sample which we trust will make at least some first-fruits of the Seminar accessible to a wider audience.

Part One is devoted to Natural Science. Stephen Carr, an agriculturalist with a lifetime of experience in Africa, incisively delineates the causes and effects of environmental degradation in today's world. The bottom line for the Christian, he suggests, is a refusal to pass on the costs of exploitation of the environment to anyone else - a refusal which has very significant effects on one's lifestyle. John Moore, a priest-scientist who has been Professor of Biology at the Universities of Dublin and Zambia, examines the anomaly of altruistic behaviour among animals supposedly conditioned by the "selfish gene". Drawing on a theology of "grace" perfecting "nature", he offers a vision of the altruism surprisingly found in the "old" creation anticipating the "new" commandment of Jesus Christ. John Dubbey, a mathematician who served as Vice-Chancellor of the University of Malawi from 1987 to 1991, draws on Christian faith as a source for illuminating the role of creativity in mathematics. He argues that a biblical understanding of

---

[6] A complete list of the Faith and Knowledge Seminars 1990-97 may be found at the end of this book.

humanity provides a basis for taking a creative approach in mathematics which is fruitful in scientific advance. Patrick Whittle, a physicist and a specialist in physics education, explores the relativity of time and its implications for Christian belief. Finally, David Mundy, who specializes in the use of information technology in developing countries, suggests that the new possibilities offered by computer technology raise very human questions concerning accountability. Here the Christian understanding of he human condition opens up useful perspectives.

Mundy's work already takes us in the direction of Social Science, the field with which Part Two is concerned. Garton Kamchedzera, a lawyer, examines the concept of social trust as the basis of the United Nations Convention on the Rights of the Child. He finds that social trust is supported by Christian teaching and practice, though Christians have not always accepted its implications for attitudes to children and young people. Where Christianity may have a critical role to play, however, is as a source of the altruism which is required if the rights of the child are to be enforced. Fulata Moyo steps on to perhaps the most critical frontier of knowledge of our time: that presented by the AIDS epidemic. While not dodging difficult questions of theodicy raised by AIDS, she concentrates on developing a call for integrity in the Christian church as a means of combatting the disease. If faith can provoke advances at this frontier of knowledge, then what a great deliverance that will be for the rising generation in Africa! James Tengatenga offers a sharp critique of the civic education which has been attempted as Malawi seeks authentic democracy. Rejecting a "top-down" approach, he turns to indigenous traditions of song, dance and faith as the channels through which the concerns and aspirations of the people could take political effect. Church life, and the hope engendered by Christian faith, have a key role to play, Tengatenga suggests, in building up the social capital on which a successful democracy depends. Finally, Jonathan Newell, a military historian, offers an historical case study of one of the thorniest questions of Christian ethics: when, if ever, is the Christian justified in using violent means to achieve laudable goals. The tools of the historian are wielded to increase our understanding of the circumstances which led Bishop

Charles Mackenzie, leader of the first Christian mission to be established in Malawi, to take up arms in order to "protect" the Mang'anja from Yao "raids". Newell suggests that Mackenzie's struggle with this issue is of relevance in Africa today as Christian workers not uncommonly find themselves in situations of civil war.

Part Three brings us to the Humanities. Kings M. Phiri, a historian, takes a long view of black and African history and grapples with the experience of suffering by which it is marked. Christian faith, he suggests, provides resources for coming to terms with the pain of the past and for making some sense of the African experience. Kenneth Ross attempts a cross-disciplinary study by examining the structure of scientific revolutions, with reference to the influential work of Thomas Kuhn, and suggesting that paradigm shift in scientific advance might be a helpful model for understanding what is involved in Christian conversion under conditions of modernity. Martin Ott, a theologian and anthropologist, is determined that the strictly policed frontier between Christian faith and artistic engagement should be broken down so that each may enrich the other. With particular reference to the work of the Ku Ngoni Art Craft Centre at Mua, Ott makes a plea for the incorporation of the visual arts in church architecture and liturgy in Malawi. Isabel Apawo Phiri writes out of a deep engagement with African women's experience of Christian faith. She tackles head-on the question of whether Christianity has been liberative or oppressive in its impact on African women? "Both" is the honest historical answer but Phiri goes on to offer her own liberative reading of the Christian faith from an African woman's perspective. Klaus Fiedler, a mission historian, examines the relationship between missionaries and colonialism in 19th and 20th century Africa. He admits that missionaries were "children of their times" and, by and large, worked not unhappily within the colonial framework. Case studies, however, soon explode the myth that missionaries were no more than the religious wing of colonialism and show that they had their own quite distinctive agenda which was at odds in important respects with the colonial enterprise.

It will be apparent that this is a book of unusual diversity. It ranges widely across the whole field of knowledge, focusing on certain critical points along its vast frontiers. Some of the chapters are consciously interdisciplinary. Others represent the concentrated application of the tools of a particular discipline to a well-defined problem. What all have in common is the two-way traffic between Christian faith and academic commitment. The book will fulfil its purpose if it shows that such interchange is fruitful in securing Christian integrity, in promoting scientific advance, and in strengthening the contribution of the academy to society as a whole.

Part One:
Natural Science

1. Stewardship of the Environment and the Pressures of the Modern World: Is There a Christian Response?

Stephen Carr

"Acid Rain Kills Millions of Trees"
"Minister Deplores Stripping of Forest Reserves"
"Whales in Danger of Extinction"
"Lake Malombe Fishery Critically Depleted"
"Hole in the Ozone Layer Grows Larger"
"Minister Concerned at Soil Degradation in Dedza"

Just a few of the headlines in the local and international press that highlight the fact of the accelerating degradation of our planet's environment. At the same time they also highlight the fact that there is a growing awareness and concern about that degradation. So far, that concern is felt by a small minority of the world's population, and an even smaller group of people is prepared to take any counter-balancing action which would impinge upon their own lifestyle.

This chapter will briefly review some of the major manifestations of environmental degradation, examine the principal causes and discuss the relationship of some biblical teaching to these issues.

What Degradation?

Perceptions of the reality of increasing environmental degradation will vary widely between different groups of people. A fisherman at Lake Malombe or in Labrador who can no longer make a living because of the collapse of fish stocks, a woman in Chiradzulu who can no longer find enough firewood, or a farmer whose soil is now so poor that it will no longer produce a reasonable crop, will have a quite different perception to a farmer in a remote, thinly populated area of Zambia or the owner of a luxury ranch at the foot of America's Rocky Mountains. Despite these differences, the past twenty-five years have witnessed a growing awareness of the major changes that are taking place in many parts of the world. Increasing numbers of people recognize that these changes are having a negative impact on the environment in which we and our descendants will have to live. Some of these developments are listed below in a rough order of their reversibility:

a) the loss of species. Many hundreds of species of plants animals and birds have become extinct in the past quarter century. Thousands more species are expected to disappear over the next twenty-five years. This is an irreversible loss of biological diversity;[1]

b) the loss of the world's forests. Trees have been cut down ever since man started farming and building houses, but as we know all too well, in Malawi, the rate of deforestation has accelerated exponentially this century. The great tropical forests are being destroyed at the rate of eleven million hectares per year and there is little evidence that they can be replaced in the foreseeable future;[2]

c) the degradation of soil resources because of overuse and misuse. The steady decline in crop yields in Malawi is the evidence of the decline in soil fertility. This is a result of regularly removing crops from the land and not returning anything to it, combined with the damage done to the soil by constant exposure to the elements.[3] Unfortunately the problem is not confined to Malawi;

d) the pollution of groundwater, rivers, lakes and oceans by industrial and agricultural waste. This has caused the collapse of some aquatic populations and endangers the health of whole communities;[4]

e) the pollution of the air from industrial fumes and engine exhausts. This is not only leads to human illness and death, but to the

---

[1] Jules Pretty, *Regenerating Agriculture,* London: Earthscan, 1995.

[2] Matti Palo and Jyrki Salmi, *Deforestation or Development in the Third World?,* Helsinki: Finnish Forest Research Institute, 1987.

[3] A.R. Saka, R.I. Green and D.H. Ng'ong'ola, *Soil Management in Sub-Saharan Africa: Proposed Soil Management Plan for Malawi,* Lilongwe: Malawi Ministry of Agriculture, 1995.

[4] David W. Pearce and Jeremy Warford, *World Without End,* New York: Oxford University Press, 1993.

destruction of large areas of forest and the loss of millions of fish as a result of acid rain,5

f) the disappearance of major fish stocks from over-fishing; and

g) the possibility of long-term climatic instability brought about by global warming. This is expected to result in human suffering from more intense storm, flood and drought events.[6]

What are the Causes?

Humanity has caused some degradation of the environment since the time when populations stopped living by hunting and gathering. Civilizations have died out because they so damaged their environment that they could no longer sustain their lifestyle. But these were small, localized phenomena and the widespread destruction of the world's natural resources started less than two hundred years ago and then speeded up rapidly in the past fifty years. What are the fundamental reasons for this?

Broadly speaking, the two main causes have been the industrial revolution and population growth. Both of these have resulted in a rapid increase in the demand for natural resources and both have produced ever-increasing volumes of noxious wastes. There are a great number of facets to both of these factors which are quite outside the range of this chapter, but it is important to understand that both factors are responsible. An industrial revolution with a current world population the same as that of two hundred years ago would have brought about considerable exploitation of natural resources and pollution, but would have left the world's forests, oceans and farmland in much better condition. Rapid population increase without an industrial revolution would have been hard on forests and farmlands, but would have avoided widespread chemical pollution and inter-regional

---

[5] Diana E. Weil, *The Impact of Development Policies on Health: a Review of the Literature,* Geneva: WHO, 1990.

[6] John Gribbon, *Hothouse Earth: The Greenhouse Effect and Gaia,* London: Black Swan, 1990.

exploitation. Any allocation of blame for degradation and any search for appropriate strategies for the future must take both of these major factors into account.

What about Poverty and Wealth?

It is important to grasp the fact that poverty alone does not necessarily cause environmental degradation. The indigenous people of the Kalahari desert, the Central African forests, the Amazon basin and the Arctic lived in harmony with their environment for many centuries, but were also poor by modern standards. If Malawi today had its 1900 population of about one million, the environment would be far less degraded, even if that population had the same low level of income available to the present population. In Malawi's case, it is rapid population growth, not poverty, which has resulted in the degradation of its soil, forest, water and fish resources. Is there then no connection between wealth, poverty and environmental degradation? There certainly is, but not in a simplistic form of poverty causing degradation and wealth avoiding it. Two examples will serve to illustrate their more complex inter-relationship.

The first is of the maldistribution of wealth within a country. In Botswana a small wealthy elite, comprising 0.6 percent of all cattle farmers, receives 50 percent of beef export revenues and has taken over large areas of grazing. This has forced the rest of the population to over-graze the remaining communal land and thereby seriously degrade it. In Central and South America a small elite controls much of the farmland, forcing poor people to cultivate fragile areas and degrade them.[7] In Malawi the extremely unequal distribution of wealth has resulted in only a small minority of farmers being able to purchase fertilizer to use on their maize. As a result more land has to be cultivated and the soil is degraded by constant monocropping without inputs.

---

[7] Herman Daly and George Foy, *Allocation, Distribution and Scale as Determinates of Environmental Degradation,* working paper 19, World Bank Environmental Department, Washington D.C., 1989.

The second is the maldistribution of wealth between nations, which allows wealthy countries to preserve their own environment at the cost of other, poorer nations. Thus, Japan consumes two-thirds of the world's traded timber and half of the world's imports of tropical hardwoods.[8] Japan's fishing fleets scour the seas of the world to provide protein for its population and thereby preserves its own environment from the by-products of factory-style fish farming. The import of energy, food, luxury goods (ivory, tropical fish, other natural products) may all be used to enhance the environment of a wealthy nation at the expense of the environment of a poor one. The traditional theory of comparative advantage has not taken into account the environmental costs of trading in natural resources.

So poverty per se does not necessarily lead to any environmental degradation, but serious inequalities of wealth certainly can.

Where Does Most of the Blame Lie?

Is the small group of wealthy nations or the great mass of poorer people responsible for the current situation? This is a highly emotive issue and the available figures can be manipulated easily to suit political positions. So 80% of the world's cars are in North America, Europe and Japan; energy consumption per capita in Canada is twenty-four times greater than that in Africa; the wealthy countries produce about 50% of man-made carbon dioxide emissions. But deforestation, soil degradation, the extinction of species, urban pollution and the uncontrolled release of noxious chemicals is much more widespread in the poorer countries, and within ten years it is the poorer countries which will be producing the major part of the greenhouse gases which are expected to lead to global warming.[9] Allocating blame is complicated. What is quite clear is that wealthy countries are in a far better position to slow the pace of environmental degradation than are very poor people. Wealth can be used to clean up industrial processes, provide alternative sources of energy, buy out surplus

---

[8] Pearce and Warlord, *World Without End*.
[9] Gribbon, *Hothouse Earth*.

producing farmers and replant forests. Poor people do not have those options. Clearing forest in the United States earns some foreign exchange and could be stopped tomorrow with little impact on the economy or the population. A ban on tree-felling in Malawi would mean no fuel, no building materials and no new farmland for a growing population. A total ban on fishing in the North Sea would have virtually no impact on the diet of the majority of people in Europe. A similar ban on Lake Malawi would result in widespread hardship.

Rich or poor, there are costs that have to be paid if the degradation of the environment is to be slowed down and more sustainable life-styles developed. And therein lies the rub.

Who Pays the Cost?

A striking feature of the past twenty years has been the reluctance of communities to pay for the cost of preserving the environment or reversing damage already committed. The cost is all too frequently passed on to someone else. This can take three broad forms:

a) passing the cost to another group in the same community. An example of this is air pollution in large cities. The rich do not want serious curbs on the use of motor vehicles, so they do not support legislation to drastically reduce private car use in cities. To avoid the pollution, they move out into the surrounding country and enjoy good quality air. The poor, who do not own cars and cannot afford to move out of the city, carry the cost of the degradation of their environment in terms of a loss of health, welfare and comfort;

b) passing the cost to another country. This takes many forms. Examples include lowering the cost of the production in one country by dumping untreated waste products into the atmosphere or rivers, which then cross international borders and damage another nation's environment. Acid rain from the United States and Britain, damaging the forests of Canada and Scandinavia, provide one of many examples.[10] Another is the clamour in the United States to preserve

---

[10] P. Harter, *Acidic Deposition: Ecological Effects,* London: International Energy Agency, Coal Research, 1988.

the Amazonian forest in order to absorb carbon dioxide from internal combustion engines, whilst the U.S. preserves one of the lowest petrol prices in the developed world and thereby encourages increased carbon dioxide output; and

c) passing the cost to the next generation. This is the most widespread practice at present and applies across the world. By taking far more than its reasonable share of the world's capital resources, this generation is deliberately passing the cost to the next. So today's Malawian toddlers will find a much smaller stock of trees, fish, birds, animals and fertile soil available to them when they grow up, than was available to their parents when they were born. The same applies on a global basis, when our grandchildren will have had their capital of clean air, water, forest, animals and plants seriously diminished by our over-consumption.

Large numbers of people in the world are therefore faced with two options. The first is to continue to draw on the world's natural resources at an unsustainable rate and do all in their power to ensure that someone else pays the bill. This represents the current situation. The second is to start paying a realistic price for air, water, timber, fuel, food and industrial goods, which reflects the social costs of production. Such calculations of costs are in their infancy and have, on the whole, been rejected by governments and the general public. So President Reagan staunchly resisted attempts by the Environmental Protection Agency to clean up factories because it would have raised prices and undermined his claim that "Americans had never had it so good". Likewise, a referendum of the German public on introducing a maximum speed limit of 100 km per hour, and so bringing about a major saving in the massive pollution damage to Germany's forests, resulted in a rejection of the speed limit. Forests were not deemed worth the inconvenience, so let the next generation have fewer forests. This is not confined to industrial or developed countries. Almost nowhere in the world do farmers pay a realistic price for irrigation water. In consequence, that resource is being used at an unsustainable rate and large areas of irrigated land are being rendered useless by over-watering with cheap water. The next generation will have to pay the cost in a greatly reduced area of irrigated agriculture and higher food prices.[11]

The bottom line is inescapable. A more careful stewardship of the environment can only be obtained at a cost. In a developed country this means paying a lot more for energy, wood, industrial products, food and water. This, in its turn, means an erosion of currently unsustainable high standards of living. In a poorer country like Malawi it involves both higher costs and more work. The latter would result from more careful husbanding of the soil, more intensive methods of production, more effort in planting trees and restoring degraded ecologies. Over all of this is the social cost of a major effort to slow down the rate of population growth. China, with its one child per family policy, is the outstanding example of a country which faced up to this responsibility and whose people have paid a great social cost for the sake of their children and grandchildren.

Where is Any Link with Christian Teaching?

"God created humanity in his own image," states Genesis. An image or symbol is not the same as what is symbolized, otherwise humanity would be identical with God. But the image resembles and reflects what is imaged. One aspect of God's nature is that God, as Creator, understands what God is doing, sees it as a whole and is concerned that it should be good. Human beings, amongst all living creatures, have the ability to grasp the inter-relationships and inter-dependence of various aspects of the created order, and alone have the power to maintain a balance between them, to the benefit of the rest of the living things with which we share this planet. This concept of our being fellow-workers with God, in ensuring that the created order remains "good", is a far cry from an attitude which assumes that all other creatures simply exist for the benefit of humankind. The idea that humans have a responsibility to work with God in bringing creatures to their full potential is diametrically opposed to the current widely held

---

[11] Robert Repetto, *Skimming the Water: Rent Seeking and the Performance of Public Irrigation Systems,* Washington D.C.: World Resources Institute, 1987.

philosophy that it is everyone's right to exploit the world's natural resources for their own personal benefit.

The sense of stewardship of natural resources as a Christian responsibility had permeated the European farming community by the 18th century, so that a tradition developed that a good fanner left his land more productive at his death than when he had received it. That concept did not survive emigration to new virgin lands of apparently limitless natural wealth, nor has it ever really taken root in the industrial community. It is only very recently that the church has given any significant thought to the implication of Christian stewardship of the created order. Its message is all too often poorly developed and inadequately researched. In the church in which we worshipped in Washington D.C. we were given a sermon on Christian responsibility towards the environment on the Sunday after the sinking of the Exxon Valdes in Alaska. Half-way through his talk the preacher assured his middle-class congregation that such a responsibility would have no impact on their standard of living. I switched off at that point.

The Bible is shot through with the concept of people being stewards on God's behalf. This ranges from mankind as stewards of the created order, to kings as stewards of their people (e.g. Deuteronomy 17:14-20) and individuals as responsible for the welfare of those less fortunate than themselves. (Leviticus 19:9-10 and many others). Likewise, the Bible makes it clear that when a steward starts to behave as if he were himself unambiguously in charge, then he will bring trouble upon himself (e.g. Isaiah 22:15-21). The corruption of the relationship with God, as imaged in the story of the Fall, leads to a corruption of relationships between people, but also a corruption of the relationship with the environment, as people see themselves as owners rather than stewards. The offer of Christ to reverse that corruption of relationships needs to be seen not only in the light of relationship with God and other people, but also in relationship to that fraction of God's creation in which we have been set.

Unfortunately, few churches have thought through the implications of the biblical teaching on the responsibility of humankind for the stewardship of the natural order under the conditions of the twentieth century. In part, this stems from a fear of the wide-ranging implications for daily living that this would involve, and the costs that many of its members would have to face. To date, the call for sacrifice for the sake of the conservation of God's creation had come more strongly from the Green political parties than from the Christian churches. There is a most urgent need for Christian thinkers to give this whole issue far more attention, so that church members can be given a clear picture of their responsibilities, the changes in lifestyle they should make and the witness they should offer. Without such leadership, Christians will continue to fail miserably as good stewards of God's creation, and a major potential ally in the struggle to slow environmental degradation will remain dormant.

There is, of course, an entirely different reason why Christians should be at the forefront of environmental concern. That is the biblical injunction of concern for others. As stated earlier, the currently held philosophy of the majority of humankind is that others should pay for our bad management of the environment, other social groups, countries or generations. Christians should be in the vanguard of those who press for greater cost-bearing by the recipients of the benefits that are obtained from the environment. Once again, the churches are mute on this subject and most Christians do not see what are their direct responsibilities in this matter. Governments are often reluctant to legislate for minimizing environmental pollution because of the unpopularity of the costs involved. Christian churches should in fact be providing a major constituency of voters for legislation which moves the burden of cost from other people to themselves.

What are the Practical Implications?

It is impossible to detail what a greater sense of Christian responsibility for the environment would involve in every situation. It will obviously differ greatly from one society to another. For many it would involve a personal decision to limit the speed of population growth by limiting their family size. For others it would mean accepting far higher prices for energy, water, wood, food and clean air. For others it would mean abstaining from the use of toxic but highly convenient products, while for many African rural people it would involve an increased workload to restore soil fertility and grow more trees. For all, it would involve bringing the light of their Christian faith to bear on the use of natural resources, combined with a willingness to pay the cost of a better stewardship of the environment and a concern not simply to pass the charge on to others.

2. The New Commandment and the Selfish Gene

John J. Moore

Self-sacrificing Behaviour among Non-Human Animals

Naturalists and wildlife enthusiasts have always been fascinated by what looks like self-sacrificing behaviour in animals.[1] The phenomenon is perhaps most strikingly illustrated in the defence behaviour of social insects. It may not be very pleasant to be attacked by bees when we interfere with their hive, but, if we can rise above the momentary pain of the stings, it is hard not to admire the suicidal intensity of the attack. For the honey bee, each stinging of a larger animal means almost certain death, since the barbed sting remains embedded in the skin and, when the bee flies away, the bee's entrails are dragged out of the abdomen. Even with termites, when we disturb a nest or tunnel, the tender, soft bodied workers move into the safety of the interior while the soldiers line the breach with their menacing jaws open, ready for instant death if necessary. Similar behaviour is often to be seen among the more familiar larger mammals. The dominant male(s) in a troupe of baboons will always confront an intruder, thus allowing the females and young to scurry away to safety.

Alarm communication is also very widespread among social animals. Many birds and social mammals have a special cry to warn their companions of the approach of a predator. If an animal notices a predator, one would think that the wisest behaviour would be to hide and stay very still. "Stotting" in some of our smaller antelopes (i.e. making huge vertical jumps with stiff tail and outstretched legs, when fleeing) seems to have a similar purpose of warning fellow members of

---

[1] The literature is widely scattered. W.O. Wilson in his *Sociobiology: The New Synthesis,* Harvard: Harvard University Press, 1975, gives an excellent summary up to that time. Matt Ridley, *The Origins of Virtue,* Harmondsworth: Penguin, 1996, competently summarises more recent advances.

the herd; but it also lets a predator know exactly where the stotter is and is thus a rather dangerous procedure.

Food sharing among adults, an obviously unselfish action, is frequent among ants and termites but it is also found, though rarely, in some of the larger animals. When a small group of chimpanzees find a fruit-laden tree they emit a loud and excited chatter that attracts any group within a few kilometres to come and join in the feast.

Perhaps the most striking cases are connected with that strongest of instincts, the reproductive instinct. Fights between males for a 'ripe' female are commonplace; but most of these fights are ritualized - "full of sound and fury" but hardly ever proceeding to the kill. When it becomes obvious which is the more dominant male, the defeated one slinks away with appropriate signs of submission and that's that. The proverb "He who. fights and runs away, lives to fight another day" would seem to dictate that it might be better for the victor to polish off today's loser - he might be the victor next year! Yet that does not happen.

Even more striking is the "voluntary celibacy" that has been observed in some animals when the food resources are not sufficient to allow all the animals in a crowded population to breed. The most usual way this occurs is by the males fighting for a territory, an area sufficient to feed his prospective progeny. Males and females who do not get a territory remain on the margins and do not reproduce. This obviously prevents disastrous overgrazing.

Fascinating phenomena like these may have often been used by clergymen (who traditionally have included some very keen and skilled naturalists among their ranks) in order to stimulate their congregations to greater efforts in their exercise of Christian love. I would like to look in a slightly more critical way at the connection between these apparent examples of self-sacrificing behaviour among non-human animals and Christ's "new commandment" of unselfish Christian love.

Altruism - How to Reconcile it with Natural Selection?

These fascinating types of behaviour I have been describing are usually referred to by biologists as altruism and they pose a great theoretical problem for evolutionary theory. Evolutionary theory, one of the major branches of theoretical biology, deals with the genetical basis for the evolutionary process. The approach is quantitative with a stress on the underlying mathematics.

If we are to deal with altruism in this rigorous way, we must first define it clearly. Such a definition may rob the notion of some of its romance and fascination, but it is necessary if we are to deal with the phenomenon in a rigorous way.

Altruism is the surrender of part of an individual's genetic fitness for the enhancement of genetic fitness in others. Fitness is a common word we use in our ordinary day-to-day speech and it usually conjures up pictures of lean, athletic young men and women. However, here, genetical or Darwinian fitness is a technical term used in quantitative genetics and evolutionary theory, and is defined as follows:

> *(Genetic) Fitness:* is the degree to which copies of an individual's genes are passed on to the next generation.

The problem of explaining altruistic behaviour within this theoretical framework is as follows. Let us postulate that a certain type of altruistic behaviour is governed by a gene (or group of genes). Further let us suppose that the altruistic behaviour involves the individual risking his life to save one or more of his fellows. By definition the possessor of this gene, if he follows the altruistic behaviour dictated by the gene, will leave behind him fewer copies of this "altruistic gene" than if he remained "selfish". The other more selfish members of his species who do not possess this gene, but who benefit from his altruistic behaviour, will leave behind more copies of their genes which favour selfish behaviour. Therefore the altruistic gene will be eliminated from the population in a few generations by natural selection.

One answer to this difficulty is the idea of "Group Selection". The whole group of animals, for example an ant, bee or termite colony, benefits from the sterility of some members of the group (i.e. the workers) and especially from their altruistic, courageous behaviour. A useful precision was introduced by Maynard-Smith[2] who defined Kin Selection as that which benefits close relatives (usually first cousins or closer, as in a hive or ant colony), whereas the term Group Selection is now confined to that favouring members of the same species who are more distantly related.

Hamilton provided a method of deciding whether a given altruistic behaviour is viable from the point of view of natural selection.[3] He tries to weigh up the genetic advantages, both to the altruist and to those animal(s) which benefit from the altruistic action. Thus, in order to make the calculation it is necessary to know how many genes are held in common by two close relatives. For siblings (same mother, same father), half of the genes are common; therefore if a brother dies before reproducing due to his altruistic efforts for his sibling, he himself will pass on no genes to the next generation; if, however, as a result of his altruistic behaviour his brothers or sisters (who also possess the altruistic gene) produce more than twice as many offspring as if they had not been helped, then, from the evolutionary point of view, the altruistic action would have been worthwhile and the altruistic gene is likely to survive or spread in the population. He refers to this as a calculation of the "inclusive fitness" of both the altruist and his close relatives who benefit.

Hamilton goes on to define Selfishness and Spite from this same point of view of Evolutionary Biology: *Genetical Selfishness* would mean that the numbers of copies of one's genes passed on to the next generation would be significantly increased at the expense of a relative whose contribution to the next generation would be lessened. He shows that such Selfishness could be favoured by natural selection.

---

[2] J. Maynard-Smith, "Group Selection and Kin Selection", London, *Nature,* Vol. 201 (1964) pp. 1045-1047.

[3] W.D. Hamilton, "Genetical Theory of Social Behaviour", *Journal of Theoretical Biology,* Vol. 7 (1964), pp. 1-52.

To complete the picture, Hamilton defined Spite from the genetical point of view. *Spite* would be where one would lessen the chance of another animal passing on its genes, but one would, as a result, also decrease one's own contribution of genes to the next generation. It is hard to show convincing examples of this behaviour among non-human animals, and of course it has proved impossible to show how it could have evolved by natural selection.

A final refinement to this approach was introduced by Trivers in his idea of *Reciprocal Altruism* which he introduced to explain what he calls "Good Samaritan behaviour".[4] It is as if there were a sort of unwritten agreement that if I perform an altruistic action for you, you will return the favour when I am in need. Most of Trivers' illustrations come from human behaviour and he found it hard to find well documented examples among animals.

Several years later Axelrod produced a mathematical proof from games' theory that Trivers' idea worked.[5] Immediately there was a resurgence of interest and a search for convincing examples amongst higher animals. For example our own vervet monkey will respond to a recorded call for help from another monkey if the voice is either that of a very close relative or if it is from a monkey which recently helped him in a similar situation, Kin Selection at work in the first case, Reciprocal Altruism in the second.[6]

Sociobiology and the Selfish Gene

In 1975 E.O. Wilson published a massive book called *Sociobiology: the New Synthesis.*[7] This was a masterly, fully documented summary of all the work which had been done up to that time on social animals, i.e. those which form groups larger than the primary family unit. However,

---

[4] R.L. Trivers, "Evolution of Reciprocal Altruism", *Journal of Theoretical Biology*, Vol. 46 (1971), pp. 35-57.

[5] R. Axelrod, *The Evolution of Co-operation,* New York: Basic Books, 1984.

[6] D.L. Cheney and R.M. Seyfarth, *How Monkeys See the World,* Chicago: Chicago University Press, 1990.

[7] Harvard: Harvard University Press.

it proved to be a highly controversial book which led to an enormous amount of conflict, both within his own University (Harvard) and internationally. The reason for this was that he attempted in his last chapter to extrapolate his findings to humans; he claimed that advances in sociobiology and neuro-physiology would enable us to deal scientifically with the origins of human ethics. These ideas were further developed in his *On Human Nature* published in 1978.[8] The apparently ultimate step in this trend was taken by Richard Dawkins in his *The Selfish Gene,* which, besides being a superbly clear exposition of modern evolutionary theory, proceeded to the ultimate limit of reductionism in this field.[9] Basing his ideas on those of Hamilton, he suggests that the best way (the only way?) of viewing the panorama of life on this planet is to focus on the gene. The drama of the evolution of new and more complex forms of life over time is adequately explained by envisaging selfish genes trying desperately to propagate themselves. Bodies (whether plant, animal or microbe) are merely instruments (extremely complex at times) to ensure the propagation of the gene. The same can be said for all the noble aspirations that poets, philosophers or theologians discourse about. They are ultimately reducible to servants of the selfish gene.

Assessment from a Christian Perspective

Not surprisingly a strong reaction to this approach has developed. Gould and Lewontin, two influential biological writers have continuously opposed the concept of the selfish gene. Even Dawkins himself states in his *The Selfish Gene* that "I never seem to get fully used to it" (the idea of the selfish gene). Very often these ideas have been taken to be an incentive to immorality and selfishness, and some teachers in the USA have reported that university students, after being exposed to these ideas, actually do behave more selfishly, at least in controlled games. However, Dawkins has insisted that his aim was not to advocate Selfishness but "to reverse it and to rebel against the tyranny of the selfish replicators" (genes).

---

[8] *Ibid.*

[9] Richard Dawkins, *The Selfish Gene,* Oxford: Oxford University Press, 1976.

Yet it must be admitted that the evidence and reasoning supporting the purely scientific concept of the selfish gene is impressive. It is often the extrapolations into the areas of moral philosophy or religion that disturb us. It is up to us Christians to see if it will fit into our world view.

The evolution of complex social systems in a number of quite distinct animal groups is fascinating in itself. There seem to have been three peaks of this development, two rather closely related in their main strategies (the bees/ants and the termites), the third radically different in so many obvious ways - human social systems.

The altruism so obvious among the social insects is very mechanical and obviously strictly determined, mainly by various emitted chemical odours (pheromones). Primate and human social systems are, however, so much more flexible and fluid. As a result the altruism that is found in humans seems even more fragile, but at the same time more full of promise.

Much thought-provoking material has been provided by the biologists, especially those specializing in the field of Primate Behaviour. Our hormonal and nervous systems are remarkably similar to those of the higher apes. Thus, while not subscribing to a facile reductionism (the human being is *nothing but* ... his limbic system ... his hormonal balance ... his gene complement, etc.), the conclusion seems inescapable that our bodily functions, our emotional reactions and our inbuilt reflexes are built on a biology that parallels in many details that of the primates.

Here we have an area of controversy and extreme positions. The behavioural scientist looks on the theologian as being out of touch with the empirical data; on the other hand the theologian considers the scientist as being one-sided in ignoring what he would consider to be the doubtful, subjective data of introspection and religious experience, not to mention the data of faith. I would prefer to develop some kind of balanced, middle position.

Gadagkar in a recent review gives the following useful table to help clarify our ideas:[10]

Consequences for the Recipient

		+	O	-
Consequences for the Actor	+	Cooperation	Weak Selfishness	Selfishness
	O	Weak Altruism	Weak Cooperation	Weak Spite
	-	Altruism	Weak Altruism	Spite

He claims that the accepted explanations of altruism by Hamilton and Trivers really explain it away; the apparent altruism among animals has in fact been shown to be just weak Selfishness. Likewise, Gadagkar denies that genuine spite has ever been found among non-human animals.

This means that humans are the only animals where genuine altruism and spite have been found. This seems to be the scientific correlate of the somewhat banal theological statement that in this visible world, sin and grace are only to be found among humans.

How, then, are we to view the apparently altruistic behaviour of the social animals, especially of the higher apes, from the point of view of our faith? The medieval theologians had a saying "Grace builds on Nature" or "Grace pre-supposes Nature". Can we not look on these examples of altruism (or incipient altruism) as a preparation for that Grace which was to be bestowed from the beginning? In line with recent thinking on the theology of grace[11] we can take this "nature" on which grace builds, not as some pre-existing state of pure human

---

[10] Raglavendra Gadagkar, "Can Animals be Spiteful?", *Trends in Ecology,* Vol. 8 (1993), pp. 232234.

[11] Karl Rahner has been very influential in the development of this new approach to grace. An excellent summary may be found in S. Schtissler Fiorenza and John P. Galvin, *Systematic Theology: Roman Catholic Perspectives,* Dublin: Gill and Macmillan, 1992.

nature (as has been rightly rejected), but as the slow development of altruism among our predecessors on this planet. It is admittedly going beyond the limits of the empirical sciences, but it is nevertheless fascinating (for me) to contemplate a divine providence programming, as it were, into living matter, on the purely biological level, (basically into its genes subjected to natural selection), the possibility of a genuine altruism developing. And yet there seems to be something unfinished about this altruism in non-human animals and hence the many efforts we have seen to "take the altruism out of altruism" as Trivers puts it.[12]

The most recent major step in human evolution which occurred with the appearance of what we traditionally refer to as the human soul (freedom and reflective thought), seems on the one hand to endanger this process of increasing altruism because of our great potential for indulging in crass selfishness, spite and cruelty. Those features of our history of which we are rightly ashamed such as genocide, total warfare, slavery, the exploitation of human beings, all make good sense from the purely evolutionary, natural selection, point of view. But when the time had come for the appearance of true human beings, right from the beginning that gift beyond all our understanding, that un-created grace of the free offer of God's self-communication in love was ours. Among its secondary effects were liberation *from* sin and liberation *for* love. The first can be interpreted as the discernment and insight needed to control our drives and emotions arising from our primate biology; the second involves the gift of the Spirit helping us to aspire to that apex of altruism, the New Commandment of love for all people.

Conclusion

Darwin at the very end of his *Origin of Species* has a sort of hymn of wonder at the magnificence of the work of the Creator revealed by his vision of the evolution of life on our planet. Cynics would say that this conclusion was written only to ensure that he would not be savaged

---

[12] Trivers, "Evolution of Reciprocal Altruism".

too severely by churchmen. Whatever the motive, I find that there is an inspiring and poetic magnificence in the words.

> There is a grandeur in this view of life, with its several powers, having been originally breathed by the Creator into a few forms or into one; that whilst this planet has gone cycling on according to the fixed law of gravity, from so simple a beginning endless forms most beautiful and most wonderful have been and are being evolved.

I thus find that my own personal approach to the findings of the socio-biologists is similar to that of Darwin and of another priest scientist - Teilhard de Chardin - who often launches into similar paeans of praise for the wonders of the evolutionary process. I have always been fascinated by the vast sweep of diversity we see among the living things of this planet, by the long vista of the successive appearances of increasingly complex organisms revealed by the fossil record. Switching to another part of my psyche I find myself sharing something of Teilhard's fascination with the Cosmic Christ: "all things have been created through him and for him ... in him all things hold together", as he quotes so often from the Letter to the Colossians (1:16,17). Theologians have wrestled and fought over the exact implication of those words, but surely this view of things as we perceive them in this scientific age, fits in with the vision of Colossians?[13]

If we join Teilhard de Chardin[14] in adopting his admittedly disputed notion of Christ being somehow the term of biological evolution, does it not seem that his New Commandment (Jn 13:34) is but the crown of

---

[13] "If the world is convergent and if Christ occupies its centre, then the Christogenesis of St. Paul and St. John is nothing else and nothing less than the extension, both awaited and unhoped for, of that noogenesis in which cosmogenesis - as regards our experience - culminates"; an idea which forms the very last entry in his personal journal. *Le Phenomene Humaine,* p. 297 in Wall's translation, Harper Torchbooks.

[14] Teilhard de Chardin, *Le Phenomene Humaine,* Paris: Edltlons de Scull, 1955.

this process, a strong plea to us to allow this altruistic trend to achieve its climactic possibilities?[15]

Exegetes like Brown[16] seem to agree that the author of the Johannine literature was thinking primarily of love within the Christian community, and a cynic might say that this looks suspiciously like the reciprocal altruism of Trivers.[17] However, the version of the New Commandment given in the synoptic gospels, "love your enemies" (Mt 5:43-48) is quite inclusive and goes well beyond any limits or biological imperatives. And yet it would seem, it is only through the spread of this Christian AGAPE that there is any hope for our war enveloped planet in this nuclear age, even, some might say, for our survival as a biological species.

---

[15] Teilhard also seems to hint at this in his conclusion to *Le Phenomene Humaine:* "Christian love ... is a phenomenon of capital importance for the science of man", p. 295 in Wall's translation.

[16] R.E. Brown, *The Community of the Beloved Disciple,* London: Geoffrey Chapman, 1979.

[17] Trivers, "Evolution of Reciprocal Altruism".

3. The Role of Creativity in Mathematics

John M. Dubbey

God creates out of nothing. Human creativity uses what is already existing and available, and changes it in unpredictable ways. I use this as a working definition in approaching the vast subject of creativity and then in applying it with respect to mathematics. If we attempt at the same time to introduce some philosophical and theological factors, the number of fundamental questions exponentiates. In human terms, what exactly is creativity? How distinct is it from other mental processes? How does creativity occur? Is there a single identifiable creative process as link between the widely varying objects of creativity? If this function exists, can it be developed or taught? How is creativity recognized or measured? What does creativity mean in mathematics? How do mathematicians create? What is mathematics anyway? Is there a theology of creativity?

Faced with a range of questions such as these in what is a difficult area for intellectual discussion, an area treated cautiously by psychologists and philosophers, I found comfort in reading a passage from Poincare, a mathematician with more to say about creativity than any other. He points out that faced with a variety of alternatives, the process of creativity is not to take the easy way of stringing any combinations of ideas together; rather the creative process is to reject all combinations except the very few which lead to fruitful ideas. I will therefore take encouragement and select from the alternatives, one combination - this is anyway the writer's prerogative - and trust that this choice will prove to have some creative value in itself.

The pattern I will present, is first a brief analysis of the problems of definition and description, then to relate the general theories of creativity which emerge to a mathematical context and add a theological postscript. Then I would like to discuss these issues in an educational context and close with some moral social implications of creativity.

The literature on creativity is generally indecisive. J.P. White, giving a philosophical analysis in 1972, attributed this to two major causes.[1] The first was the unstated but implied feeling that creativity existed as some type of mental faculty to be developed and trained if possible. Such an assumption would seem to rest on a model of the mind as some sort of machine with different parts carrying out different functions when in fact there was no logical connection between the idea of creativity and some corresponding mental compartment. Rather, one looks for examples of creativity as in the works of Shakespeare or Newton not by the mental process of the two great men, about which we know nothing, but in the quality of the work produced. This leads to the second source of confusion; that if we see creativity in terms of end products, there must exist many types of creativity each considered in the context of the particular field of work. Creativity as a faculty of mind in, say, Bertrand Russell looks quite different from that of Beethoven or Rembrandt, and we look in vain for some common thread.

This problem of differentiation is, however, denied by the Synectic School. W. Gordon in defining Synectic Theory asserts that:

(i) Creative efficiency can be markedly increased by understanding the psychological process of the operation.
(ii) In the creative process, the emotional component is more important than the intellectual, the irrational more important than the rational.
(iii) It is these emotional, irrational elements which can and must be understood in order to increase the probability of success in a problem-solving situation.[2]

We will return later to this irrational component. Clearly the Synectists are optimistic about training in creativity by their technique of joining together different and apparently irrelevant elements: the researchers on the other hand are more inclined to agree with D. Child who asserted: "the truth is, we know very little about what makes a

---

[1] J.P White, *Creativity and Education: A Philosophical Analysis*, 1972.
[2] W.J.J. Gordon, *Synectics*, New York, 1961.

creative person and even less about the determinants of creativity. Consequently, there is no clear, unambiguous and widely accepted definition of creativity".[3]

Faced with the problem of definition the emphasis in the research turns to the recognition, description, assessment and analysis of qualities related to creativity. For example, Joseph Wallas breaks down the creative process into four stages: preparation, incubation, illumination and verification.[4] Jackson and Messick distinguish four essential features of a creative work, that of novelty, appropriateness, transformation and condensation.[5] Anne Roe attempted a study of 64 eminent scientists, to determine common features.[6] Nearer to our subject, J.L. Hadamard wrote his *Psychology of Invention in the Mathematical Field* in which he attempted a study of the working habits and more personal traits of leading mathematicians.[7] Other approaches have been to define divergent thinking as a measurable quality and associate it with creativity.

These attempts are interesting and descriptive, but none take us to the heart of the matter; what is creativity and how does the creative process take place? Probably the best attempt to do this, is contained in the elegant and erudite work of Silvano Arieti *Creativity, the Magic Synthesis* which attempts a direct answer to the fundamental question, applying his thesis to creativity in the arts, science and religion.[8]

Arieti's theory is to use what he calls the *primary process* defined by Freud as generally the set of ancient, obsolete and primitive mental mechanisms relegated to the recesses of the psyche which prevail in

---

[3] D. Child, *Psychology and the Teacher,* Nottingham, 1973.

[4] J.B. Wallas, *The Art of Thought,* New York, 1926.

[5] P. Jackson and S. Messick in, *The Journal of Perionality,* Vol. 33 (1965), pp. 309-329.

[6] Ann Roe, *A Psychologist Examines 64 Eminent Scientists,* 1952.

[7] Jacques Hadamard, *The Psychology of Invention in the Mathematical Field,* London: Dover, 1945.

[8] Silvano Arieti, *Creativity: The Magic Synthesis,* New York: Basic Books, 1976.

dreams and some mental illnesses, in contrast to the *secondary process* which is the mode of functioning of the mind when it is awake, and using common logic.

Arieti observes that from appropriate matching of the primary forms with secondary process mechanisms, innovations occur. He uses the term *tertiary process* to designate this special combination of primary and secondary process mechanisms. The *tertiary process* is capable of blending the worlds of mind and matter, rational and irrational, obtaining the magic synthesis from which the new, the unexpected and the desirable emerges.

Taking these formal and psychological approaches as background, can we find creativity in mathematics? Not very often it would seem if we look at the end products, the textbooks and the publications. Here the logic flows inexorably and faultlessly from one premise to another until the theorem is proved, the result established. Nowhere do we find evidence of that irrationality, the primordial primary process of the mind, the churning of the unconscious which the experts on creativity assure us must be present. The apparent non-existence of these phenomena is, however, due much to our conventions - that the write-up of a mathematical problem at any level relates exclusively to the context of justification and hardly ever to the context of discovery. When we think of discovery we can go back to the theorists and recognize all the stages of preparation, incubation, illumination and verification. We can agree that a genuine mathematical discovery should include as features, novelty, appropriateness, transformation and condensation. But with few exceptions the mathematical fraternity does not talk much about these things. Among the exceptions I have mentioned Hadamard, without much enthusiasm, and Poincare as much more hopeful. Poincaré's essay on mathematical creation was first published in *Science et Methode* in 1908, and it is doubtful if any mathematician since has spoken so frankly and introspectively.[9]

He supplies in this essay, the famous description of his discovery of the Fuchsian functions. After intensive but fruitless sessions of

---

[9] Henri Poincare, *Science et Methode,* London: Dover, 1908.

mathematical work, attempting to put combinations together, the vital insights came to him after leaving the problem alone and in most unexpected circumstances. The major discovery that the transformations he had used to define Fuchsian functions were identical to those of non-Euclidean geometry came to him stepping onto a bus. Walking along the beach a few days later and thinking of something quite different, the idea came to him, that arithmetic transformations of indeterminate ternary quadratic forms are also identical. From these two inspirations, the theory is now developed very straightforwardly.

Poincare's explanation is as striking as his inspiration. He wonders why it is among the many products of our unconscious activity, only a few will pass the threshold of consciousness while the majority will remain below. His answer is that those combinations emerge which pass the test of emotional aesthetic sensibility.

> Now what are the mathematical entities to which we attribute this character of beauty and elegance, and which are capable of developing in us a sort of aesthetic emotion? They are those whose elements are harmoniously disposed so that mind without effort can embrace their totality while realizing the details. This harmony is at once a satisfaction of our aesthetic needs and an aid to the mind, sustaining and guiding. And at the same time, in putting under our eyes a well-ordered whole, it makes us foresee a mathematical law.

We have the subconscious and inspiration and aesthetic delight as part of the mathematical creation. This is consistent with theology. We have: "in the beginning God created the heavens and the earth," (Gen. 1:1), but also a few verses later, "so God created man in his own image: in the image of God created he him." (Gen. 1:27). What does it imply that humanity is created in the image of God? Dorothy Sayers has pointed out that between these two verses in Genesis 1, the only activity of God referred to is his creativity.[10] The implication then is that humanity resembles God as being endowed with creative ability. This is a fundamental aspect of the nature of humanity. Further, we

---

[10] Dorothy Sayers, *The Mind of the Maker*, New York, 1956.

read that God looked on his creation and declared it to be good. We have the immediate association of the creative product, the aesthetic appreciation and the moral value.

Combining then, the incentive of Scripture, the testimony of Poincare and the analysis of Arieti, I would offer three basic reasons for the encouragement of creativity in mathematics:

1. It is in the nature of humanity formed in the image of God, to create and to delight in the creation. We should emphasize not only the utility of mathematics, but its aesthetic value and the role of discovery.

2. Following the work of Popper on Falsifiability, Lakatos has demonstrated that mathematics progresses through the successive attempts to refute hypothetical conjectures by counter examples. He emphasizes convincingly the use of imaginative conjectures and counter-examples as being as necessary for mathematical development as the use of deductive reasoning.[11]

3. Creativity needs emphasis in mathematics as an antidote to that placed on deductive reasoning. The human animal is very effective in making logical inferences and has even been able to build machines to do the complex reasoning for him. It could be that the fifth generation computers will absorb all forms of mathematical analysis, as calculators have for arithmetic. The human need to supply deductive reasoning will become increasingly redundant, and the more neglected aspects of the mind will need to develop that creativity which the machines cannot supply.

Given the need for creativity in mathematics, how can it be developed? In pedagogical terms, we need to avoid syllabi and examinations which put the whole emphasis on deductive techniques. These will in any case soon became as redundant as arithmetic tests. Instead we must instill the beauty, the harmony, the generality and simplicity of mathematics. We need to encourage mathematical modelling in a diversity of applications, and look for open-ended

---

[11] Imre Lakatos, *Proofs and Refutations,* Cambridge, 1976.

problems at all levels. The processes of creation in the great mathematicians should be investigated, and one of the best practical ways to avoid the text book approach and see concepts developing, is to make more use of the history of mathematics. Pupils should be encouraged to talk and discuss mathematics, and to raise their own conjectures and refutations.

These are a few of the classroom suggestions. Arieti has some proposals for fostering creativity which are distinctly anti-classroom, but have evident educational merit. Such ideas include *aloneness* - the cultivation of ways to listen to the inner self, removed from all distractions: *inactivity*, taking time off to do nothing, avoiding routine work; *day-dreaming*, allowing the mind to stray constructively from the usual paths; *freethinking*, being in a state of readiness to grasp similarities; *gullibility*, a willingness to rule out criticism and suspend judgment; *remembrance*, the inner replaying of past traumatic conflicts in order to transform them to creativity; *alertness* and *discipline*. It is interesting that each of these features has its spiritual counterpart in the development of devotional life.

The emphasis has been on creativity as an individualistic matter simply because creation comes through individuals. It is not impossible, but rare for a committee to act creatively. Equally it is unusual for the creative person not to be strongly influenced by the ethos and needs of contemporary society. The history of Mathematics demonstrates that men of genius such as Archimedes, Newton and Gauss are effectively creative in a general context of contemporaries engaged in similar work. The work of the creator always enriches its own society and those which follow. Giving the last word to Arieti:

> Creativity is the opposite to the greedy King of Corinth of the old myth. Whatever he gets, he gives to others; whatever he gives to others, he retains. Although he will not reach the peak of the ultimate mountain, the horizons that open before his eyes are vaster and vaster. And he rejoices in his heart, knowing that his labour has not been in vain, since these horizons will be shared by millions of brothers and sisters, not just today, but as long as people will live on earth.

Thus, what remained unfinished as a cognitive ascent finds an end as an act of social love.[12]

Here indeed, is the human being as creator, born in the image of God.

---

[12] Arieti, *Creativity: The Magic Synthesis.*

4. The Physical Concept of Time and the Christian Concept of Eternity

Patrick A. Whittle

Traditional Concepts of Time and Eternity

The concept of time is as important in philosophical and religious thinking as it is to scientific perceptions of human existence and our place in the universe. Philosophers and scientists have frequently speculated about the nature of time. Plato regarded the physical world, including time, as only a secondary reality compared with the intellectual, eternal, "World of Being". Both he and Newton, whose classical mechanics laid the foundation for all modern physics, assumed that space and time are absolute. According to Ward virtually all the classical writers, including the Sunni Muslim theologian Al-Ghazzali, viewed time itself as in some sense closed or completed.[1]

Remarkably, St Augustine pointed out that before the creation of the universe, time had no meaning.[2] Thomas Aquinas regarded time as endless and one of the attributes of the eternal as being its infinite completeness. To Maimonides the eternal God was the creator of time, but still capable of interacting with creation.[3] This seems to have remained a common contemporary Christian view.

The linear concept of time extending into the indefinite past, the present and an infinite future is, according to Mbiti, a Western view, with its roots in Judeo-Christian thinking. Most traditional African cultures treated the historical past as as significant as the present, making up what may be called "Actual Time". Virtually no consideration was given to the "Potential Time" ahead in the future; what was yet to be, could not have reality.

---

[1] K. Ward, *Images of Eternity,* London: Darton, Longman and Todd, 1987.
[2] P. Davies, *God and the New Physics,* Harmondsworth: Pelican, 1983.
[3] K. Ward, *Images of Eternity.*

This kind of thinking is exemplified in most African language tenses and time reckoning systems.[4]

It seems that the Bible, the Qu'ran, and other major religions, attribute to God an existence outside of time, with post- and fore-knowledge of history of mankind, and an "eternal" changelessness. At least three different concepts of eternity have been identified by Ward:

    (i)   exclusive eternity, where the eternal has no relation to time at all;

    (ii)   inclusive eternity, revealed and consummated by time;

    (iii)   dynamic eternity, interacting with an 'endless time.[5]

Scientific and Religious Time Scales

On a human scale we tend to think in terms of our own experiences; from transitory events of seconds, to a life-time of three score years and ten. Whereas cosmologists are concerned with very large timescales in billions of years, nuclear scientists are concerned with billionths of a second. The increased accuracy with which time is now measured is illustrated by definition of the second. Originally defined from the mean solar day, it is now defined as 9,192,631,770 periods of oscillation of a caesium atom. The range of timing of some scientific intervals shown in Table 1 in the appendix, is based on a recent paper by Sutton.[6]

Religious time scales are also concerned with the infinitesimally small, and the infinitely long, extending into "eternity". The questions arise;

    (i)   is "eternity" just the upper limit of physical time, or is there any deeper religious and specifically Christian, meaning? and

---

[4] J.S. Mbiti, *African Religions and Philosophy,* London: Heinemann, 1969; cf. Augustine Muso-pole's critique of Mbiti's concept: *Being Human in Africa: Toward an African Christian Anthropology,* New York: Peter Lang, 1994.

[5] K. Ward, *Images of Eternity.*

[6] C. Sutton, "Faster than Thought: an Experimental Approach to Time", Paper read to British Association, Swansea, 1990.

(ii) how can an active God, with some human attributes, be "timeless"?

Relativistic Time

Einstein showed that the principles of Newtonian mechanics break down if an object is travelling at a high speed, approaching the speed of light. Since then, many experiments in high-speed particle accelerators have given emphatic confirmation to relativity theory. Time dilation effects may be observed to illustrate the Lorentz contraction, usually expressed as:

Where: v   is the velocity, and
       c   the speed of light,
           300,000,000 m/sec.

$$t = \frac{t_0}{\sqrt{1 - (\frac{v}{c})^2}}$$

In addition to the relativistic contractions experienced in space and time, light and time are known to be affected by gravity. Clocks sent up in rockets have been demonstrated to differ from those on Earth.[7] Modern physics can no longer accept a concept of absolute time. Einstein went so far as to say "for we convinced physicists, the distinction between present and future is only an illusion, however persistent".

The Space-Time Continuum

When time is stretched, space shrinks, and vice versa. The "twins effect" neatly and concisely described by Paul Davies illustrates this well.[8] "An itinerant twin blasts off to a nearby star, nudging the light barrier. The stay-at-home twin waits for him to return ten years later. When the rocket gets back, the Earth-bound twin finds his brother has aged only one year to his ten. High speed has enabled him to experience only one year of time during which ten years have elapsed on Earth."

---

[7] S.W. Hawkey, *A Short History of Time*. Bantam, 1988.
[8] P. Davies, *God and the New Physics*.

Relativity theory has led to the acceptance that time cannot be completely separated from space, but combined in a space-time continuum, often known as four-dimensional (curved) space. The coordinates of an object in space and time identify where it is at a given time, and this may be illustrated diagrammatically in a two- or three-dimensional representation.

Although difficult to visualize, mathematical models accurately define properties of 4-D space.[9] Feynman's "Sum over histories" method predicts statistical probabilities of a particle's position.[10]

All events associated with a given event, past or future, fall within its associated space-time cone.[11]

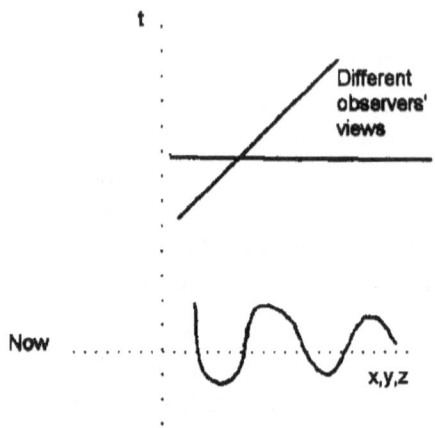

Fig. 1 Elusive events/particles

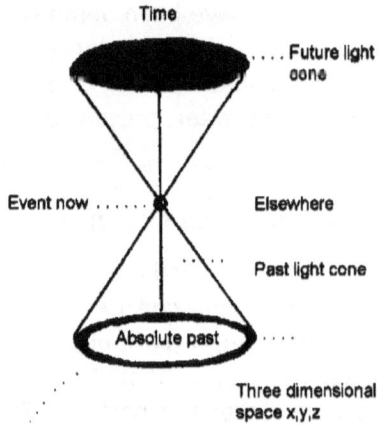

Fig.2 A "Light Cone"

---

[9] R.T. Weidner, and R.L. Sells, *Elementary Modern Physics,* Allyn and Bacon, 1973.

[10] R.P. Feynman, et *al.*, *The Feynman Lectures on Physics,* Addison-Wesley, 1963.

[11] P. Coveney, and R. Highfield, *The Arrow of Time,* London: Allen and Unwin, 1990.

Uncertainty

In 1927 Heisenberg postulated his famous "Uncertainty Principle" which is often expressed:

$$d(mv).dx \geq h$$

where: mv = momentum,
x = position, and
h = Planck's constant, 6.6×10^{-34} J-s

This means that the more precisely we know the measured value of one of these quantities, the greater the uncertainty in the other quantity. Consequently, the simultaneous measurement of position and velocity are only possible for macroscopic objects, not for particles of small mass, m. Similarly, there is a limitation to the accuracy with which we can measure energy within a given time interval or vice-versa; the life span of an atom in a particular quantum state is equally uncertain.

$$d(E).dt \geq h$$

The Uncertainty Principle demolished Laplace's postulate of scientific determinism, in which he suggested that one set of divine laws would determine the evolution of the universe. If particles were all replaced by waves, however, this random element might be eliminated, according to Hawkey, who seems to advocate a "Big Bang" creation, leading to a final "Big Crunch" ending of the universe, over a finite period of time.[12] He says "Even if the whole universe did not recollapse, there would be singularities in localized regions that collapsed into black holes. These singularities would be end of time for anyone who fell into a black hole".

The Arrow of Time

Eddington pointed out that the increase of disorder in the universe, with time, or the irreversibility of natural events (physicists know it as the Second Law of Thermodynamics), is evidence that time is

---

[12] S.W. Hawkey, *A Short History of Time*.

unidirectional. This forward direction has come to be known as the 'arrow of time' and Hawkey identifies three pointers to it: in addition to (i) the pointer of increasing thermodynamic disorder, he cites (ii) the psychological pointer of our memories of the past and not of the future, and (iii) the pointer from cosmology's expanding universe.[13] In his recent book, Coveney also draws on the evidence of irreversible chemical changes, many non-linear mathematical models of biological cells, and clock mechanisms, to firmly establish an argument for the one-way nature of time.[14]

Davies, however, regards the arrow of time as a naive concept, despite the obvious assymetry of time, past and future. He states that the difficulty of defining "now" (in space-and-time) makes it impossible to define "future". His view is that change occurs because things move about through space, in time; but time itself is there, not moving. Our perception of time-flux he claims to be a psychological phenomenon, in the mind, rather than in physical reality.

Polkinghorne apparently sympathizes with Davis' position when he asks, "Is our experience of time an illusion?"[15] He seems to revert to the deterministic position, however, in maintaining that if we really properly knew the present, we would retrodict the past and predict the future.

The Biblical View of Time

The Bible is a history book, in the sense that it describes, from the Creation onwards, God's dealings with the human race, and provides some insights into its future. Although the actual timing of events is not always precisely stated, there are clear references to the evolution of the Earth, the development of civilizations (and their downfall), divine intervention in the person of Jesus Christ, and the expectation

---

[13] *Ibid.*

[14] P. Coveney, and R. Highfield. *The Arrow of Time*.

[15] J. Polkinghorne. Time. God and Creation", Paper read to British Association, Swansea, 1990.

of his return in judgement before the "end of the age" (Hebrews 9:26-28).

Whereas the temporal nature of humanity is emphasized, the eternal nature of God is equally stated. God is clearly placed outside of the human time limitation, and yet can interact with the physical and living world. The gospel offers the "hope of eternal life, which God, who does not lie, promised before the beginning of time ... " (Titus 1:2-3). God has full knowledge of the past, and of the future (Isaiah 46:9-11). God is unchanging in his nature (James 1:17), but is given many human attributes in the scriptures, if we take them literally. Jesus Christ, in his earthly life, was subject to all the limitations of humanity, but is now no longer subject to them, being already "in heaven", which is clearly stated to be "eternal" (2 Cor 5:1).

Christian Views of Time and Eternity

Boethius, in the sixth century, speculated about how God could possess, at once, the complete and perfect knowledge of the past, and of the future. Aquinas pointed out that since time implies change, if God is perfect, he cannot change, so he must be timeless. Polkinghorne has suggested that our modern views of indeterminism and the dynamical theory of chaos do not clash with an eternally changeless God who demonstrated dynamic perfect-ion.[16] He postulates a "dynamic theory of chaos where there is unpredictability of systems unfolding within an envelope of predictability". The picture is of God knowing all the future possibilities, not the actual future. My own view is that if God is outside of time, he also knows the actual future.

The human attributes which the Bible, Jesus, and Christians, all give to God, are necessary for mere humans to grasp something of the nature of an infinite being, and to enjoy the privilege of communion with God. They do not imply that God is subject to the limitations of space and time. In a previous paper I referred to the interaction between the

---

[16] *Ibid.*

physical and the spiritual worlds, from the time-bound finite to the timeless infinite.[17]

Christians interpret God's timelessness in different ways. Are prayers for the dead a recognition of divine time reversal? Is Christian prophecy an example of God's fore-knowledge being made known? The central act of divine forgiveness seems to me to embody the process of rectifying human error through a "providential" unfolding of events through which God is able to somehow put a Christian back on the right track. Faith in God's ability to know all the possibilities, and to be able to put right the past, are implicit in seeking his present favour and future guidance.

The concept of "eternal life" in John's gospel is generally interpreted by Christians to mean a new quality of life "now" and also in the after-life. This implies a transition from the physical to the spiritual which might be the basis of another treatise, dealing with some aspects of our perceptions of heaven.

---

[17] P.A. Whittle, The Physical Concept of Energy in Relation to Christian Belief and Experience", Faith and Knowledge Seminar No. 4., Chancellor College, University of Malawi, 1990.

Appendix

Table 1: Range of Timing of some Scientific Intervals (after Sutton):

The age of the universe	450000000000000000	Seconds
The age of the Earth	130000000000000000	
The death of dinosaurs	1000000000000000	
Time for light to come from Andromeda	10000000000000	
Time since earliest homo sapiens	900000000000	
Average human lifetime	2100000000	
One year	10000000	
One week	600000	
One hour	4000	
100 metres race	10	Seconds
Human brain reflex	0.1	
Biological systems	0.001	
Life-time of a muon (stable particle)	0.000022	
Life-time of a pion	0.0000001	
Time for light to travel one metre	0.000000001	
Time for light to travel one centimetre	0.00000000001	
Life-time of a charmed meson	0.0000000000004	
Time for light to cross an atom	0.0000000000000000001	
Time for light to cross a nucleus	0.00000000000000000000001	Seconds

5. Accountability: Living Our Faith?
An Information Systems Perspective

David Mundy

1. Introduction

After a thirty-year period of authoritarian dictatorship under Kamuzu Banda, in 1994 Malawi emerged as a democratic republic. The catalyst for the process of transformation in Malawi was the publication in March 1992 by the Roman Catholic Bishops of Malawi of a Pastoral Letter entitled *Living our Faith*.[1] Significantly the Bishops called for the Banda regime to become accountable, to establish democratic structures through which public officials could be held responsible for their decisions and their actions: "Accountability is a quality of any good government. People are entitled to know how their representatives fulfil their duties. No disrespect is shown when citizens ask questions in matters which concern them."[2] As Kenneth Ross notes, "this call for accountability to the people marked the beginning of a process of democratization which was to transform Malawian political life during the coming two years."[3]

---

[1] *Living our Faith,* Pastoral Letter of the Catholic Bishops of Malawi to be Read in Every Catholic Church on 8 March 1992; later published under the title *The Truth Will Set You Free,* Church in the World 28, London: CIIR, 1992; also in Kenneth R. Ross, *Christianity in Malawi: A Source Book,* Gweru: Mambo, 1996, pp. 203-215.

[2] *Ibid*, p. 10.

[3] Kenneth R. Ross, "The Transformation of Power in Malawi 1992-1994: the Role of the Christian Churches", in Kenneth R. Ross (ed.), *God, People and Power in Malawi: Democratization in Theological Perspective,* Blantyre: CLAIM, 1996, p. 25.

On 16 May 1994 Parliament, sitting in an emergency session, enacted a new Constitution approved by the National Consultative Council.[4] Section 13 of this new Constitution outlines principles of national policy:

> The state shall actively promote the welfare development of the people of Malawi by progressively adopting and implementing policies and legislation aimed at achieving the following goals—
>
> (o) Public Trust and Good Governance
>
> To introduce measures which will guarantee accountability, transparency, personal integrity and financial probity and which by virtue of their effectiveness and transparency will strengthen confidence in public institutions.

While accountability is clearly on the national political agenda in Malawi, it is also on the international political agenda. From the early 1980s. with successive Conservative governments in the UK and two Republican administrations in the USA, public sector reform has been a constant theme in both countries.[5] In the UK a series of White Papers and government reports has attempted to increase the accountability of public officials in public sector organizations, both in terms of their use of tax payers' money *(Financial Management Initiative,[6] Next Steps,[7] Compulsory Competitive Tendering)[8]* and of the quality of the public services delivered *(Citizen's Charter).*[9] Since the fall of the Berlin Wall in 1989 and the end of the Cold War, western bilateral donors

---

[4] *Malawi's Constitution* [Online]. http://www.malawi.net/constitution.html. [25 September 1997]

[5] David Farnham and Sylvia Horton, "Public Service Management: A Review and Evaluation", in D. Farnham and S. Horton (eds.), *Managing the New Public Services* (2nd ed.), Basingstoke: Macmillan, 1996, p. 268.

[6] *Efficiency and Effectiveness in the Civil Service,* London: HMSO (Her Majesty's Stationery Office), 1982.

[7] K. Jenkins, K. Caines and A. Jackson, *Efficiency Unit: Improving Management: The Next Steps,* London: HMSO, 1988.

[8] *Competing for Quality,* London: HMSO, 1991.

[9] *The Citizen's Charter: Raising the Standard,* London: HMSO, 1991.

have used their financial support of developing countries to impose changes on the structure of governments in developing countries.[10] These changes may be summarized by the term "good governance", of which accountability is one aspect. Good government, and hence accountability, is now seen both by western bilateral donors and by multilateral donors as a necessity for reducing poverty and improving the quality of life in developing countries.[11]

However, the act of adopting a new Constitution and changing the structure of governance does not of itself make Malawi a truly democratic republic. In particular, it does not guarantee that the public officials in public sector organizations can be held responsible for their decisions and their actions. The democratic structures may now be in place, but democratic attitudes and behaviours are not learned overnight, nor can they be imposed from outside. Although the new Constitution makes explicit reference to the need for public officials in public sector organizations to be accountable, there is no guidance either for the form that this accountability should take or how it is to be realized. Nor can it be assumed that this accountability should follow the practices of the governments of the western bilateral donors. As Hofstede points out, the multi-dimensional socio-economic context in which a system of accountability exists, defines not only the symbols used in that system of accountability, but also the objective of the system of accountability.[12] Thus, in many public sector organizations, the symbols defined by the system of accountability relate to money and the objective of the system of accountability is to demonstrate the financial probity of the public officials engaged in financial transactions in the public sector

---

[10] Mark Turner and David Hulme, *Governance, Administration and Development: Making the State Work,* Basingstoke: Macmillan, 1997, pp. 229-231.

[11] World Bank, *World Development Report 1997: the State in a Changing World,* New York: Oxford University Press, 1997; *Eliminating World Poverty: A Challenge for the 21st Century,* London: HMSO, 1997.

[12] Geert Hofstede, *Cultures and Organizations: Intercultural Cooperation and its Importance for Survival,* London: HarperCollins, 1994, p. 155.

organisation. However, alternative systems of accountability can be envisaged; the objective of these systems is to demonstrate that there has been no negative impact on the natural environment; the symbols defined by such systems of accountability relate to aspects of the natural environment rather than to money. Clearly, then, there are choices concerning systems of accountability; that which may be appropriate in the context of industrialized nations such as the UK or the US may be inappropriate in the context of a particular developing country such as Malawi.

For democracy to survive outside a small privileged elite in Malawi it must be founded on popular norms and values which inform these choices for systems of accountability. Clearly education has an important role to play in fostering 'popular democracy'. But if, as Ross puts it, democracy is to move beyond rhetoric to reality,[13] this education process must both challenge existing practices at all levels of society and encourage the search for and adoption of new practices which, *inter alia*, enable public officials in public sector organizations to be held accountable for their decisions and their actions. During the education process two fundamental questions must be addressed: first, what are relevant systems of accountability within the context of public sector organizations in Malawi, and, second, how are effective and sustainable systems of accountability to be realized in public sector organizations in Malawi.

The thesis of this chapter is that the Christian church is well placed to play a leading role in this education process. Accountability is both a theme within the Christian scriptures and a practice in the early Christian church. Evidence of this accountability in the Christian tradition is presented in section 3; to place this evidence within a theoretical framework, Soft Systems Methodology (SSM)[14] is used to present both a conceptual model of accountability and a conceptual

---

[13] Kenneth R. Ross, "A Practical Theology of Power for the New Malawi", in Ross (ed.), *God, People and Power in Malawi*, p. 252.

[14] Peter Checkland and Jim Scholes, *Soft Systems Methodology in Action*. Chichester: Wiley. 1990.

system for realizing accountability in section 2. Finally, in section 4, some factors impeding the realization of accountability are discussed.

2. Systems of Accountability

There is little disagreement over the meaning of the adjective *accountable* from which the term *accountability* is derived:

> responsible to someone or for some action;[15]
> responsible; having to explain or defend one's action or conduct;[16]
> bound to give account, responsible; explicable.[17]

At face value, from these definitions, the accountability of public officials in public sector organizations might be seen simplistically as the right of individual citizens to castigate public officials for their failings; in short to blame the public officials for those decisions and actions which adversely affect the citizens. Thus, a mother might blame a public official in the Ministry of Education when her daughter is denied admission to a particular secondary school and might blame a public official in the Ministry of Health when that same daughter is denied an immediate consultation with a specialist. However, this is a very narrow view of accountability inasmuch as it fails to take into account the systemic context surrounding the decisions made and the actions taken by the public officials in a public sector organisation, in particular the 'whys' and 'wherefores' of those decisions and actions. This view is also undemocratic since it reduces accountability to a contest between competing citizens; potentially this could lead to public officials in a public sector organisation being accountable only to those citizens with the most 'power', be that political, religious or financial.

So what is accountability? A broader view of accountability which takes into account some of the systemic context is evident in the management literature, particularly that related to management by

---

[15] *Collins Dictionary of the English Language,* London: Collins. 1979.

[16] *Chambers 21st Century Dictionary,* Edinburgh: Chambers, 1996.

[17] *The Concise Oxford Dictionary of Current English,* Oxford: Oxford University Press. 1976.

objectives. For example, Armstrong links the accountability of managers in organizations with issues of responsibility and authority:

> [Managers] have full *responsibility* for what they and their department and unit does. They are delegated *authority* to make decisions within certain parameters. And they are *accountable* to their superiors for the results they have obtained.[18]

Implicit within this view of accountability is the concept that an organisation has objectives, and that the decisions made and the actions taken by managers within that organisation should be consistent with those objectives. For example, an objective of the Ministry of Health might be to reduce infant mortality. The accountability of the public officials in the Ministry of Health relates to how their decision making and action taking has helped to achieve this objective; that is, to what extent their decision making and action taking has contributed to reducing infant mortality.

But organizational objectives are not 'given', as Walsham states:

> The view which attributes corporate goals to an organisation is incorrect - only the people who together constitute the organisation have goals.[19]

Thus, there is some group in the organisation, probably the most powerful, who have set the organizational objectives against which the outcomes of decisions and actions will be assessed and to whom the decision makers and action takers are accountable. For public sector organizations this group is likely to be the politicians. And in many organizations it is possible to go back beyond this powerful group to ask to whom this powerful group are themselves accountable; in other words, from whom do this powerful group derive their power? In the case of public sector organizations in a democracy, the politicians derive their power from the electorate, to whom they are accountable through the ballot box.

---

[18] Michael Armstrong, *Management Processes and Functions,* London: Institute of Personnel and Development, 1995, p. 81.

[19] Geoff Walsham, "The Application of IT in Organisations: Some Trends and Issues", *Information Technology for Development,* Vol. $^4/_2$ (1989), p. 636.

So, to whom are the public officials in a public sector organisation accountable for their decisions and their actions? And how are these public officials to be held accountable for their decisions and their actions? The answers to these questions may now seem not as straightforward as was first imagined. These fundamental questions must be answered before the public officials can be held to account. In this section, systemic answers to these questions are explored through the use of SSM's root definitions:[20]

A root definition in SSM expresses the essential purpose of a particular system of human activity in terms of six elements (referred to by the mnemonic *CATWOE*):

- C: the customers or clients who are the beneficiaries (or victims) of a transformation process *T*
- A: the actors who undertake *T*
- T: the process of transforming an input entity into an output entity
- W: the worldview which makes *T* meaningful in context
- O: the owner of *T* who could stop it
- E: the environmental constraints outside *T* which are taken as given

In a participatory democracy there are at least two distinct systems of human activity, one at the level of broad political intentions and the other the level of specific purposes consistent with those political intentions. At the higher level of broad political intentions the system of human activity is concerned with legitimation of policy; for example in a Ministry of Health a possible transformation process could be *the need for popular policies on health and health-related issues to improve the health of citizens = => that need met*. The six CATWOE elements of a system of human activity for this transformation process could include the following:

---

[20] Checkland and Scholes, *Soft Systems*. pp. 35-37.

C: citizens

A: elected politicians

T: the need for popular policies on health and health-related issues to improve the health of citizens = => that need met

W: improvement of the health of citizens is an important political goal

O: citizens

E: appropriate resources can be made available to formulate popular policies

In this system of human activity, the owners (citizens) give the actors (elected politicians) authority to define policies consistent with the shared worldview; in a participatory democracy the actors might be expected to consult with the customers (citizens), through mechanisms such as the publication of green papers, to determine what policies are most appropriate. Thus, at the very least, the elected politicians are accountable to the citizens for the ways in which the decisions they make and the actions they take contribute to meeting the need for policies consistent with the shared worldview.

At the lower level of specific purposes, the system of human activity is concerned with the implementation of policy; examples of four possible transformation processes *T* in the Ministry of Health could include the following:

sick patient ==> cured patient

a local population ==> that population more healthy

need to reduce infant mortality ==> that need met

need for information about health and health related issues ==> that need met

Using the last example of a transformation process given above, the six *CATWOE* elements of the root definition might be as follows:

- C: the local population, in particular those members of historically disadvantaged groups who have previously not been served by the state health sector
- A: the public officials in the state health sector responsible for public service delivery
- T: need for information about health and health-related issues = => that need met
- W: improved access to information about health and health-related issues allows the local population to exercise more choice about their life styles, thereby improving the local population's health and reducing the cost caused to society by unnecessarily poor life styles
- O: the elected politicians responsible for the Ministry of Health
- E: information about health and health-related issues on topics relevant to the local population is available and is accessible to the local population

In this system of human activity, the owners (elected politicians) give the actors (public officials) authority to effect the transformation; thus the public officials are accountable to the elected politicians. However, indirectly through the relationships of delegated authority between owners and actors in both systems of human activity, the public officials are also accountable to the citizens for the extent to which their decisions and their actions cause the need for information about health and health-related issues to be met. Thus, two dimensions of accountability are immediately evident: *downward accountability* in which the public officials are accountable to the public and *upward accountability* in which the public officials are accountable to the politicians.[21]

---

[21] Ewan Ferlie, Lynn Ashbumer, Louise Fitzgerald, Andrew Pettigrew, *The New Public Management in Action*, Oxford: Oxford University Press, 1996, pp. 202-215.

A third dimension of accountability - *outward accountability* - is evident from the environmental constraints surrounding the transformation process. Although the root definition does not indicate *how* the actors are to undertake the transformation process, in practice it is likely that there will be several environmental constraints on the decisions they may make and the actions they may take. Examples of common environmental constraints include legal, ethical, moral and cultural restrictions. Implicit therefore in the sixth *CATWOE* element, environmental constraints, is a set of restrictions which must be observed by the actors in their decision making and action taking. The actors, in this case the public officials in a public sector organisation, are accountable to the 'regulators' of these restrictions, in particular the judiciary, professional associations and, in some nation states, the religious authorities.

The three dimensions of accountability to which the public officials in a public sector organisation are subject are shown in the diagramme below:

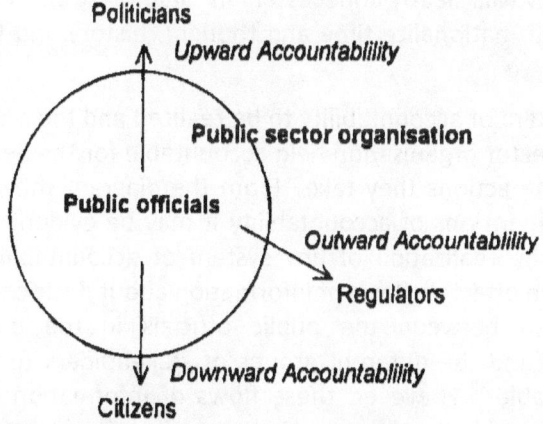

With three different dimensions of accountability, it is inevitable that there will be occasions, perhaps frequent, when the public officials in a public sector organisation are simultaneously subject to multiple accountabilities for their decisions and their actions. In particular, there is the distinct possibility that these multiple accountabilities may lead to conflicts of accountability in which a decision made or an action taken to satisfy the interests of one group of stakeholders does so at the expense of another group of stakeholders.

During the era of Kamuzu Banda, *upward accountability* was clearly the dominant dimension: the public officials in public sector organizations in Malawi were accountable to the Malawi Congress Party, and ultimately to the Life President himself, from which the public sector organizations derived their legitimacy. Numerous examples of this *upward accountability* in the Banda era exist: the requirement that female employees in the public sector organizations, Kamuzu's *Mbumba,* should attend regular practices of traditional dancing during work time, and the use of government vehicles to transport *Mbumba* to Party rallies are but two. In sharp contrast, the dimension of *outward accountability* was severely limited by the restrictions on the freedom of association and by Kamuzu Banda's own statements that encouraged members of certain public sector organizations, in particular the Malawi Young Pioneers, to view themselves above the law. Moreover, the dimension of *downward accountability* was clearly unnecessary in "an omniscient regime with a divine right to nationalize time and thought, history and the political will".[22]

How is a system of accountability to be realized and the public officials of a public sector organisation held accountable for the decisions they make and the actions they take? From the diagram shown above of the three dimensions of accountability it may be evident that, at the very least, the realization of any system of accountability depends crucially upon effective flows of information about decisions made and actions taken between the public officials in the public sector organisation and the different groups of stakeholders to whom they are accountable.[23] However, these flows of information do not just happen by accident; they must be designed, implemented and maintained if accountability is to be realized. Moreover, effective

---

[22] P.T. Zeleza, "Totalitarian Power and Censorship in *Malawi", Southern Africa Political and Economic Monthly,* Vol. 8/11 (August 1995), p. 33.

[23] Armstrong, *Management Processes and Functions,* p. 80.

systems of accountability are more than just systems that disseminate information. Here, SSM's activity models are used to explore the realization of systems of accountability.[24]

SSM's root definitions are used to derive one or more activity models. Each activity model, if realized, would achieve the transformation process described in the root definition. At the highest level, an activity model comprises four distinct activities (see diagram below). At the core of the activity model is the activity representing the transformation process itself; this activity transforms the input entity into the output entity. The *monitoring activity* gathers information about the output entity produced by the transformation process. This information is compared against criteria previously defined by the

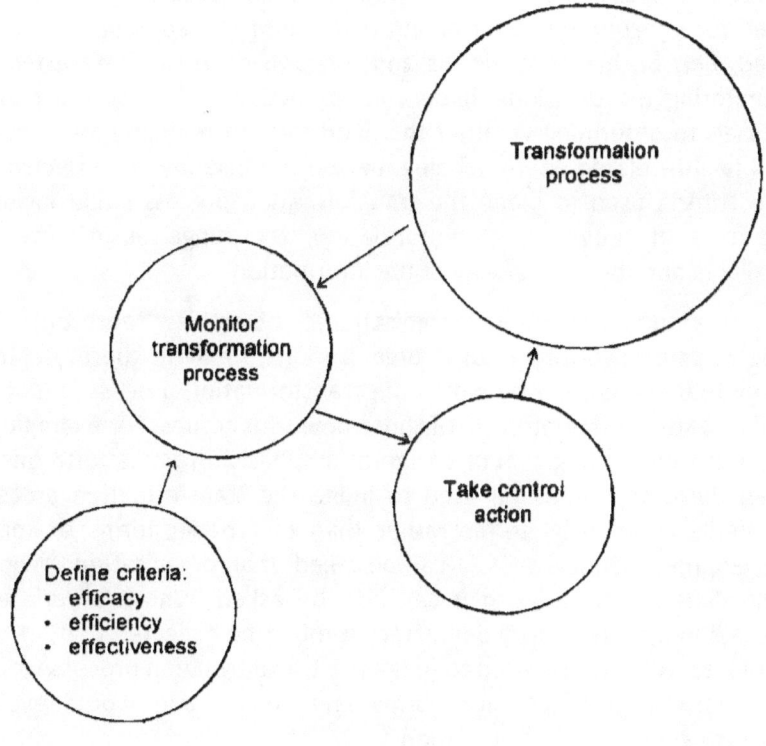

---

[24] Checkland and Scholes, *Soft Systems,* pp. 38-41.

standards activity. Finally, the *control activity* decides upon and then ensures implementation of corrective action on the transformation process based on the result of this comparison. Thus, the *monitoring activity* and the *control activity* represent a 'feedback loop' in which information about the output entity produced by the transformation process is fed back, to stimulate control of the transformation process itself.

The monitoring activity, the standards activity and the control activity of the activity model provide a model for realizing a system of accountability for the transformation process. A group of stakeholders to whom the public officials in a public sector organisation are accountable can use these three activities to hold the public officials to account. For example, using the transformation process given earlier, *need for information about health and health-related issues ==> that need met*, both the politicians and the public may be interested in monitoring the decisions made and the actions taken by the public officials to determine whether the need for information about health and health-related issues is being met both efficiently and effectively. The criteria used to judge the transformation process could include the cost of providing the information, the range of information available and the accessibility of the information.

As indicated previously, organizational objectives represent the interests of powerful groups in organizations; similarly, therefore, it is likely that the criteria by which the transformation process is judged will also reflect the interests of those powerful groups. For example, if the most powerful group places great emphasis on 'value for money', then the criteria may be used to judge the transformation process primarily in financial terms rather than in broader terms of social development. Thus, just as it can be asked of an organisation, 'Whose objectives are these?', so it can also be asked 'Whose criteria are these?' In a participatory democracy it might be expected that, at the very least, the criteria used to judge the transformation process would take into account popular norms and values, and would evolve through a process of participation.

The criteria need not relate solely to the output produced by the transformation process. The criteria may also relate to the broader outcomes of the transformation process or indeed to the inputs of the transformation process. Similarly, the control activity need not relate solely to the transformation process; other aspects that can be controlled include both the inputs to the transformation process and the objectives and criteria of the transformation process itself; changing either of the latter would be expected to lead to changes in the transformation process itself. Indeed, the whole cycle of transformation, monitor and control can be thought of as an organizational learning process in which *problems* detected in the transformation process become *opportunities* for learning how to improve the transformation process.[25]

Clearly there are a number of important issues which must be addressed if a system of accountability is to be realized. First and foremost a system of accountability is inextricably bound up with the monitor and control activities - the review process - that are an expected part of any transformation process occurring in an organisation. Without a suitable review process, the transformation process, once initiated, cannot be 'kept on track'; the existence of the review process assumes that there are clear objectives for the transformation process to achieve, and that suitable performance indicators exist which can be used to 'measure' the trajectory of the transformation process with respect to these objectives. Second, a system of accountability is a process which requires the active participation of the stakeholders. For the participation to occur, the stakeholders require information about the performance indicators which they can understand and require opportunities to exercise control over the transformation process. This has two implications: that for the information disseminated to stakeholders to be useful it must be as relevant, complete and timely as possible, and that the dissemination of information to stakeholders does not in itself realize a system of accountability. Realizing a system of accountability has,

---

[25] Penny *Hackett, Introduction to Training,* London: Institute of Personnel and Development, 1997, pp. 152-167.

therefore, a cost - the cost of gathering data about performance indicators, the analysis of these data, the subsequent dissemination of this information and the potential intervention of stakeholders in the transformation process.

All this suggests that a system of accountability does not come into existence by accident, but is the product of a process of development and implementation. In many organizations the realization of new systems of accountability has been accompanied by the introduction of new information systems to manage the gathering of data about performance indicators, the analysis of these data and the subsequent dissemination of this information.[26] The realization of these new information systems is often through the introduction of information technology. However, of itself, the introduction of information technology into an organisation does not increase the accountability of the organisation to its groups of stakeholders. In particular, it is far from clear that extension of access to the Internet into previously disadvantaged communities, increases democracy and accountability.[27] Indeed, the inappropriate use of information technology in an organisation may be a barrier to accountability, for example by reducing access to information to those stakeholders who are computer literate or by serving the interests of one group of stakeholders who can provide the necessary resources to develop and implement such information systems at the expense of other groups of stakeholders who have no access to such resources.

3. Accountability: a Christian Theme and a Christian Practice

It might be considered unlikely that the concept of accountability which has risen to prominence in the last two decades of the

---

[26] Brian Blundell and Alex Murdock, *Managing in the Public Sector*, Oxford: Butterworth-Heinemann, 1997, pp. 47-48.

[27] Vivian Sobchack, "Democratic Franchise and the Electronic Frontier", in Ziauddin Sardar and Jerome R. Ravetz (eds.), *Cybetfutures: Culture and Politics on the Information Superhighway*. London: Pluto Press, 1996, pp. 77-89.

twentieth century should also be found as a theme in the Christian scriptures and as a practice in the early Christian church. Although the direct evidence for accountability as a theme and as a practice is relatively limited, by taking a systemic approach it is possible to gather indirect evidence which points to accountability.

There are just four places in the Christian scriptures where the phrase 'give account' occurs: Matthew 12:36, Luke 16:2, Romans 14:12 and I Peter 4:5. With the exception of the occurrence in Luke's Gospel (which forms part of the parable of the shrewd manager), the remaining three are all concerned with the future judgement of humanity by God. It is very clear from these three occurrences that humans are directly accountable to God for their thoughts, words and deeds. Furthermore, it is clear from the occurrence in the apostle Paul's letter to the Romans that it is not only the nonbeliever who has to give account - something which is evident from the other two occurrences - but also the Christian believer. Of course, this sense of the accountability of each man and woman to God touches the heart of the Christian message: although God blames us for our wrong doing He goes beyond this to provide a way forward - "Once you were enemies of God ... But now He has reconciled you ..." (Colossians 1:21-22).

The context surrounding the occurrence of the phrase 'give account' in the Letter to the Romans bears further examination since it also indicates that a believer may not hold a fellow believer to account - "therefore let us stop passing judgement on one another" - and, going further, that a believer should avoid acting in a way which hinders a fellow believer - "make up your mind not to put any stumbling block or obstacle in your brother's way" - suggesting that the believer should avoid behaviour which could encourage another believer to want to hold him accountable. Of course, associated with this denial of accountability between fellow believers is Jesus' own injunction to His disciples to forgive one another (Matthew 18:21-22). The process of reconciliation between God and men and women is the model of the process of reconciliation between fellow believers.

Indirect evidence in the Christian scriptures for accountability can be inferred from the relationships involving deferred authority. Three such relationships are examined here: that between God and Jesus Christ, that between Jesus Christ and the apostles, and that between God and Christian believers. Each of these relationships is explored using SSM's root definitions to investigate the possible accountability relationships between the different groups of stakeholders.

Supremely Jesus Christ is an example of delegated authority, authority derived from God Himself. In terms of a system of human activity, the six *CATWOE* elements of a root definition to describe Jesus' earthly ministry could include the following:

- C: The human race; more specifically, the men, women and children of 1st century Palestine
- A: Jesus Christ
- T: The need to reconcile the human race with God = => that need met
- W: The human race is separated from God and needs reconciling with Him if it is to enjoy His favour
- O: God
- E: Only God can bring about the reconciliation between the human race and Himself

To whom was Jesus accountable during His earthly ministry? Clearly He was accountable to God: at His baptism God shows his acceptance of Jesus (Mark 1:11) and Jesus Himself indicates His acceptance of this accountability relationship by choosing to do God's will (John 5:30), even to death itself (Mark 14:36).

Was Jesus accountable to the men, women and children of 1st century Palestine? To investigate this further, it is useful to subdivide this group of stakeholders into the disciples, the religious leaders, and the 'ordinary' people. Evidence that Jesus did not hold himself accountable to the disciples can be inferred from His rebuking of Peter (Mark 8:31-33). The religious leaders of the day - the Pharisees and the Sadducees - clearly wanted to make Jesus accountable to them, but He refused to be accountable to them (Mark 2:23-28). What is particularly interesting in the exchanges between Jesus and the religious leaders is the way in which He undermines the criteria they use for judging Him. Indeed, from the perspective of systems of human activity, it appears that the religious leaders have appropriated for their own use the criteria that only God Himself can use; that is, they have 'borrowed' criteria from a different system for use in their own system. It is difficult to find evidence to suggest that the 'ordinary' people attempted to hold Jesus accountable, or that He held Himself accountable to them. There is of course considerable evidence that throughout Jesus' ministry He healed the 'ordinary' people, but there is nothing to suggest that this was motivated by a sense of compulsion arising from accountability rather than by His love for them.

The apostles were given delegated authority by Jesus both during His earthly ministry (Mark 3:13-19) and after His resurrection (Matthew 28:16-20). In terms of a system of human activity, the six *CATWOE* elements of a root definition to describe the apostles' ministry after receiving the Great Commission could include the following:

- *C:* The human race; more specifically, the men, women and children of 1st century Palestine
- *A:* The apostles
- *T:* The need to make disciples = => that need met
- *W:* The human race is separated from God and needs reconciling with Him if it is to enjoy His favour
- *O:* God
- *E:* Only God can bring about the reconciliation between the human race and Himself

The apostle Paul explains the accountability relationship surrounding an apostle (1 Corinthians 4:1-5): apostles are God's servants and are accountable to Him, not to believers (or even non-believers). In the letter to the Galatians Paul recounts that he rebuked the apostle Peter (Galatians 2:1114) for his inconsistency regarding Jewish traditions and Christian practice. This suggests that the apostles were accountable to one another, but it is worth noting that the criteria for this accountability is that of "acting in line with the truth of the gospel". The apostles also delegated their authority to others, in particular the seven 'helpers' (Acts 6:1-7). The limit of the delegated authority is clearly stated in verse 2 - "the daily distribution of food".

Finally, through the gifts of the Holy Spirit, Christian believers have been given a form of delegated authority by God (1 Corinthians 12:7-11). Later on in this same letter, the apostle Paul makes this delegated authority clearer (1 Corinthians 12:27-31) - "you are the body of Christ and each one of you is part of it". So to whom are Christian believers accountable? From the direct evidence it is already clear that believers are accountable to God Himself. And it is clear that God does not require complex information systems to discover the outcomes of the decisions made and the actions taken by believers as the story of Ananias and Sapphira graphically indicates (Acts 5:1-11). While the indirect evidence suggests that believers are not accountable to one another, Jesus does indicate that a believer who has been sinned against can bring this to the attention of the sinning believer (Matthew 18:15-17), while Paul instructs Timothy to admonish publicly elders who have sinned (1 Timothy 5:19-20). The purpose of this admonition is not to apportion blame but to restore believers to the fellowship (Galatians 6:1).

The criteria for accountability are summed up by Jesus as "love the Lord your God with all your heart and with all your soul and with all your mind and with all your strength" and "love your neighbour as yourself" (Mark 12:29-31). Additionally, He and the apostles warn about judging fellow believers - that the criteria used by one believer to judge other believers will also be used by God to judge that believer (Luke 6:37; James 4:1112).

The main conclusion that can be drawn from this evidence is that accountability is a theme with which the Christian church should be familiar. First, if the Christian church in Malawi has been true to its apostolic foundation in the Christian scriptures, then accountability is a contemporary practice, not only through the confession and repentance of individual believers but also through the discipline of those believers holding positions of responsibility in the Christian church. Second, that the criteria for accountability are not arbitrary and are not determined by individual believers; they are based on God's own exacting standards. Third, that accountability for the individual believer is not so much about blame but is about a process of self-learning: recognizing sin and, with the Holy Spirit's help, identifying ways to avoid it in the future.

4. Barriers to Realizing Accountability

Three categories of barriers to the realization of systems of accountability can be identified: conceptual barriers, socio-political barriers and technical barriers.

Failure to perceive accountability from a systemic perspective will inevitably lead to the important issues of accountability being explored in insufficient depth. Answers to fundamental questions such as who is accountable to whom and what criteria are to be used may be partial or flawed. The monitor and control activities required to realize accountability may be poorly planned or absent. As a result there is a 'gap' between the rhetoric of accountability and the reality of accountability: claims are made that systems are accountable but in reality the accountability is partial. For example, lack of clarity over the objectives of a system may make it difficult or impossible to agree on meaningful criteria for accountability.

The social-political interests of powerful groups of stakeholders may subvert a system of accountability through the imposition of criteria consistent with a particular set of objectives which are not universally held, or by deliberately restricting the information that is disseminated to other groups of stakeholders and the opportunities available to other groups to exercise control over the system. Again, this can lead to a 'gap' between the rhetoric of accountability and the reality of accountability.

Finally, the information disseminated to stakeholders must be in a form that is useful to them, enabling them to plan control activities. Clearly if the stakeholders are unable to understand the information made available to them, and do not understand the procedures of the control activity, there is again a 'gap' between the rhetoric of accountability and the reality of accountability.

Part Two:

Social Science

6 The Rights of the Child in the Christian Context

Garton S. Kamchedzera

[Jesus said to them], "Let the little children come to me, and do not hinder them, for the kingdom of heaven belongs to such as these."... And he took the children in his arms, put his hands on them and blessed them (Mark 10:14-16).

And whoever welcomes a little child like this in my name welcomes me (Matthew 18:5).

Introduction

Special human rights for children are necessary, not only because children are people too. The more important justification is that children are vulnerable and dependent people.[1] There is international consensus that such rights are necessary. The Convention on the Rights of the Child 1989 (CRC) has enjoyed an unprecedented endorsement in international law making and application.[2] Regional groups and states have taken steps to adopt and implement the international standards that are contained in the CRC.[3]

---

[1] Garton Kamchedzera, "Access to Property, the Social Trust and the Rights of the Child", PhD, University of Cambridge, 1996, p. 38. The work is forthcoming as a monograph.

[2] The CRC was adopted unanimously by the General Assembly on 20 November 1989 and received a first day record response on 26 January 1990 when sixty-one states signed it. On 2 September of the same year, the CRC entered into force and a World Summit on the Survival, Protection and Development of Children, attended by most world political leaders called for the CRC's "earliest possible ratification". There are only the USA and Somalia still to ratify the Convention.

[3] The Organisation of African Unity: the Charter on the Rights and Welfare of the Child 1990; the Organisation of American States: the Additional Protocol to the OAS Convention on Human Rights in the Area of Economic. Social and

The Convention's wide support has been possible because of its incontestable aims. The Convention has two main aims. The first is to facilitate the survival, development, participation and protection of all children.[4] The second aim is to achieve intra- and inter-generational equity by guaranteeing the security of subsequent generations through the improvement of the welfare of present children.[5] This chapter notes some controversy about the rights of the child. It explains the ideological foundation of the rights of the child as enshrined in the CRC and examines its aims and strategic principles. The discussion occurs within the context of Christianity as a discourse and a practice. The founding principle is that both the CRC and Christianity imply and advocate the social trust and not contract doctrine. This chapter further observes that the rights of the child, as a discourse, poses challenges to Christianity as practiced in many churches. The conclusion is that Christianity and the rights of the child are mutually reinforcing.

Confusion about the Rights of the Child

Despite the Convention's wide acceptance, the use of the term "right" has often caused controversy.[6] It is sometimes questioned whether

---

Cultural Rights, 28 *I.L.M.* 161 (1994)+, especially Article 16; the European Parliament: The European Draft Convention on the Exercise of Children's Rights, *The International Journal of Children's Rights*, 3. 134-143. Countries with constitutions reflecting the CRC include Bolivia. Brazil, Colombia, Malawi, Namibia and the Republic of South Africa. Uganda has adopted a CRC-based children statute and there are strong indications that many countries will enact similar laws.

[4] UN Centre for Human Rights and UNICEF, "Overview: The Convention on the Rights of the Child", 'Information Kit', New York, United Nations Centre for Human Rights and UNICEF, 1990.

[5] On Intergenerational equity: Edith Brown Weiss, *In Fairness to Future Generations and Sustainable Development: International Law, Common Patrimony, and Intergenerational Equity*, New York: Transnational Publishers, 1989, especially chapters 1 to 4.

[6] W. Lucy, "Controversy About Children's Rights", in D. Freestone (ed.), *Children and the Law: Essays in Honour of Professor H.K. Bevan,* Hull: Hull

children can realistically be subjects of rights. Proponents of this argument assert that rights in history have been a result of struggles. Even some strong advocates of the rights of the child accept that rights "of course, are never given but fought for".[7] O'Neil powerfully argued that it is more helpful to emphasize the obligations of adults rather than the rights of the child.[8] Parents, including some Christians, have often wondered whether the language of rights does not polarize children against their nurturers. It was Hafen who worried about "abandoning youth to their rights".[9] In the United States of America certain conservative Christians, among others, have prevented the ratification of the CRC not only because it is a UN document, but also because certain parents feel threatened by what is perceived as a child rights project.[10] In African and Asian traditions, the cultural relevance of the rights of the child is questioned. The language of rights is, further, not common in the Christian Church.

There are two main reasons for the controversy about the rights of the child. The first is failure to appreciate that the rights in the CRC are a codification of historically and philosophically different categories of need-based rights and that, as such, the categories of human rights are never closed. The second is a failure to comprehend the nature, extent and purpose of the rights of the child.

University Press, 1990, at 213; M. King, "Book Review", *International Journal of Law and the Family,* 7(1993), 139-141.

[7] M.D.A. Freeman, "Taking Children's Rights More Seriously", in Philip Alston, Stephen Parker and John Seymour (eds.), *Children, Rights and the Law,* Oxford: Clarendon Press, 1992, pp. 52-71.

[8] Onora O'Neil, "Children's Rights and Children's Lives", in Alston, Parker, and Seymour (eds.), *Children, Rights, and the Law,* at pp. 24-42, especially pp. 35-40.

[9] Bruce Hafen, "Children's Liberation and the New Egalitarianism: Some Reservations About Abandoning Youth to their Rights" (1976), *Brigham Young University Law Review,* 605.

[10] The USA has signed the CRC, but it will require concerted effort and education to achieve ratification of the document under USA law.

The Dominance of Contract Doctrine or Liberal Individualism

There are different discourses of human rights. The rights of the child cannot be explained by the current dominant human rights discourse which is based on contract doctrine or liberal individualism. That conception places emphasis on civil and political rights as well as individual autonomy.[11] Christianity, for its part, has long existed in a context dominated by superior status and contract doctrines. Jesus Christ's social ministry involved advocacy for the rights or needs of the weak or marginalized members of society.[12] In the incarnation, Jesus opted for meekness[13] and identified Himself with the weak, the poor and the oppressed.[14] Patriarchical-based superior status in the then Jewish society, for example, resulted in inequities against women, certain sick people, and the poor. Alexander, for example, notes that the fatherless, widows, and foreigners each have in the Bible "about forty verses that command justice for them"[15]

Often, the practice of Christianity has played a challenging, transforming or compensatory role against superior status and contract doctrines. In Europe, for example, Bossy has observed that

---

[11] Issa Shivji, *The Concept of Human Rights in Africa,* London: Codesria, 1989, especially chapters 1 and 2.

[12] E.g., His statement of His job description at the start of His public ministry in the synagogue at Nazareth when He read from Isaiah (Luke 4:18-19); Other many passages include Matthew 25:31-46, Matthew 11:2-6.

[13] Paul saw that as a challenge for every Christian: Philippians 2:5-11.

[14] The salvation news was prophesied and announced as the birth of a child (Isaiah 9:6-7 and Luke 1:26-38, among other biblical passages); His parents were too poor to bring a proper purification offering (cf: Luke 2:24 and Leviticus 12:6-8), He became a refugee and then an immigrant in Galilee (Matthew 2:13-15 and 19-23), He had no home of His own during His Ministry (Matthew 8:20).

[15] Quoted by Ronald J. Sider, *Rich Christians in an Age of Hunger: A Biblical Study,* Downers Grove: Inter-Varsity Press, 1984, at 70.

Christianity achieved a "social miracle" when Christians focussed on communitarianism amidst social inequalities.[16]

The Deficiencies of Contract Doctrine

The Enlightenment promoted contract doctrine. The dominant discourse in Anglo-American and European thought became social contract and Locke[17] and Rousseau[18] were, then, influential. The "movement of progressive societies", observed Maine, had "hitherto been a movement from Status to Contract"[19] The individual, rather than the family, was regarded as the "unit of which civil laws took account"[20] The individualization of society has since increased and social cohesion is under threat.[21] Wills, reason, actions and individual autonomy are central to a contract-based conception of rights. The contract-based conception of rights, also referred to as a Kantian conception,[22] insists that a right "comprehends the whole of the conditions under which the voluntary actions of one person can be harmonized in reality with the voluntary actions of every other person, according to universal law of freedom"[23] Kant required a right to co-

---

[16] See John Bossy, *Christianity in the West: 1400-1700,* Oxford: Oxford University Press, 1985, chapter 4.

[17] John Locke, *Two Treatises of Government,* edited by Mark Goldie, London: Everyman, 1993.

[18] Jacques Rousseau, *The Social Contract; and Discourses,* translated by G.D.H. Cole, revised and augmented by J.H. Brumfit and John C. Hall, London: Dent, 1990.

[19] Henry Summer Maine, *Ancient Law: Its Connections with Early History of Society and its Relation to Modern Ideas,* London: John Murray, 1906, at 174.

[20] *Ibid.*

[21] Michael Schluter and David Lee, *The R Factor,* London: Hodder and Stoughton, 1993 and Lawrence M. Friedman, *The Republic of Choice,* Cambridge, Mass.: Harvard University Press, 1990.

[22] Kamchedzera, "Access to Property", at 38.

[23] Immanuel Kant, "The Science of Right", in M.J. Adler (ed.), *Great Books of the Western World: Kant,* Chicago: Encyclopedia Britannica, 1990 at 397-398.

exist with "freedom of the will of each and all in action"[24] The aim of a contract-based conception of rights is to achieve liberty, equality and egalitarianism.

Liberty and equality are deficient as processes that can facilitate human rights for all human beings. Regarding children, for example, only those with sufficient mental, physical and economic capacity would qualify as subjects of human rights. Theories of rights that exclude many children, Campbell has correctly remarked, manifest "intellectual and moral limitations"[25] because children are human beings too. Rights are "valuable resources"[26] or "political trumps"[27] and it seems unfair that some should be regarded as without human rights. MacCormick has strongly argued that the philosophical problems encountered by conventional theories of rights, when such theories are applied to children, illustrate that children's rights pose a good test case for any "credible theory of rights"[28] A credible theory of rights therefore must not insist that a right holder should be able necessarily to make claims and exercise choices as some proponents of child rights have posited.[29] It is also not feasible to expect most children to fight for their rights. To require children to fight for their rights is to conflate "the rights of the child" with "rights of children"[30]

---

[24] Ibid., at 398.

[25] Tom D. Campbell, "The Rights of the Minor: as a Person, as a Child, as a Juvenile, as a Future Adult", in Alston, Parker, and Seymour (eds.), *Children, Rights and the Law,* 1-23, at 4.

[26] R. Wasserstrom, "Rights, Human Rights and Racial Discrimination" (1964), *Journal of Philosophy,* 628, at 628-629.

[27] Rights entitle an individual to be treated with dignity even if such treatment is not utilitarian: Ronald Dworkin, *Taking Rights Seriously,* London: Duckworth, 1977, at xi and chapter 7.

[28] Neil McCormick, *Legal Right and Social Democracy,* Oxford: Oxford University Press, 1982, at 154.

[29] One such proponent: John Eekelaar, "The Importance of Thinking that Children Have Rights", in Alston, Parker, and Seymour (eds.), *Children, Rights, and the Law,* 221-235, at 228.

[30] Kamchedzera, "Access to Property", at 46-47.

A child might possess legally enforceable rights despite difficulty to enforce similar rights as group rights for children. It is also useful to appreciate that political struggles for rights by oppressed groups have, in many cases, not involved exclusively the oppressed. Some men, for example, have participated in the struggle for women's rights.

Contract doctrine has in any case been limited by social trust notions to mitigate injustice. Even Adam Smith, the influential free market advocate, recognized that freedom of contract is limited by the demands of law and justice. Every person, Smith wrote, "so long as he does not violate the laws of justice" ought to be "left perfectly free to pursue his own interests in his own way".[31] The Copenhagen Declaration on Social Development calls for "appropriate programmes that would entitle and enable people living in poverty and the disadvantaged" to participate "fully and productively in the economy and society".[32] Every jurisdiction has laws that control competition for access to resources, access to markets, contract relations, the protection of third parties, and the protection of the public.[33] For children, altruistic actions from other social units are necessary.

Christianity is insistent on the importance of altruism as a manifestation of faith.[34] Individualism though still dominates the wide operative context of Christianity. The Enlightenment observation is still valid that the child is still regarded as lacking in the "first essential of an engagement by Con-tract".[35] The Parable of the Good Samaritan remains a challenge for society to address the vulnerability and dependency of children. The importance of the child in Christianity

---

[31] Adam Smith, *Wealth of Nations: An Inquiry into the Nature and Causes of the Wealth of Nations*, ed. E. Cannan, London: Methuen, 1930, at 184.

[32] A/CONF.166/9 19 April 1995, Commitment 1(e).

[33] Kamchedzera, "Access to Property", pp. 250-262.

[34] E.g., the Biblical neighbour principle (Luke 10:25-37), the exhortation to love one another (John 13:34-37).

[35] This is Maine's phrase: Maine, *Ancient Law,* at 173.

cannot be overemphasized. Jesus identified the child as the model of the faith attitude and practice that is required in Christianity.[36]

Rights and Responsibilities

The relationship between rights and responsibilities also causes confusion and it is likely to generate greater confusion within the Christian Church where the importance of personal and collective responsibility is stressed. Regarding the rights of the child, the confusion has been exacerbated by certain child rights advocates who emphasize rights alone. Rights and duties, however, are interdependent. For every person's right, there is a corresponding duty on another person, group or institution.[37] Rights, further, are not unlimited. They are limited by the human rights of others. An individual's human right must be curtailed when it begins to infringe the human rights of another. The enjoyment responsibility for every right holder commences when the exercise or use of that right might conflict with another person's or subject's right. Too much rights talk without appropriate emphasis on responsibilities is dangerous and confusing. Glendon, who is echoed by Etzioni[38] among others, has criticized excessive "rights talk" in the USA because in

> its essence concerning responsibilities, it seems to condone acceptance of the benefits of living in a democratic social welfare state, without accepting the corresponding personal and civic obligations. In its relentless individualism, it fosters a climate that is inhospitable to society's losers, and that systematically disadvantages care takers and dependents, young and old. In its neglect of civil society, it undermines the principal seedbeds of civic and personal virtue.[39]

---

[36] E.g., Matthew 18:2.

[37] Wesley Newcomb Hohfeld, Some Fundamental Legal Conceptions as Applied to Judicial Reasoning", 23, *Yale Law Journal (1913-14)*, 16.

[38] Amitai Etzioni, *The Spirit of Community: Rights, Responsibilities and the Communitarian Agenda*, New York: Crown, 1993.

[39] Mary Ann Glendon, *Rights Talk: The Impoverishment of Political Discourse*, New York: The Free Press, 1991, at 14.

The arguments in favour of responsibilities, as Eekelaar[40] and Howard[41] have pointed out, do not necessarily negate the importance of rights for individuals and communities. Communities are composed of individuals who interact with each other and each of whom has separate entitlements. A community, further, might have class rights.[42] The African Charter on the Rights and Welfare of the Child unlike the CRC, stipulates that children too, have responsibilities subject to age and ability.[43] The context of Christianity also requires responsibilities for children to their parents.

Children are required in Christianity to obey and honour their parents.[44] The concept of the rights of the child is therefore acceptable in the context of Christianity so long as able children take up appropriate responsibilities.

The Gradual Emerging Need for a Social Trust

A century has passed since Maine made his celebrated statement that "progressive societies" had moved from status to contract. There has since then been a gradual movement from contract to social trust. Political buzzwords such as transparency, accountability and good governance all imply some elements of a trust.[45] The rights of the child provide a very good illustration of the necessity of the social trust. The

---

[40] John Eekelaar, "Family Justice: Ideal or Illusion? Family Law and Communitarian Values" (1995), *Current Legal Problems*, 191 at 194.

[41] Rhoda E. Howard, *Human Rights and the Search for Community*, Boulder: Westview Press, 1995, especially chapter 8.

[42] Will Kymlicka, *Liberalism, Community, and Culture*, Oxford: Oxford University Press, 1989, especially Chapters 7 - 10.

[43] Article 31. The responsibilities are to parents, families, nation, the international community and other legally recognised units.

[44] Ephesians 6:1-3.

[45] Garton Kamchedzera, in Joanna Lewis, Peggy Owens and Louise Pirquet (eds.), *Human Rights and the Making of Constitutions: Malawi, Kenya, Uganda*, Cambridge: University of Cambridge African Studies Centre, 1995, pp. 28-33.

social trust is also compatible with the loving and caring tenet within Christianity. "A social trust is a relationship of altruistic interdependence to overcome a need."[46] Interdependence, rather than equality and contract, comprise the foundation of a social trust. Cotterrell has attempted to describe a social trust as: trust in a broad moral sense: involving reliance, in social relationships or other people's good will, solicitude and competence; or confidence that the general expectations in familiar social circumstances will not be frustrated.[47]

The Existence of the Social Trust

The social trust is not a new idea and has existed in many societies. In many African societies, for example, property relations were based on social trust. Asante, writing in 1965, claimed that property concepts in Ghanaian customary law were impressed with the "trusteeship idea".[48] Underlying basic conceptions of property law was the notion of the "ancestral trust". Property was vested in the living for the benefit of themselves and generations unborn.[49] This view of the ownership of natural resources is similar to Christianity's perception that the world belongs to God and human beings are but stewards who must share with those in need.[50] A similar notion has now become the organizing tenet of international environmental law. Frequently endorsed in international environmental law is Burke's statement that there is "not only a partnership between those who are living, but also between

---

[46] Kamchedzera, "Access to Property", at 39.

[47] Roger Cotterrell, "Trusting in the Law: Legal and Moral Concepts of Trust", 46 *Current Legal Problems, Part 2: Collected Papers*, (eds. M.D.A. Freeman and B.A. Hepple), 1993, at 75.

[48] S.K.B. Asante, "Fiduciary Principles in Anglo-American Law and the Customary Law of Ghana: A Comparative Study" (1965), *International and Comparative Law Quarterly*, 1144.

[49] Ibid., at 1145.

[50] Genesis 1:29-30 as read with passages such as Isaiah 1:16-17, Luke 10:29-37, Luke 3:11 and many others.

those who are dead and those who are to be born"[51] Cribbet has argued that a property owner is responsible for the interests of posterity.[52] The Aboriginal concept of "dreaming", furthermore, is now gaining respect. Gray has observed that:

> There is increasing evidence on all sides that we are slowly recognising some concept of trust in relation to the natural environment. The gathering perception of stewardship emulates something of the greater humility expressed in the Australian Aboriginal's orientation towards resources. We may be starting to have a more cogent sense of obligation than ownership, and this realisation, is of course, the necessary precursor of a new equilibrium with our environment.[53]

There is evidence that the social trust is being promoted in certain societies. Reich has argued that there is need for a more inclusive concept of property rights that protects the economic rights on which certain people depend.[54] The fiduciary position of the Government has been recognized in Australia[55] and Canada.[56] New Zealand has taken steps to resuscitate the indigenous ways of social trust-based ownership of property.[57] The Philippine Supreme Court has held that

---

[51] Edmund Burke, "Refections on the Revolutions in France 139-40, in *Two Works of Edmund Burke*, London, 1905, at 368.

[52] John Edward Cribbet, "Concepts in Transition: the Search for the New Definidon of Property" (1986), *University of Illinois Law Review, 1* at 40.

[53] Kevin Gray "Equitable Property" *Current Legal Problems, Part 2: Collected Papers,* 155-214, at 204.

[54] Charles Reich, The New Property", 73, *Yale Law Journal,* (1963-64), 733, especially at 738-39.

[55] *Mabo v. Queensland* (1992) 175 C.L.R. 1, at 51 per Brennam J.

[56] *Guerin v. The Queen* (1984) 13 D.L.R. (4th) 321.

[57] New Zealand has passed legislation to facilitate the more inclusive ownership of property especially regarding land for Maori: The Te Ture Whenua Maori Act, Maori Land Act, No. 4 of 1993.

children can enforce their interests and the interests of posterity against wasteful state actions.[58]

The Social Trust and Social Cohesion

Societies that had strong social trust conceptions within their socio-political structures were characterized by a strong sense of social cohesion among its members. Allot observes that "it is the normal case that in African customary laws, a person's family or kinship group was responsible for his actions, at least habitually participated in any proceedings that called those actions into question".[59] The concept of shared responsibility led to a conclusion by Gluckman that immovable and movable property helped to maintain "social community among the Barotse".[60] The apparent social cohesion in African and other societies has tempted others to claim a holy conception of trust. Adigun, for example, claimed that Africa had a workable conception of social trust that must be promoted and that the property-based narrow Anglo-American conception[61] of trust must be dropped. "It is our contention, he asserted, to show that we have in our system a better concept of trust. The concept does not permit such inequality in social wealth as to lead to hunger, homelessness, and depression.[62]

Adigun, however, idealizes the current legal significance of the social trust in African societies. First, traditional and social functionaries are now under the overriding power of the state whose system of government is not based on social communality as in indigenous African societies. Second, the current position of the trust in African

---

[58] *Minors Oposa v. Secretary of the Department of Environment and Natural Resources* (DNR) 33 *I.L.M.* 173+.

[59] A. Allot, *The Limits of Law,* London: Butterworths, 1980, at p. 66.

[60] Max Gluckman, *The Ideas in Barotse Jurisprudence,* Manchester: Manchester University Press, 1972, at pp. 113-140.

[61] Which has been held to apply to private law relations only: *Tito and Others v. Waddell and Others* [1971] 1 Ch. 106.

[62] Olayide Adigun, *Cases and Texts on Equity, Trusts, and Administration of Estates,* Abeoulcuta: Ayo Sodimu, 1987, at 251.

societies should not be idealized because the communalism of African societies is disintegrating. The collective nature of African societies has been adversely affected by the cash economy which promotes individualism. Studies by Chanock,[63] Rwezaura,[64] and Snyder[65] show that patriarchal powers colluded with colonial capitalism to control children and women and consequently altered property relations. Remains of authentic customary law relating to communalism still exist, but effort must be made to counter the adverse effects of the cash economy. Both the modern state and the cash economy, however, were ushered into Africa by Christianity. Christianity therefore can be said to have contributed to the weakening of the social trust in African societies. Ironically, Christianity's neighbour principle and the exhortation to love a neighbour as one loves herself or himself, remain potentially strong catalysts for the reinvigoration of the social trust on which the implementation of the CRC depends.

The Need-Based Generations of Human Rights

The CRC's dependence on the social trust is illustrated by the rights it contains. The CRC is a codification of three interdependent and interrelated generations of human rights, all of which are need based. Much of the controversy about the rights of the child is partly a result of insufficient appreciation that the CRC is a codification of three categories of human rights that are historically-specific in origin. Each generation of human rights arose because of society's perceived needs. As aspirations though, human rights are futuristically ideal. The need-based origin of human rights imply that the categories of human rights cannot be closed.

---

[63] Martin Chanock, *Law, Custom and Social Order: The Colonial Experience in Malawi and Zambia,* Cambridge: Cambridge University Press, 1985.

[64] B.A. Rwezaura, *Traditional Family Law: A Case Study of the Kuria Social System,* Baden: Nomos Verlagsgesellschaft, 1985.

[65] Francis Snyder, *Capitalism and Legal Change: An African Transformation,* New York: Academic Press, 1985.

The first generation of human rights is a product of the Enlightenment, when social contract and liberty were the dominant philosophical goals. Social contract theory influenced political and legal thought during the English Revolution of 1688, the French Revolution of 1789 and the American Declaration of Independence of 1776. The individual's reason and freedom were the perceived needs that resulted in the various Bills of civil and political rights.[66] The child was still regarded as lacking the legal and contractual capacity. It must be underlined, however, that social contract did not create civil and political rights; it merely attempted to explain the basis of those rights. Instead of social contract and liberty, the CRC addresses the child's vulnerability and dependence. Such vulnerability and dependence are the basis for the CRC's civil and political rights.[67] Many of such civil and political rights require the participation of the child who is able to form and express her or his opinions.[68] Tengatenga has noted that "the youth" in Christian churches "feel ignored, excluded, exploited and marginalized"[69] He warns of a "potential time bomb"[70] The

---

[66] England: The Bill of Rights 1689; the USA: The American Declaration of Independence 1776; France: the Declaration of the Rights of Man and the Citizen 1789.

[67] The ground breaking international instrument here is the International Covenant on Civil and Political Rights 1966. Examples of such rights include the right to a name and a nationality (Art. 7), identity (Art. 8), the right not to be discriminated against (Art. 2), freedom to form and express opinions (Arts. 12, 13 and 14), freedom of association (Art. 15), protection of privacy (Art. 16), safeguarding the rights of minorities and indigenous populations (Art. 30).

[68] Article 12.

[69] James Tengatenga, "Young People: Participation or Alienation?: An Anglican Case", in Kenneth R. Ross (ed.), *God, People and Power in Malawi: Democratisation in Theological Perspective*, Blantyre: CLAIM, 1996, pp. 107-123, at p. 119.

[70] *Ibid*.

implementation of participation human rights for children would improve the quality of belonging to the Church for all its members:[71]

Economic, social and cultural human rights are often referred to as belonging to the second generation of human rights. Their importance was partly a result of the two world wars and general economic and social misery. Economic, social and cultural rights were until the 1960s, associated with socialism and certain capitalist states were not keen to promote these rights. There is now broad acceptance of these rights.[72] Others however still find it useful to link these rights not to socialism,

---

[71] Meaningful association with a congregation, as Tengatenga implies, must be harnessed by a relevant sense of ownership or belonging on the part of all members. For children, such participation, of course, must be according to age and ability; but it must be allowed and encouraged as children can easily be sidelined because of their social status. Those congregations that run participatory Sunday school programmes for young children, for example, are well-liked by children who attend the classes. A church that merely focuses on adults and treats children as appendages cannot develop a free sense of belonging in its children. The participation of the young in congregations, however, requires that the children's concerns, suggestions and opinions are taken into account in the planning and implementation of church activities. A sense of belonging for church young people will increase if such young people feel listened to and their interests included rather than ignored or marginalised. Many congregations would indeed enrich the quality of their church lives if young people were allowed to design and implement their own church projects or even lead the congregation at selected times or according to appropriate events. Access to leadership roles at an early stage would also help prepare future church leaders better. E.g., cf. footnote 6.

[72] The ground breaking international instrument on this is the International Covenant on Economic, Social and Cultural Rights 1966, Un. Doc. A./6316 (1966). Countries such as Britain that did not approbate these rights now do so: Britain, for example does not "regard them as an inferior order to civil and political rights", UN Human Rights Commission, UN Doc. E/CN.4 1988/SR.23, at 9, per a British Government representative.

but to Roosevelt's New Deal and his declaration of the four freedoms.[73]

Economic, social and cultural human rights do not contradict but rather supplement civil and political rights.[74] Some of the early international standards on the subject were on the rights of the child. The League of Nations Declaration on the Rights of the Child was adopted in 1924.[75] It was initiated by a remarkable woman, Eglantine Jebb who also founded the Save the Children Foundation. The Declaration contained obligations on society for the economic, social, and cultural well-being of the child.[76] A mare elaborate Declaration was passed in 1959.[77] That Declaration foreshadowed the CRC and contained economic, social and cultural rights[78] as well as civil and

---

[73] Cynthia Price Cohen, "The Relevance of Theories of Natural and Legal Positivism" in M.D.A. Freeman and P.E. Veerman (eds.), *The Ideologies of Children's Rights,* Dordrecht: Martinus Nijhoff, 1992, 53 at 56. Roosevelt's freedoms were: the freedom of expression, freedom of worship, freedom from want and freedom from fear: F. Newman and D. Weissbrodt, *International Human Rights: Law, Policy and Process,* Cincinnati: Anderson Pub. Co., 1990 at 362-363.

[74] Vienna Declaration and Programme of Action on Human Rights 1993, 32 I.L.M. 1661 (1993)+.

[75] League of Nations, *Records of the Fifth Assembly,* Geneva: League of Nations, 1924, at 177.

[76] To give the child necessary means for normal spiritual and material development (Principle 1); to feed the child (Principle II); to nurse the sick child (Principle II); to help the backward child (Principle H); to reclaim the delinquent child (Principle II), to shelter and succour the orphan and waif (Principle II), to give priority relief to the child during times of distress (principle II); to help the child to earn a livelihood (Principle IV); to protect the child from every harm and exploitation (Principle IV), to bring up the child in the consciousness that the child's talents must *be* devoted to the services of others (Principle V).

[77] UN Doc. A./4059 (1959).

[78] E.g., social security, (Principle 4), health (Principle 4), housing (Principle 4), recreation (Principle 4), love and understanding (Principle 6), and education (Principle 7).

political human rights[79] intended to facilitate "happy childhood".[80] In all circumstances, the child was to be "among the first to receive protection and relief"[81] The best interests of the child were to be a primary consideration in all matters concerning children.[82] There were rights for special treatment, education and care for the child who was physically, mentally or socially handicapped.[83] There were also rights for the protection of the child in situations of disadvantage.[84] The CRC continues the tradition of the 1959 Declaration by enshrining economic, social and cultural rights which are all incontestable in the Christian context.[85]

Critics regard economic, social and cultural human rights as too broad to be realized. It is difficult, the critics argue, to identify an individual who can bear the corresponding duties. Thus Wald asserted that the courts "cannot order that the world be free of poverty or that children have adequate health care"[86] The CRC, nevertheless, recognizes that duties to implement the rights of the child are not merely on the individual, but on all social units. The centrality of the individual is,

---

[79] E.g., name and nationality.

[80] The Preamble.

[81] Principle 8.

[82] Principle 7.

[83] Principle 5.

[84] From abuse (Principle 9), neglect (Principle 9), exploitation (Principle 9), cruel treatment (Principle 9), discrimination (Principles 1 and 10).

[85] E.g., the right to health (Art. 24), social security (Art. 26), adequate standard of living (Art. 27), education (Arts. 28 and 29), leisure, recreation and cultural activities (Art. 31). There are also rights on protection from abuse (Art. 19), protection of the child without a family (Art. 21), protection of disabled children (Art. 23), protection from disabling child labour (Art. 32), protection from drug abuse (Art. 33), protection from sexual exploitation (Art. 34), protection from sale, trafficking and abduction (Art. 36), protection from torture and deprivation of liberty (Art. 37) and protection from armed conflicts (Art. 38).

[86] Michael S. Wald, "Children's Rights: A Framework for Analysis" 12, *University of California Law Review*, 255 (1979), at 260-265.

therefore, dwindled under the CRC. Instead, individuals as well as parents, nuclear families, extended families, states, the international community and other social units all have duties to nurture the child. The relevant question is how to implement the child's intrinsic economic, social and cultural rights. The duties implied by the CRC are not mere supererogatory duties or "imperfect obligations" because once institutionalized, imperfect obligations become specific instrumental duties.[87]

The CRC further reflects the philosophy of third generation human rights.[88] Third generation human rights involve co-operation and interdependence, both among states that are not economically advanced as a group, and among all states. It is thought that the third generation human rights have emerged out of the plight of the third world countries which "have been exploited for many decades" and where underdevelopment is dire.[89] The most important third generation human right is the right to development which is enshrined in Malawi's constitution.[90] The essence of the right to development is that all human beings have a right to benefit from the fruits of comprehensive economic, social and cultural development that is based on the respect for human rights and the participation of all members of society.[91] One stated aim for the CRC is to "promote social progress and better standards of life in larger freedom".[92] The Church in many countries, including Malawi, has participated in the quest for

---

[87] Even O'Neil, "Children's Rights and Children's Lives", who disagrees with the use of rights as applied to children, agrees with this point, at 27.

[88] E.g., the right to survival and development in Art. 6.

[89] H.S. Kibola, Some Conceptual Aspects of Human Rights: the Basis of the Right to Development in Africa", paper presented to the African Seminar on Human Rights to Development, National Institute of Development, Research and Documentation, University of Botswana, Gaborone, 24-29 May 1982, at 6.

[90] Section 30.

[91] Declaration on the right to Development, UN GA Resolution No. 4 of December 1986, preamble.

[92] Preamble.

social progress and larger freedom.[93] There is, however, need for a greater realization of the dignity and potential role of children in such processes.

The Convention's Aims and Strategic Principles

The CRC's overriding aims and strategic principles all imply a social trust which could be easily achieved within the Christian context. The CRC's two aims, to facilitate the survival, development, participation and protection of the child, and, to promote intra- and inter-generational equity both imply interdependence and altruism for children. The CRC's main strategic principles further reinforce the point that the rights of the child depend on the existence and-practice of a social trust. The CRC has two main strategic principles. The first is that the best interests of the child should be paramount in all matters relating to children. The second principle is called "first call for children" and it means that the lives and moral development of children should have a first call on society's concerns and capacities and that children should be able to depend upon the commitment in good times and in bad, in normal times and in times of emergency, in time of peace and in times of war, in times of prosperity and in times of recession.[94]

Compliance with these principles reflects the caring attitude of a social unit. These principles are, however, poorly followed in families, villages and churches. They are ignored in the exercise of discretion, inheritance matters, collective enterprises, the performance of public duties and the management of pooled resources.[95] There is need for fiduciary principles to be applied in all these areas for the benefit of children.[96] There are three fiduciary principles in the common law. The

---

[93] See, for example, Ross (ed.) *God, People and Power in Malawi.*

[94] Javier Perez de Cuellar, in a message to an international meeting on the rights of the CRC, Lig-nanano, Italy, September 1987, also quoted in UNICEF, 'Information Kit', at 8.

[95] Kamchedzera, "Access to Property", chapter 4.

[96] *Ibid.*

first is that those in positions of ascendancy must not place themselves in circumstances where personal interests might conflict with duty. The second is that resources must be managed with reasonable prudence. The last is that a fiduciary must act fairly towards all beneficiaries.

Jesus' requirement for shepherding responsibilities requires compliance with such fiduciary principles.[97] A right-oriented approach helps "shepherds" and all those in positions of trust to regard children as subjects that have entitlements to be fulfilled. Shepherds, in Jesus' sense, must also be altruistic. One moral reason for the principle of first call for children is that the way society treats children "reflects not only its qualities of compassion and protective caring but also its sense of justice, its commitment to the future and its urge to enhance the human condition for coming generations".[98] Such societal attributes are required by and can be available from Christianity.

Christianity and Altruistic Actions for Children

The CRC provides that "the child, by reason of [her or his] physical and mental immaturity, needs special safeguards and care, including appropriate legal protection, before, as well as after, birth".[99] Such special safeguards require communitarian and altruistic actions by all social units, at least for children of tender age. Parents and families are given the primary responsibility to nurture children.[100] The state, the international community, and other social units are required to support the role of parents and families for the best interests of the child.[101] The other social units include churches. The teaching of Jesus

---

[97] John 21:15-17.

[98] Javier Perez de Cuellar, in a message to the international meeting on the Convention on the Rights of the Child, Lignano, Italy, September 1987, also quoted in "Quotable Quotes", in UNICEF, 'Information Kit'.

[99] Preamble.

[100] E.g., Articles 5, 9 and 27.

[101] Participation of the child's parents (e.g., Article 5 of the CRC which requires recognition for parental guidance and Article 27(2) of the CRC which

Christ already requires a social trust, but superior status and contract doctrines are dominant even within churches.

The enforcement of the rights of the child largely requires altruism for children. The CRC's own stipulated mechanism is not satisfactory. States and other "competent bodies" are required to submit reports to the Committee on the Rights of the Child.[102] The mechanism provides an opportunity for monitoring and evaluation. The African Charter on the Rights and Welfare of the Child goes further to provide for a mechanism through which individuals can petition the OAU's Committee on the Rights of the Child.[103] The Charter, however, is yet to receive strong backing from many African countries. The Charter also lacks a strong institutional implementation framework which the CRC enjoys.[104]

---

recognises the tenet that parents have the primary responsibility to ensure the child's right to an adequate standard of living); the role of the nuclear family (Article 10 which stresses the importance of family reunion and Article 20 which requires special protection for a child without a family); the extended family (e.g., Article 7 which calls for the due respect of the responsibilities, duties and rights of extended family members); public and private bodies (e.g., Article 3 which states that public and private bodies must regard the best interests of the child as a primary consideration); NGOs (e.g., Article 45 which provides for representation for non-governmental organisations in the implementation of the CRC); states (e.g., Article 2-13, 14-46, 47-53 of the CRC all expressly refer to state parties to the Convention while the remaining few make implied reference to states); and the international community (e.g., Article 23(4) require states "in the spirit of international cooperation" to promote the exchange of information for the benefit children with disabilities, Article 24(4) stipulates that states must encourage international cooperation for the child's better health, and Article 28(3) requires international cooperation for the child's education.

[102] Article 44.

[103] Also Article 44.

[104] It is still to enter into force because of lack or signatures to it.

The altruism implied by both Christianity and the CRC may be captured by the Chichewa terms of *chithandizano* or *umunthu*[105] . The Commission on Global Interdependence captured the significance of *chithandizano* or *umunthu* when it stated that the:

> quality of life in society depends to a great extent on its members accepting a duty to care for their neigbours. Its sense of community and well-being are enhanced when more citizens are imbued by a spirit of care and concern for other citizens, whether deriving from African tradition, the Moslem obligation of hospitality, or the practice of other cultures ... The instincts of caring and compassion provide the impulse for humanitarian action - and for sharing with those less advantaged - that all societies need. In addition to motivating people to undertake voluntary action, the citizen's instinct of care can be a catalyst for action by official agencies.[106]

Many religions try to achieve *umunthu*. Christianity, however, has the advantage of accepting that all human beings are fallible and have to rely on the graceful regeneration from God for sustainable altruistic actions. Jesus requires that a person must be born again.[107] Paul and other New Testament writers stress the importance of regeneration and Christians are expected to live as new creatures who have the help of the Holy Spirit.[108] Christianity presents such possible regeneration as a result of God's grace and not mere human endeavours. If sufficient Christians were truly regenerated for good works, children and other vulnerable groups in society would benefit.

---

[105] South Africa is now advocating for a moral philosophy called *ubunthu*.

[106] Commisssion on Global Governance, *Our Global Neighbourhood,* Oxford: Oxford University Press, 1995, at 53.

[107] John 3:3.

[108] E.g., Roinas 6:1-14, 2 Corinthians 5:22-25, Ephesians 2:10, Ephesians 4:22-24, Philippians 3:111,1 John 3:11-24. James 2:14-19,1 Peter 2:4-12 and Jude 20-23.

Conclusion

Both the rights of the child and Christianity as discourses and practices assume and promote the social trust or interdependence. Both, however, remain dominated by contract doctrine or liberal individualism. The biblical tenets on altruism and the need for regeneration are nevertheless clear.

Christians and society are required to practice love and care especially for the vulnerable. True love and care for the vulnerable would help address the needs of children. Coincidentally, the rights of the child are need-based aspirations that society must achieve for the benefit of all children. In many cases, such as the participation of children, the rights of the child can enrich the Christian Church's altruistic and inclusive work for the benefit of the child. Human shortcomings are, however, inevitable and the needs of all children may not be achieved if their welfare is left to individuals. Christianity stands out among religions to offer an answer to human frailty and self-interestedness: God-worked regeneration. The Bible is clear that such regeneration is enough for good fruits or work that can benefit the vulnerable such as children.

7. The AIDS Crisis: A Challenge to the Integrity of the Church in Malawi

Fulata Lusungu Moyo

Prologue

> Africa is home to more than a tenth of the world's people, yet it has 64% of the world's AIDS cases according to WHO. The agency forecasts that by the late 1990s, 15 million people in Africa will be infected with the Human Immunodeficiency Virus or HIV, which causes AIDS and for which there is no known cure. Because nearly all adults develop the fatal symptoms of AIDS within 10 years of infection, WHO estimates that a fourth of black Africa's work force will be wiped out within 20 years. And the average life span in Africa, once expected to reach 60, will fall to just 47 years, according to the World Bank.[1]

When the above was predicted in the early 1990s, it seemed just speculation but the reality of it has become what Dick Day[2] described as *Africa's Death Sentence* - worse than the above predictions. In Malawi, according to Hakan Byrkman, a policy specialist quoted in the Human Development report, the HIV/AIDS epidemic reached its peak in 1992.[3] 12% of Malawi's population is infected (population 12 million people). Between 20-33% of women who give birth in urban hospitals are HIV positive. 20 to 25% of the sexually active population are estimated to be HIV positive. 20% of reported AIDS cases are youths aged 15-24 (five times as many young women as young men). 70% of women with HIV are estimated to be between 15 and 24. By the year 2022, a quarter of Malawi's population (almost 2.5 million people) will have died from AIDS. Moreover, the United Nations Population

---

[1] *Los Angeles Times Magazine,* 1 March 1992, pp. 12-16.

[2] Dick Day is the co-ordinator for SAFE! (Sub- Saharan Africa Family Enrichment!), a non- governmental organisation. He is also Associate Professor in Human Ecology, University of Malawi.

[3] *Daily Times,* 8 July 1992, p. 13

Division has revised the life expectancy figure for Malawi from 45.5 in 1996 to 41.1 at present, to take into account the impact of AIDS.

AIDS does not become an issue of faith at the frontier because it is a greater killer than other diseases. "Many more people die of motor accidents in the United States than of AIDS. More women die of breast cancer. In the Third World, widely though AIDS has spread, it is not the greatest killer. More children die of tuberculosis than of AIDS."[4] Though it may not be the greatest killer, AIDS attacks the family, therefore, will ultimately be like the Flood, if not checked. Like the Holocaust, the Bugandan Martyrdom and other phenomena in the life of the Church, AIDS "projects us into a *kairos, a* time of decision, testing and change after which nothing will be the same any more".[5] We do not have the answers to the questions that the AIDS situation raises about life and death but we are challenged to offer some thoughts about Christian integrity in the face of AIDS. How do we interpret God and his purpose in this AIDS-torn world? How does the Church help the AIDS-torn Sub-Saharan Africa apply the liberating gospel of Jesus Christ to our present situation? AIDS challenges the very integrity of the Church. Whither the Church's message of God's justice in safeguarding the vulnerable youths and adult singles? What about the Church's message regarding the chastity of marriage? This chapter looks at sexual intercourse as the major mode of transmission. This is because of its concern for the integrity of the Church, part of which deals with the Church's call to holiness which directly affects behavioural patterns of people.

This chapter has four major sections. The first section deals with facts about AIDS; the second raises some of the issues that have contributed to making the AIDS epidemic such a crisis as it is presently; the third gives some of the reasons why the Church could be strategic in helping deal with AIDS and why it has not been so effective in carrying out this mission; and the fourth is a short conclusion and some suggestions to the Church and its ministry.

---

[4] Ronald Nicolson, *God in AIDS?,* London: SCM Press, 1996, p. 5.
[5] *Ibid.*

What is AIDS? Some Hard Facts About HIV-Infection and AIDS

AIDS stands for Acquired Immune Deficiency Syndrome. This is the late stage of infection with HIV (Human Immunodeficiency Virus). It is *acquired* because it is not genetically determined; it *is immunodeficiency* because it brings about a severe depletion of immune system cells, that is, the cells that defend the body from infections; and it is a *syndrome* because it is an illness which presents itself in various forms. Once the virus (HIV) infects a white blood cell, it literally turns the cell into a virus-producing factory. The virus becomes a part of the cell's genetic composition, ensuring that it will remain part of the infected person for life. While immediately after one is infected, one becomes very infectious, the theory of "dynamic infectivity" has it that the longer individuals are infected, the more infectious they become. This arises because increasing quantities of virus are present as decreasing numbers of T4 lymphocytes (small white blood cells that orchestrate and/or directly participate in the immune defence) are found in the blood. As the body's T4 cell population is increasingly depleted by the virus, the immune system becomes less able to fight other infectious viral, parasitic and bacterial agents present in the body.[6] The infected person thus becomes susceptible to a wide range of the so-called "opportunistic" infections, such as tuberculosis or pneumonia, which rarely occur in persons with normal immune systems. Persons infected with HIV are both infected and infectious for life. Even when they look and feel healthy they can transmit the virus to others.

Soon after one becomes HIV-infected, one may develop fever, enlarged lymph glands, skin rash or cough. This response ranges from four to twelve weeks after one is infected. Some people have a rare delayed response of up to six months or more. This early response to infection is usually followed by a long symptom-free interval which

---

[6] Shepherd and Anita Moreland Smith, *Christians in the Age of AIDS?*, Wheaton: Victor Books, 1990.

may last for many years. After 10 years or so, the infected person will most likely develop symptomatic HIV disease (AIDS) which will often be indicated by various opportunistic infections. This will result in death. So symptomatic AIDS is really the end stage of a disease process which began long before we see people who are physically ill.

How does a person become HIV infected?

Scientific research shows that there are three modes of HIV transmission. For the purposes of this paper transmission through HIV-contaminated blood, blood products, or tissues, re-used syringes, needles and from an HIV-infected mother to her new born baby will not be discussed. Transmission through sexual intercourse, whether homosexual or heterosexual is the main concern of this discussion as it affects behaviour. When you talk of holiness,[7] you talk, in this case, of something that is part and parcel of what the Church is.

Prevention is More Possible than Cure:

Since 1981 when the first AIDS cases were diagnosed in America, 1985 in Malawi and late 1980s in South Africa, there has been a very rapid spread of this disease worldwide. To be realistic with this worldwide pandemic, it is actually wiser to talk about the HIV infection rather than AIDS which is only the last part of the whole problem. Since its first diagnosis, it was clear that AIDS had no cure: once infected, forever infected until death. While medical specialists worked on trying to find a cure or even a vaccination and are still working on it, the best solution has to do with avoiding infection.

Public awareness campaigns and provision of condoms were the two strategies used by African governments and international donors in the first efforts to combat the epidemic, but increasingly the attention has shifted to education, both formal and informal, focusing specifically on programmes that reach children who are not yet at risk,

---

[7] I use holiness to mean being Christ-like in attitude and behaviour - "To act justly and to love mercy and to walk humbly with your God." (Micah 6:8b).

in the hope that the up-coming generation can remain largely AIDS-free before it is too late.[8]

The above shift from awareness campaigns and provision of condoms to education was because in a country like Malawi where sexual behaviour is a matter of strict privacy, the public awareness campaigns produced minimal results in the face of a very rapid spread of the HIV infection. Moreover condoms are not as risk free as they have generally been presented. The failure rate of condoms in preventing HIV infection varies from 5 to 30%. Since the risk of acquiring HIV infection is defined in terms of "risk behaviour",[9] the solution to this problem therefore, has to do with dealing with the risk behaviour. In the case of this chapter, risk behaviour for contracting HIV infection has to do with sexual behaviour. In an age where sex has become permissible among the youth and adult singles, and more common outside marriage for married couples, how do individuals and organizations deal with this sexual behaviour? Secular organizations cannot help because they have no set of spiritual values. The only answer, one would hope, is found in the Church. But as it is, even with about 63% of the Malawian population claiming to be Christian, the HIV infection rate is still rising.

What has gone wrong?

1. For most Malawians, they will continue to engage in sexually immoral behaviour until they cannot hide it any more. They will only stop such risky behaviour when someone finds out since their guiding principle is shame rather than guilt. As .long as such secrecy continues, there will be no change. Because AIDS has such a long incubation period some may chose to persist in this risky behaviour until one or both partners begin to show signs of illness. Moreover, people refuse

---

[8] E.g. Moira Chimombo, *Why Wait?/Family Enrichment Secondary Curriculum, Unit 1,* Zomba: SAFE!, nd.

[9] Anyone, of any age, race or sexual orientation, who has had one or more sexual partners whose

HIV status is unknown, has participated in risk behaviour.

to be tested for HIV until they start to exhibit signs of illness which has served only to aggrevate the overall situation of AIDS and HIV.

2. According to the "True Love Waits" programme for University students,[10] in every human being there is the need to be accepted, approved and loved. These are needs that are usually not addressed.

The Need for Acceptance

Everyone has an essential need to be accepted. The need to be part of a group that accepts and trusts us is a fundamental to our physical and psychological health. Sometimes sex is used as a tool to gain acceptance. Many young women will give in to sex because they desire to be accepted by their boyfriends. Some men will also give in to sex because of the same pressure of wanting to be accepted. They feel that if they refuse then these boyfriends/girlfriends will reject them. This pressure might be made even worse if they feel that their families do not accept them. This problem can only be solved by the Church and its Gospel of God's acceptance of each one of us despite our sinfulness.

The Need for Approval

Apart from acceptance, every person needs approval from other people. We want people in our family and our social group to like us. Often our self-esteem is based on the approval that we get from others and people would go to almost any lengths to gain approval. How valuable are you? The Church is supposed to have a message and a life that can help people try to calculate their worth, knowing that God loves them so much, even with all their failures and shortcomings.

The Need for Affection

Deep in each one of us, there is the desire to be loved and to be able to love. When that love is not found at home (in the family) individuals

---

[10] Rendell Day, 'Tree Love Waits", Trainers of Trainers by Baptist Mission in Malawi.

will often try to find it in the "wrong place". This need is something that often people are not aware of. But some may seek to meet this need through sexual activity.

With the above needs and many misconceptions and myths about sexuality, the Church that is true to its call to be light and salt to the earth can help the youth, adult singles and married couples to develop self-control despite the above issues. To come to a point where individuals with their human dignity (affirmed strongly that they are in God's image and that their life is worth so much because the only Son of God died for them so as to liberate them) will be able to choose to resist the charm of the crowd and the temptation of easy rewards. They will choose to slow down so they do not miss all the wonderful happenings on the way to their destination. To have the best in life takes some self-control and discipline. To develop this attitude in people, the Church has to preach and live its holiness gospel, otherwise the AIDS chains will never be broken in Africa as well as in the whole world.

3. With urbanization, the traditional family structure has been destroyed and no other structure has been established to take up the issue like sex education that the traditional family addressed. With urbanization and the economic pressures the parents have no time to "parent" their children. So the children grow up and become youth who are basically influenced by the media and peer pressure.

> Traditional values and the family unit have been impacted by the rapid changes undergone throughout Africa. Norms of sexual behaviour have changed. Pre-marital and extra-marital sex have greatly increased leading to a dramatic rise in the incidence of STDs and exponential growth of AIDS.[11]

According to John S. Mbiti, the African has been severed, cut off, pulled out and separated from corporate morality, customs and traditional solidarity and has no firm roots any more since the rapid change that Africa has been caught up in has uprooted him/her but

---

[11] Dick Day, "Abstract, International School Project", and "Why Wait?/Family Enrichment, A Proposal for the Ministry of Education", on Malawi, p. 3.

has not necessarily transformed him/her.[12] The coming of Christianity, it has been argued, did not deal with African sexuality,[13] that is partially why Africans do not know how to express their sexuality even in the midst of the AIDS pandemic. This is where the real challenge to the Church in Africa comes in - while there has been a preoccupation in recent years with trying to make Christianity real to Africans as regards their culture, the AIDS crisis has not been seriously considered as a context from which we cannot escape. AIDS in Sub-Saharan Africa has become part and parcel of our culture so that contextual theology[14] needs to consider it along with the other cultural aspects. This kind of reorientation might help sort out the problem of whether there really is an African sexuality which was neglected by the missionaries whom we have readily blamed, and how, if there is such a thing as an African sexuality, we can address it so as to make a spiritually sound contribution to combatting AIDS. Such an exercise will also help develop human dignity as a basis for every decision and action in the Church as well as the community at large.[15] This would help change people's attitude about sexuality. From an attitude that says "Sex outside marriage is natural and feels good" or "Sex is the ultimate fulfillment and if you have not done it you are really missing out", to an attitude that respects human dignity and counts the cost of every decision before it is acted upon. On the other hand, it might also help the Church understand sexuality with its positive values as well as its negative ones.

---

[12] John S. Mbiti, *African Religions and Philosophy,* London: Heinemann, 1969, pp. 24 and 219.

[13] Sexuality in this paper has to do with what one is and how that affects one's sexual behaviour as an expression of intimacy between two people of the opposite sex. Cf. D.H. Field, "Sexuality", in S.B. Ferguson and D.F. Wright (eds.), *New Dictionary of Theology,* Leicester: Inter Varsity Press, 1988, pp. 637-638.

[14] In very simple terms, contextual theology tries to make Christianity real and meaningful to people in their particular situation.

[15] As *Why Wait?* says, people must understand that they are special, because they are made in the image of God.

Whatever one uses as the basis of constructing one's sexuality, it is clear that the issue of human dignity is not restricted to Christianity only. Most African cultures value human dignity so that at the end of the day, what Christianity does is affirm this with its teaching about male and female being created in the image of God.

> It is very important ... that the church should provide reliable information about sexual practices which may lead to AIDS. This is especially important in Africa where in areas church ... (has) more access to more people than any other institutions in the continent. But our sex education should go beyond merely warning against AIDS, or against premarital pregnancy or any other dangers. Sex education needs to be about more than what we must avoid. Children need to be brought up with healthy sexual attitudes from the beginning. They need to learn a positive attitude towards their bodies and themselves, and not merely warned against the dangers of sex in their teens. This is not because children are often targets of paedophiles and child abusers and thus need to know what sex is all about, but because they are already, in their own way, thoroughly sexual beings.[16]

With AIDS, most people have adopted an attitude of just warning against sex. So such people would advise the youth against those sexual practices that would put one at risk from AIDS, so their advice would involve the use of condoms. This is probably because these people, like so many others, are not courageous enough to talk about chastity. Maybe because they have not been able to deal with their own sexuality themselves.

To Preserve its Integrity, the Church Must be Christ-like, Compassionate and Holy

The Church has a mandate to proclaim clear moral standards in all areas of life, including sexuality. In light of the often ambiguous and morally confusing messages from the mass media and other areas of influence, and the lack of sex education in the home, churches can

---

[16] Nicolson, *God in AIDS?*, pp. 100-101.

make a significant contribution to the moral development and health of society.[17]

Of course, different groups of people in Malawi have different bases of the construction of their sexual behaviour but with about 63% of the Malawian population professing Christianity, it becomes justifiable to claim that the Church is strategic in addressing this problem.

> Christians have a responsibility to provide reasoned, sensible, achievable standards of sexual behaviour which may help the various societies and cultures of the world to provide the basis for personal and family stability which we have lost.[18]

If the Church is not just a structure with the symbol of the Cross but the body of the compassionate and holy Christ, then it should take up the AIDS/HIV challenge and make the difference as it brings hope where hope was gone. The Church has to continue the work the Master began in this world of toil and snare; to continue preaching the gospel to the poor, proclaiming freedom for the prisoner, recovery of sight to the blind and release to the oppressed. Where poverty in Africa is one of the reasons why some women take the risk of selling their bodies for money, what message does the Church have to such people? Will the Church be like Christ and extend love to even the outcasts in society like prostitutes and tell them that God, who created them with dignity, loves them? Church leaders have mostly sent the outcasts running deep into the dungeons of hopelessness because of their judgmental attitude, prejudice and intolerance of failure and their wrong view that weakness or failure shows lack of spiritual commitment.

The Church can no longer define AIDS as God's punishment. Like the Phalombe disaster,[19] so many innocent people die of AIDS. Some because of sexually promiscuous partners, some children who are

---

[17] *The Church's Response to the Challenge of AIDS/HIV: A Guideline for Education and Policy Development,* MAP International, 1991, p. 27.

[18] Nicolson, *God in AIDS?, p.* 103.

[19] In 1991, more than 200 human lives were lost when a massive rockslide took place at the Phalombe side of Mulanje Mountain.

born HIV-positive, and the few that contract HIV infection from reused syringes. How can a loving and just God punish the innocent? This problem of theodicy can no longer be dealt with by hiding in the understanding that God's dealings are mysterious. That explanation works only for those who can distance themselves from the problem, not for those who are fully involved in the pain. Yet church leaders themselves have often not lived what they have preached, if they have preached it at all! Why should the Church maintain the attitude of the scribes and the Pharisees (John 8:3-5)?

The Church has not proclaimed freedom for the prisoners. Many church members are deeply enslaved by sinful behaviours, and they wish they could behave differently but they cannot. Youths who have misunderstood their sexuality and have sold their bodies to sex outside marriage, girls who are sex slaves of older men some of whom are even church leaders, single and married women who, not knowing that they are worth much more that what their male counterparts have made them believe, have given in to sex pressure so as to gain positions of influence and high status; married men who have extra-marital relationships that enslave them so much so that they fail to be the kind of husbands and fathers that God intended them to be ... What about the homosexuals? What message does the Church proclaim concerning them? Does the Church just condemn them or does it continue ignoring them as if they do not exist? How does the Church proclaim freedom to such people when the church leaders have not understood the truth that sets people free, the truth of God's deliverance through Jesus Christ? The Church itself has been conformed to the standards of this world instead of being transformed by the renewing of their minds (Romans 12:1-2). The Church has proclaimed the negative message about sexuality (thus laying down the "do's and don'ts" too burdensome to be carried out) without looking at its creational intent, that it is an intrinsic and important aspect of humanness.

> By promoting a sense of guilt about sexual desire the church has been responsible for a great deal of harm in the world for many centuries and ruined many lives. Almost all of us are aware of sexual desires. The church has made us feel that this is sinful. The

church has created the impression that it disapproves of all sexual behaviour.[20]

Sexuality remains a taboo which is not talked about in most churches. Those who venture to talk about it are often misunderstood to be not morally upright. With this attitude how can the Church help fight against this pandemic? Freedom comes when truth is known. Freedom, even for the AIDS victims as they experience God's forgiveness and wholeness, as the Church helps the AIDS victims to forgive themselves and to be forgiven by their partners, their freedom will be deepened as the victims are helped to open up and confide in some people: expressing their fears and their hope.

When so many people are blinded by the confusing messages of this world: that sex is permissible in this revolutionary age, that women are sex objects created to attract the men and fellow women in cases of the gays, that sex outside marriage is not different from sex within marriage; the Church has to have a clear message about its stand backed up by what God says in the Bible. The Church has to have a clear definition of chastity as regards singles as well as married couples.

> Chastity refers to the faithfulness to the biblical standard for sex in relationship, to purity of thought and intent, and to avoidance of anything that cheapens or debases the self and others. It is more than abstinance from sexual activity outside marriage. It is a matter of living fullness of life as God intended.[21]

Can the Church preach the above truth that opens the eyes of the blind so that they see? Are the church leaders in a position where they can help the men especially married men to see that women were also made in the image of God and thus they should treat them with due respect and bury their wrong attitudes that make them look at their wives as tools that are made to serve them? Most male church leaders have been proponents of such wrong attitudes that have made it impossible to have men and women as companions supporting each

---

[20] Nicolson, *God in AIDS?*, p. 106.
[21] *Ibid.*, p. 29.

other in a self-sacrificing kind of love that looks not at one's own interests but rather thinks of the other more than the self. If there was companionship in marriage, there would be faithfulness, which would ensure a stable family that is the basis of a stable and righteous nation where youth, adult singles and married couples realize what is best for themselves and for each other.

Yet, as we see, the Church has not proclaimed release to the oppressed. In this AIDS crisis in Malawi, more and more women die of AIDS because their male counterparts have been involved in risk behaviour to selfishly satisfy their desire for pleasure. Culturally it is permissible for men to be unfaithful to their wives and physiologically it is easier for a man to pass the HIV infection to the woman. In the same way, innocent children die or suffer as uncared for orphans. In some cases after the woman has suffered the hurt of being cheated by her husband, she has to go through the pain of nursing the AIDS-dying husband before she has to finally die herself and leave her children as orphans. While unfaithfulness is enough injustice to her, the injustice mounts even higher as her dying husband refuses to be honest with her about what is killing him. Does she not have a right to know at least? Wouldn't knowing about what it is that happened, that which brought about the mess that she finds herself in *not* by her own choice, help her to go through all that she has to go through? Can the Church not break these chains of injustice as they help the man to open up and be honest with his wife? Can the Church not help the woman forgive her husband and be saved from bitterness? Can the Church not go as far as to offer healing in all this process.

The Church should also help break the Malawian taboo of not speaking about death to the dying. In Malawi, it is easier to 'assure' someone who is obviously dying that she/he will be well again than to talk about death and how one can go through it. Through his life, suffering, death and resurrection, Jesus offers healing which is holistic: spiritual, psychological, physical and social. So too can the Church, as a body of Christ, offer the above healing. The Church can practise faith healing for the AIDS victims who have faith enough to be healed apart from the healing which comes from the forgiveness of sin. Unfortunately in most cases the Church through its leaders and members has shown attitudes that inhibit openness among those members who are HIV positive. The fear of rejection makes the HIV infected person not open up to others, even Christians, so they end up in an attitude of denial and withdrawal because that is the only way they feel they can be accepted, approved and loved. If only the Church can help people open up and still have the assurance that they are loved, accepted and approved despite their HIV status, this would be an even more meaningful and deeper healing than the physical healing that otherwise preoccupies many Charismatic Christians.

Conclusion

As one becomes more and more devastated by the AIDS pandemic in Africa and the reality of increased cases of sexual promiscuity, one realizes that what has gone wrong is the understanding of sexuality. If it were the fear of AIDS, then we would be talking of chastity among the youth, adult singles and married couples. There can be no basis for sexual morality if there is no basis for human dignity. If, and only if, human beings, both male and female, would come to a realization that they were created in the image of God, both male and female, and that sexuality was created as part of humanness and that it was good, then we would be talking of hope in Africa. Hope that someday even before Christ returns, AIDS will be a thing of the past like any other scare that at one point in time had a solution and was no longer a scare. Since AIDS is a behavioural problem, proposed solutions will not be effective unless they change the behavioural patterns of people.

Sexual behaviour is very complicated because it is so private that sometimes it is only the two individuals involved that know about it so that if it is a problem it would be difficult to solve it. The training of church leaders should involve them taking courses in sexuality, Family Studies and communication which hopefully would help equip these leaders with skills that would help them present a meaningful gospel to their people. More than that, one would hope that these leaders would be able even to live the gospel that they preach. Since Africans are notoriously religious[22] and a majority of Africans profess Christianity, one would still hope that these theologically "trained" church leaders can impact the rest of their communities. There is hope as God's message becomes real in the life of an individual and the Holy Spirit makes the reality of God's salvation through Jesus Christ a reality in someone's life, the Holy Spirit then transforms the attitude of the one affected to a point where one lives not to satisfy selfish desires but lives for Christ and Christ crucified. This would entail that there is integrity in the Church. If this happens then the following becomes meaningful as regards sexual purity:

> Drink water from your own cistern, running water from your own well. Should your springs overflow in the streets, your streams of water in the public squares? Let them be yours alone, never to be shared with strangers. May your fountain be blessed, and may you rejoice in the wife of your youth. (Proverbs 5:15-18)

Suggestions to the Ministry of the Church

In general, the Church has to take up the challenge to give sex education to their youth, adult singles as well as married couples. I am aware that in some cases the Church in Africa has realized that as a church, it has AIDS and it has started being involved but in cases where it is still naive about this, it has to work hard and make the context of AIDS a reality that affects its presentation of the gospel. The Church should present sex education that does *not* only present the negative standpoint thus attempting to change behaviour out of fear for the consequences, rather it should present it within the positive intentions of the Creator that it was good. It should also present not only the physical aspects of sex but also the emotional, mental and spiritual - making clear what the Bible says about sexuality. This will help the members to have a true understanding of their sexuality and their human dignity which already has a very great impact on one's attitude towards sex. Moreover the Church in Africa should help people to

---

[22] J.S. Mbiti, *African Religions and Philosophy*, p. 4.

develop behavioural attitudes based on truth with love and not on shame.[23]

The Church should also equip itself with facts about HIV/AIDS. Whatever new developments there are, the Church should be in touch. In this context, the Church should have educators and counsellors who are "full of the Spirit" and full of knowledge about HIV/AIDS issues. These counsellors and educators should be relevant to different groups that are found in the Church: youths, adult singles and married couples. At this note, therefore, our faculties can make a vital contribution. What is the meaning of God's forgiveness to someone who after committing sexual sins has to die of AIDS? Can there be reconciliation even when one's HIV-status is not changed? Can there be a pursuit of holiness even in the case of someone who is essentially condemned to die - of AIDS? What would be the meaning of God's healing in this case? If God does not delight in human sacrifice, how does the Church interpret the death of the innocent partners and children who have to die of AIDS because of the irresponsibility of others? The Church seem to have no answers to these questions but it could look into the following suggestions:

For the Youth

1. The Church should help the youth to be accepted, approved and loved so that they develop a sense of belonging and they become part and parcel of the decision-making bodies. They should be taken seriously not as stupid 'good for nothings'.[24]

2. They should be equipped with the right information about sexuality through special programmes, church sermons etc.

---

[23] If you ask many people in Malawi about what helps them abstain from such behaviour as having sex outside marriage, if they are honest, they will tell you that it is more of the shame that they feel if caught than the guilt that comes with wrong behaviour.

[24] James Tengatenga, "Young People: Participation or Alienation?", in K.R. Ross (ed.), *God, People and Power in Malawi: Democratization in Theological Perspective,* Blantyre: CLAIM, 1996, p. 114.

3. They should have a support system of some kind for the HIV infected, the orphaned and those who otherwise are under peer pressure for sex. This support system can also help those youths who have been sexually active and need God's message of forgiveness and renewal.

4. Church leaders and others must be urged to live so as to be models for these young people.

5. There should be fora for the youths to discuss issues that affect them.

6. The Church should involve the young people in other activities like sport so as to keep them busy and profitably harness their excess energy which otherwise would be used destructively.

7. Help these young people to develop meaningful and pure relationships amongst themselves.

For Adult Singles[25]

1. The Church should recognize that singles face great pressures to be sexually active. It should develop a sexuality programme that is designed to respond to such deep and genuine pressures.

2. Train singles in the development of skills which will help them live in chaste relationships. Skills that will promote self-discipline, and that will help develop intimate relationships without sex.

3. Help singles develop support systems that encourage and honour chastity and promote healthy lifestyles.

4. Train counsellors that can be involved in pre-marital counselling that will prepare couples to develop a complete relationship, emotionally, physically, psychologically and spiritually.

5. In pre-marital counselling, encourage the couple to go for an HIV test so as to know their HIV status for realistic planning for their future.

6. Form support systems for the HIV-infected so that they still feel loved, accepted and approved.

---

[25] Adapted from *The Church's Response to the Challenge of AIDS/HIV*, p. 29.

For Married Couples

1. Provide marriage seminars on personal intimacy and faithfulness in marriage especially helping them understand that love is not a feeling but a commitment. All married couples should know the danger of HIV infection from sex outside marriage.

2. The Church should offer the moral and spiritual guidance for setting the standard of faithfulness in marriage relationship through sermons, teachings and other media.

3. The Church in Africa should encourage married couples to spend more time together even by simple efforts like encouraging couples to sit together during worship in church in those churches where up to now men sit separately from women. (i) This will help both men and women not to feel ashamed of each other (but identify with *each* other freely). (ii) It will also help those who are single to know for sure who is not single so as not to fall prey to the already married. Most of the time it is very difficult to know whether a man is married. This would help the young girls and single women to avoid "hoping"[26] for a man who is already married.

4. Set up support groups for couples who face HIV infection so as to provide the emotional, spiritual and physical support.

5. Where one spouse is HIV-positive, promote full disclosure of the infection to the other spouse, and where appropriate, to an expanded, caring community.

The Malawian experience shows that most Malawians will live with hope as long as they do not know the reality of their HIV status if HIV positive. They will suspect that they are HIV positive but they will be hopeful that probably they *are not* HIV positive. The moment most of these HIV positive individuals know for certain that they are HIV positive, they will die very fast because they will immediately give up on life. So the Church in Malawi faces the challenge of giving these hopeless individuals the hope that can only come from the reality of

---

[26] Hoping is a University of Malawi colloquialism, meaning secretly loving someone in the hope
that a love affair develops between you and the person for whom you hope.

God's love and Christ's liberation from their guilt, and their predicament. Perhaps the Church in Malawi should avail itself of the possibility of applying Christ's healing ministry to the Malawian community - emotional, physical as well as spiritual healing. What does the Church do if an HIV infected person comes forward and proclaims their faith in God's healing - that they believe that God can touch them and change their HIV status to negative? While looking into this challenge, the moving challenge in this chapter lives on - the Church has to affirm through and through - in its life and ministry, that chastity, not mere abstinence is a priority even as "Prevention is more possible than Cure!"

8. Singing, Dancing and Believing: Civic Education in Malawi Idiom

James Tengatenga

Nowadays the chief comes with his own dancers and his own song. When is he going to listen to our village songs? The crocodile that eats our cattle down the river, the hippo that devastates our crops, the tax burden that sends our young men scurrying into the hills in fear of the tax collector, and the thugs who rape our women. His dancers are going to sing our song? Know our problems? Feel our pain?

Until the "mbumbas" learn to sing our song and dance our dance, they cannot feel the village pain.[1]

Amene amva mmimba ndamene atsekula chitseko! *(It is the one who feels the pain who takes the measures to alleviate the pain!) [Malawian saying freely interpreted]*

"Civic education on what?", I was recently asked by a theological student when I told him I had been invited to speak about civic education. The understanding behind the question is that there is civic education for health issues, civic education on agriculture: generally any dissemination of information is understood as civic education. This reflects that most of us do not know what civic education is all about and much less how it is done. To this extent the whole area of civic education is a frontier of knowledge which we must explore, especially when it comes to what role our faith has to play in it. It is the intention of this chapter to make a move towards this frontier. Many models have been proposed and used but they seem not to have yielded the desired results. Are there other means that can be used to achieve the end?

---

[1] Hesse Mhango, *Mbumbas, feel the village's pain!,* Nyasanet, 7 November 1996.

The Need for Civic Education

Ife tonse? ... Boma! [All of us are? ... the Government!] (Repeat).

I am not campaigning for the Malawi Congress Party and neither am I poking fun at the Old Days. I would like us to think about what that slogan meant. Was it a statement of fact or was it a cry for recognition - a wish - a desire of the people?

During the Kamuzu era when the Malawi Congress Party Convention was about to meet and when it was in session we all gave our allegiance to the party and also pledged our agreement with and endorsed all the resolutions to be made at the convention *in toto*. In fact, even the delegates to the convention were already in agreement with whatever the powers that be brought before them. Our conventions were an endorsement of the party line all the time, at all cost. In that, we lived the lie that we all were involved in the decisions. *Ife tonse ... Boma!* meant endorsement of the Kamuzu *et al.* line. Kamuzu and his group were us and we were them. That was the claim we made whether we realized it or not. Because of this none of us can claim innocence about the abuse meted on us by the Kamuzu regime. *Ife tonse Bomar* was a pledge of complicity in the abuse. We thus had conspired to sell ourselves to the regime. We had sold our birthright by our complicity and self-deception. This was the extent of the psychological imprisonment of the populace by the regime. Kamuzu *et al.* did what they did in our name, with our permission.

This is what participatory democracy is all about: participation by representation! Isn't this the essence of Rousseau's social contract? Did we know our birthright, I wonder? I am of the opinion that we sold out because we were ignorant of our birthright and the system used the ignorance. The Bible says, "In the time of ignorance God forgave but now he has set judgement in Jesus Christ" (Acts 17:30).

Maybe it was not ignorance but that the chief brought with him his singers and dancers and they mesmerized us and we got taken in to the extent that we forgot our song and began to sing the strange song in our own land. But this time it was not our song and neither was it our dance. Even the land was no longer ours and neither were we free, we now belonged to Kamuzu. Yes, we sang with gusto, *"Zonse zimene nza Kamuzu Banda"!* [everything belongs to Kamuzu Banda]. Yes, we participated in Kamuzu's government. However, we are agreed that we did not *really* participate. We have also noted that now that we are free to participate we don't or rather by our apathy we give the government the idea that we have given them our endorsement. The powers that be are not wrong to make that assumption because apathy can be interpreted as endorsement of the status quo especially when we are supposed to know our birthright.

I am suggesting that the goal of civic education is to enlighten us as people about our birthright. What I would like to tackle in this chapter is the means by which we want to achieve that goal. In so doing I ask that we turn the direction of our sight inward and look at ourselves as civic educators.

I would like to suggest that we learn again the importance of song and dance as modes of both participation and civic education. In order to understand this I would like to return to Hesse Mhango's allusion to song and dance which I quoted at the head of this chapter. What Mhango was saying is not a novelty in Malawi folklore. Women sing about their troubles and other goings-on in society at the mortar as they pound their grain, *Gule Wamkulu* songs are also ongoing commentary on the goings-on in society, a means of imparting knowledge and inculcating morals and a means of rebuking both ordinary people and the village leaders. The messages received are taken seriously and where action needs to be taken it is taken. The needs and plight of the people are heard in their songs. Civility and morality are learnt therein. The regular *Mganda/Malipenga* dance visits from *Boma* to *Boma* [village to village; more like from club to club] are thus more than just song and dance. They are also a means of transmitting and sharing the stories of our people and their society. The trust level in these ways of communication is incredible. They can sing and dance very strong words to the powerful with impunity. Social capital is what this is based on. If the people can sing their own song and dance their own dance we will be a long way towards making democracy work.

In the Kamuzu era we had given room to the Leviathan *(a la* Hobbes) to police our trust. In fact we had let the monster act on our behalf. We had invested our trust in Leviathan and thus not only abdicated from involvement in the maintenance of democracy but we also gave Leviathan the right to become a god-like creature with omniscience and we stopped thinking, became frozen, atomized and isolated. We had not realized what North noticed that,

> if the state has coercive force, then those who run the state will use that force in their own interest at the expense of the rest of society.[2]

Leviathan ate up most of the other creatures and thus negatively impacted his biosphere! Elsewhere I had referred to this as us having fallen for Kamuzuist psycho-social engineering.[3] We were so dehumanized that in everything we gave deference to the Boma. Fredland has observed that:

> A political system which is dependent upon "one person, one vote" cannot operate when most of the potential voters see themselves as very much second class citizens and unworthy of the respect that a full-scale citizen deserves.[4]

The Aim of Civic Education

The time of ignorance is gone and here begins the work of civic education. The form of civic education I am suggesting is a form where people themselves regain their selfworth and their birthright and so participate effectively in their government. This is particularly so when there is a democratic dispensation which has not only to be savoured but also to be consolidated, nurtured and *sustained* by the growth of those institutions which make democracy work commonly known as civil society or the third sector (between family and government). The

---

[2] Robert Putnam, *Making Democracy Work: Civic Traditions in Modern Italy*, Princeton: Princeton University, 1993, p. 165.

[3] "Democracy in Malawi Two and Half Years On", unpublished address given at PAC General Council, January 1997.

[4] Richard Fredland, "Democracy and Deference", [unpublished notes] 8/97.

assumption here being that democracy will not work unless we have a vibrant civil society which civil society in turn fosters and/or engenders a civic minded ethos in society based on popular participation.

Some people have argued that civic education also has the aim of continuing the election euphoria. I would argue that that is not the business of civic education. That is the business of jingoism: Whip up the people's emotions and keep them excited! Euphoria by its nature is ephemeral, it does not last and thus cannot be maintained. If the aim of civic education is to keep and maintain it, it will be a chasing after the wind, an exercise in futility. My contention is that civic education has a more serious goal than just that. Democracy is not elections. Elections are the minimum requirement for a democracy and at that they must also be free, fair and regular. If seeking to maintain high percentages of voting is the goal of civic education we might as well stop now! Elections are part of the democratic ethos but they can become a mockery of democratic processes: A pilgrimage to the holy shrine of the voting cubicle, every so often, to abdicate by voting in a new or the same Leviathan! What I believe is a worthwhile exercise is to seek to maintain the interest in matters of government and governance in the people. To elicit in the people the commitment to participation which is theirs as responsible stakeholders.

This obviously begs the question of paradigms. How can we effectively accomplish the task of civic education? What paradigms will be most useful? To put it differently: Which way should we go to accomplish our goal?

The Educators

Before I tackle the issue of paradigms it is important to talk about the actors in this enterprise. The Government has been seen by some as one of the providers of this service, in fact the constitution of Malawi has a section to this effect. The government can, but whether it does is another thing. Leviathan will not have this as a priority on its agenda. If anything, Leviathan will turn it into propaganda - a tool for its own ends. The democratic state can be appropriated by the elected officials and they will use civic education to limit the responses of the people.

They, too, can create powerlessness by limiting choices and ask us to vote for either A or B. We would not know what happened to C, D, etc. Civic education can become the way to disempower people by inculcating that the responsibility of a democratic citizen is only to vote.

It has also been argued by some that the Education System in the country is the place. The Civics course in the curriculum is supposed to do it. If Leviathan is so pervasive, as the Kamuzu version of it was, it would, where it was attempted, be propaganda and for the most part it was not even attempted for fear of saying the wrong thing! One also wonders whether the classroom setting would be conducive to civic education which I believe is distinct from, though related to, civics.

I suppose that it is the realization of these dynamics that gave rise to the need for NGOs to take it upon themselves to provide this service. NGOs have the money and the personnel (and the ideologies) to do this work. However, they too have assumptions and limitations that do not augur well for the enterprise. These will be discussed as I tackle the paradigms.

The Church has also seen civic education as part of its business. Can the Church really do it? Is it not wandering into areas it shouldn't? In Malawi, where it is the most ubiquitous institution, to ignore it would be to ignore an important player and the one institution that touches all levels of society. It is in touch with the remotest parts of the country and commands the respect which opens doors. It is for this reason that some NGOs will not bypass the Church in their undertakings. Another reason for the Church's involvement is that it has a tendency to be neutral. Inculcating morals and civility is supposed to be part of its very nature. Respect of the dignity of persons is at the heart of the gospel. In its new ecclesiological forms it has emphasized the fostering of small ecclesial communities. It is thus in the business of community formation which in turn helps participation.

The Church in its life and teaching believes that every human being is made in the image of God and thus responsible and accountable to God and fellow human beings. This accountability is the one that leads to acts of altruism. We are responsible for each other as Christians. This responsibility is intended to help the Christian not to fall into sin. For this reason Christians are enjoined not to neglect meeting together, which meeting together is for helping each other not to sin (Hebrews 3:12-13). Civic education is, in this context, a means of helping one another to know our responsibility in society and so be able to call each other to account. In matters of faith one is not called to account for what one does not know.

The Church's teaching on the gifts of the Spirit helps the church not to despise the contributions of its members, however insignificant they may be (Rom. 12:3-8 and I Cor. 12). To that extent then, civic education is a matter of transmitting faith responsibility. Some of the writings of the prophets are diatribes against the abuse of power and authority by the rich and the powerful. Every Christian is expected to turn their sister or brother when they see them going astray. Paul says that one who turns a sinner from his/her ways saves the sinner and oneself. In the Epistle of James we are told that anyone who knows what is right to do and does not do it for him/her it becomes sin (Jas. 4:17). Therefore apathy and noninvolvement would be sin in this case.

Christian teaching says that we are stewards of God's creation. Stewardship has to do with good governance. This responsibility is both individual and collective. The Christian community is made up of brothers and sisters who are responsible one for another and are preoccupied with the common good. In the Christian community none is supposed to be in want: the strong are to help the weak and selfishness is sin and thus not acceptable.

Trust is another of the prized values of Christianity. Civic education has to do with building a community of trust. In this way the paths of Christian catechisis and civic education meet.

Civic education as one of the democratic processes is never finished. There is a continuous need for it as the life situations and needs change. The only time when civic education will cease to be needed is when human beings become perfect. This, Christian teaching says, will never be a state of being in this age but will be experienced at the consummation. As Karl Barth observed there is never a time, in this age, when the Church is not required to give its "No". A vibrant civil society is one that is a constant learner and one that has to keep striving for a perfect society until utopia is achieved. To keep at it in the face of the despotic tendencies of those in power and apathy on the part of the governed is an act of faith and an act based on hope - the hope that transformation of society and of individuals is a possibility. The Christian hopes and knows that they have a hope that does not disappoint (Rom. 8:24-25).

I realize this is painting a rosy picture of the Church. We all know the other, yes the darker, side of the Church where it consorts with Leviathan. All the same, I still believe that the Church is a site for civic education and that civic education is a matter of faith. It too has things to learn as its paradigms have been known to be authoritarian, domesticating and to anathematize dissent. It too suffers from a superiority complex - a know-it-all complex, especially reflected in its justice and peace activists.

Some Paradigms

The following paradigms are seen to be new and an improvement on the old ones which suggested that the recipients knew nothing and the educator knew everything - the old *tabula raza* theory. The job of the educator was seen as pouring knowledge into empty vessels and the people were to do as they were told. The new paradigms suggest that the educator acknowledges the knowledge and wisdom of the people s/he works with. However, for me it is this acknowledgment which is the source of the problems for these new paradigms. There seems to be an inherent patronization in them. Most of them suggest *coming down* to the people. Even when it is referred to as blending or being one with the people, one can't help but notice the condescension. As such I propose one which I believe takes care of the problems. Even as I propose it I realize that it too will be superseded in due course. I will thus present a critique of the current (new) paradigms in turn and at the end propose a way forward.

Initiator

This is the paradigm of the civic educator as the initiator. The educator sees a need among the people and responds to it by coming in with an initiative. It is the idea of the kind of intervention which is like the proverbial shot in the arm. The educator has the silver bullet that will do the job. The noble aim is to initiate and then leave the rest to the people. The initiative gives them something which they do not already possess. To illustrate this here are the objectives of PAC's civic education programme. Attention should be paid to the words in italics.

1. To *instill* a spirit of participation in people, especially in encouraging women to be fully involved and emphasizing the importance of having them in leadership positions.
2. To *make* people aware of their rights and responsibilities in a democracy, and in particular their role in democracy at the local level.
3. To *develop* structures that can sustain democracy at a local level through the action and involvement of people in their own communities.
4. To *educate* all citizens, irrespective of party affiliation, religion, ethnic group, or any other distinction, about their role in a democratic Malawi.[5]

What is clear in this is that PAC has an agenda to push. It has the truth which it wants to *instill* in the people about which it wants to *make* people aware so as to *develop* structures and so *educate all* citizens. The people are expected to be recipients of these goods. They have nothing to contribute to the enterprise. The assumption is that PAC knows the needs of the people and can articulate them more than the people can. PAC sends its officers and other hirelings like me to go over to the people to do the job. Obviously we are so sophisticated that we use the language of bringing that extra something which is missing in the community: the silver bullet. The silver bullet is with PAC!

---

[5] James L. Cairns and G.S. Dambula, *Gwira Mpini Kwacha: Civic Education to Build Local Democracy,* PAC Trainer's Manual, 1996, p. iv, [my italics].

This is true not only of PAC. Many NGOs, even though they will not admit it, operate on this paradigm. They see themselves as initiators, both in the sense of being the impetus and catalyst,[6] and in the sense of the African traditional rites of passage.[7] To this Jahn's words (said in reference to relations between the super powers and Africa in the 1960s) are an apt critique:

> And the one who is addressed, the African, is asked no questions. Freedom? Equal rights? "Yes, but only when you have been baptized in the name of Christianity, in the name of democracy, in the name of civilization, in the name of economics, in the name of communism ... according to the particular faith in question. For all these gods are the children of the one who says: "I am the Lord ... and thou shalt!"
>
> Plans are elaborated, programmes made, books written as to what should be opened up, in what direction it should be led but the Africans are for the most part ignored. Nearly everyone who writes, speaks, arranges, recommends - disposes of them, because he thinks: "I am ... and thou shalt! "[8]

Yes, the chief brings his dancers and they sing their own song!

This has also led to connecting civic education with advocacy. Advocacy sounds like an innocent word but it too has connotations of someone acting on the other's behalf. Who will the advocate be and whose song will they sing? In this case we are talking of someone, like

---

[6] The word catalyst is important here. A catalyst helps the process of change but itself remains unchanged. Ferment is the word that has gained currency with its connotation that the ferment by its nature changes in the process. See Kenneth R. Ross, "Not Catalyst but Ferment: The Distinctive Contribution of the Churches to Political Reform in Malawi 1992-1993", in Matembo S. Nzunda and Kenneth R. Ross (eds.), *Church, Law and Political Transition in Malawi 1992-94,* Gweru: Mambo, 1995, 2p. 31-42.

[7] In initiation rites the initiands have nothing to say: they receive the wisdom handed down to them. They have no right to say anything: they receive and to talk back is the height of disrespect and culpable for punishment.

[8] Jahnheinz Jahn, 1961 cit. R. Fredland, "Recipient Fatigue", [unpublished notes] 7/97.

an NGO, speaking on behalf of the people. The assumption being that the people do not have the necessary skill, hence their need for an advocate who would then speak to Leviathan or any other potentate. It may be that the advocates see themselves as teaching by example. However, if civic education has been so effective as to enable the people themselves to be their own advocates able to articulate their needs and grievances this would obviate the need. Trusting the advocate to do it for you is as good as trusting Leviathan. If the advocate is one of them or some from among themselves that would be a different thing for it will be the people speaking (hopefully!).

Connected to this is *lobbying as* a new option in civic education. It too should be a goal in civic education. If the people are articulate they can do it themselves. They can also take the option of sending representatives to do it for them. The aim of civic education would be to produce these lobbyists from among the people.

Facilitator

Another popular word in civic education is facilitator. The paradigm is that of the educator who acknowledges the wisdom of the people, in fact goes out of his/her way to find out what the people know and what their needs are. The facilitator is then supposed to facilitate the process of identification of needs and skills inherent in the community and those that are lacking. The facilitator comes in because s/he sees that people are not organized enough or coherent enough and thus sees the task as that of facilitating the organization of the community. Because s/he has contacts or knows the systems and structures of power s/he can open some doors for the people. The facilitators see their job as that of helping direct the discussions and pointing to new possibilities where necessary.

The problem I see with this paradigm is that the facilitator is most likely involved in self-deception. I am not saying this in a pejorative way. Let me put it this way: Do the people see you as *facilitator* or is that your view of yourself? Most likely they see you as *initiator!* If that be the case then the whole work will not be what is intended and so will the results.

There seems to be a naïveté in this approach which assumes that the people are willing and trust each other enough to make collective action work. Trust and reciprocity are important elements in any collective initiatives; especially in Malawi where community has been so destroyed and the level of trust is very low. So to come and identify the needs and begin facilitating community organization is already doomed to failure because the mindset in the community is that of one person for oneself and Leviathan for us all. The situation which prevails is like that which Game Theorists have called *the tragedy of the commons, the logic of collective action and the prisoner's dilenzma.*[9] Says Putnam,

> This quandary does not arise from malevolence or misanthropy, although those sentiments may be fostered by its grim denouement. Even if neither party wishes harm to the other, and even if both are conditionally predisposed to cooperate - I will, if you will - they can have no guarantee against reneging, in the absence of verifiable, enforceable commitments. Worse yet, each knows that the other faces the same predicament. "It is necessary not only to trust others before acting cooperatively, but also to believe that one is trusted *by* others". In such circumstances, each finds cooperation irrational, and all end up with an outcome no one wants - unharvested corn, overgrazed commons, deadlocked government.[10]

---

[9] See Putnam, *Making Democracy Work*, pp. 163-64: The tragedy of the commons is one in which

everyone is unwilling to have their use of the common meadow limited for the common good. The dismal logic of collective action is one in which every worker would benefit if all struck simultaneously, but whoever raises the strike banner risks betrayal and so everyone waits hoping to benefit from someone else's foolhardiness. The prisoner's dilemma is one in which the temptation to defect is strong. If both remained silent, both prisoners would be let off lightly, but unable to co-ordinate their stories, each is better off squealing no matter what the other does.

[10] Putnam, *Making Democracy Work*, p. 164.

No wonder civic educators have come out frustrated at the fact that they do not get the desired results even though it had been evident that they had animated the people enough.

Partner

Another paradigm is that of partner. It is believed that the partner model projects the partner as someone who is humble enough to acknowledge that s/he does not have the answers and that s/he is not initiating anything and neither is s/he facilitating anything. The educator is a partner with the people. The people will play a greater part in their education. The partner becomes part of the people and uses their wisdom and means of inculcating the virtues. This is now common language in the Church and in NGO circles. There is a willingness to learn as one teaches. *A partner assumes equality and believes that their contribution is as good as that of the local people.*

I believe that this paradigm runs into problems precisely on this last point. It is imperative that the educator accept that s/he has ideas but that those ideas may not even be necessary as the people themselves already have valid ways which the partner would need to learn and identify with before they can earn the freedom to compose their own song and choreograph their own dance among the people. Equality is not something that can be assumed. A stranger is always a stranger until they earn the right to be treated as equals. It is not a given, it is earned by immersion in the ways of the people. Granted this takes a long time and does not always fit in with our impatience and the requirement to write reports for whoever it is who pays for the civic education programme. To that extent even the partnership paradigm ends up being patronizing as well, albeit unintended. I, however, believe that this paradigm is on to something hence my proposed way forward takes off from it.

Song and Dance: The New Paradigm

> Come dance with me,
> Hear my song and learn what I can do.
> Come dance with me
> So that you can know who I am.

> Come dance with me
> And you will earn the right to speak about and (maybe) for me.
> If my song becomes your song and my dance your dance,
> You can speak with me.[11]

> **Mlendo abwera ndikalumo kakuthwa** (Don't despise a stranger they may actually bring the solution to our problem! [literally a sharp knife]) [Chichewa saying freely interpreted]

Am I suggesting a new paradigm? I would not presume to do such a thing. My humble submission is that we need to go back in order to go forward: the new is in the old. Back is the way to the future. We *cognoscenti* need to accept that what we know is "new" knowledge. New in the sense of novel and exotic. It makes no sense to most of the people in the village. This to me accounts for the frustrations that we modernists experience when our efforts at conscientizing and educating seem to fall on stony ground. We need to learn from the people and use their methods and not impose our new pedagogics which are so alien and alienating. As elders in the village usually say in response, "*Nzakusukulu zimenezo. Taima tikuuze zenizeni*" (That is book knowledge; let us show you the real thing). Another critique is that most of our civic education scratches where it does not itch. The problem with our leaders is that they are usually absentee leaders, and thus outsiders and so are most of us who presume to be civic educators. We come with our own songs and dancers and ignore the ways of the people. In fact we, in our ignorance, assume that the people's songs and dances are purely aesthetic. We do not realize that they go beyond the aesthetic to the ethical.

Our songs are about democracy and participation, which are very nice words and ideas to which all will assent. But that is still our song, not their song - participation in our dance and not the people's dance. The democracy and participation we are talking about is that which is dictated by the West and its institutions. They expect Africa to do overnight what took them many centuries to achieve. Malawi's, and

---

[11] James Tengatenga, *"Sing and Dance with Me"*, a poem composed for this chapter.

indeed most of Africa's democracy is in its *infancy* but civic educators want to give it advice which is suitable for a *teenager* or an *adult!* Unless we learn the people's song and dance their dance we will scratch were it does not itch. Graduates of our civic education ToT's will come out with new knowledge and that is what it is going to be, new and exotic with no connection to the ways of the people - alien to the people and also highlighting our alienness. To that extent we will alienate the people.

If we are not careful as civic educators we will suffer the same fate that the politicians suffer. The politicians elicit not participation but cynicism and apathy. In poor countries like Malawi there are other needs that are important to the people. The most important is subsistence. What do I eat and how do I get a good price for my crop and how do I circumvent the middleperson who rips me off. The important issues are local issues and if there is to be participation at all it is participation at the local level not in the big Government.

As indicated earlier the game theory is played out to the full. Everyone expects Leviathan, the donor, the NGO, the Church to do something for them. These organizations are supposed to be nonpartisan and impartial and are seen as the providers of the amenities and the goods. That's what they exist for: to free the people to go on with their (selfish?) pursuits. The people do not trust the politicians or any of the community leaders. What makes us believe that they will trust us? They will use us and clap for us as we sing our song and dance our dance. They may even join in but it will remain our song and our dance and will never be theirs. There is no shortcut except through what Putnam calls social capital.[12] These are reciprocal relationships of trust and collective action. This is not easily acquired; it is earned by immersion in the community and is based on trust and social links.

NGOs and other civic educators assume that politics are important for the people hence our preoccupation with the political. But the important thing for most of the people is their survival. In that sense then, economic issues are important for the people. Only when there

---

[12] Putnam, *Making Democracy Work*.

is serious attention to their economic needs will their attention be led to the political which is inherent in the economic. This is where the pain is. We need to ask ourselves the question: If you were hungry and your family were hungry, would talk about political participation be important to you? Would you see your future tied up in politics? Would you have the time and energy to devote to such pursuits? Chances are that one would rather be involved in what will satisfy one's survival needs - the economic. Organization of groups around their needs for survival, their needs for markets to sell their produce and their need to organize over against the exploitative middlepersons will in turn be organizing for political ends. This is what social capital is all about - building communities of trust working towards the common good.

Our politicians have been shrewd. They have played on our lack of trust. They have used *the tragedy of the village common* and *the prisoner's dilemma* as the game theorists have taught us. It is the place of civic education to help build the social capital. I am here suggesting that anyone interested in civic education in Malawi (and Africa) should invest in building social capital "and all these things shall be added unto you". I am therefore suggesting that we concentrate on encouraging and sponsoring choral and dance troupes and encouraging the composition of songs about society and about the people themselves. Says Putnam about social capital:

> Networks of civic engagement, like the neighbourhood associations, choral societies, cooperatives, sports clubs, mass-based parties ... represent intense horizontal interaction. Networks of civic engagement are an essential form of social capital: The denser such networks in a community, the more likely that its citizens will be able to cooperate for mutual benefit. Why, exactly, do networks of civic engagement have this powerfully beneficial side-effect?[13]

He goes on to answer his question by suggesting that these work because they reduce the chances of defection since all people will

---

[13] *Ibid.*, pp. 173-174.

have a stake in working together and thus they foster reciprocity. He further says,

> Networks of civic engagement facilitate communication and improve the flow of information about the trustworthiness of individuals. Networks of civic engagement allow reputations to be transmitted and refined as the past behaviour and present interests of potential partners, while uncertainty reinforces dilemmas of collective action. Thus other things being equal, the greater the communication (both direct and indirect) among participants, the greater their mutual trust and the easier they will find it to cooperate.[14]

In this way people can work together against their elected officials because they know that they will stand together. They can have a say in who their representative is going to be over against the party's nominee whom they may not want. In this way they may choose a people's person who will be invested with their trust to represent them. As long as the people are divided and there is no trust among them they cannot act collectively. Their participation will be that of fulfilling what they consider an enforced obligation.

Social capital will help them to trust each other enough so as to choose from among themselves their own representatives, advocates and lobbyists. Only in this way can we topple the old guard of politicians who have oppressed us for so long. As the cry has been heard on the Nyasanet,

> *We need a new political tradition and we'll only achieve this by having a new breed of politicians,* politicians whose primary goals should be to serve the electorate not to be served or to enrich themselves and their friends.[15]

If our aim is to help create a new political tradition we would do well to pour our resources and energies into encouraging the people to find their singing voice and dancing feet. So they can sing their song again

---

[14] *Ibid.*, p. 174.

[15] Fukula H. Nyekanyeka, Nyasanet, 6 November 1996, original emphasis.

and the chief can listen to the village woes. We will do well to invest in social capital.

This applies not only to the NGOs but also to the Church. The Church being a specialist in building community, it has to call on its tradition to be

an effective civic educator. As I indicated before, the Church is a community of moral people and a morality making community. If it lives up to this it cannot only be a teacher by word but also by example. The advantage that the church has over the other organizations in this is that it already operates at the grassroots with local operatives. The leaders of local prayer houses or outstations are normally local people who need not be introduced to the community. If they speak about the local situation they would speak from the gut which no other person, even the pastor, is capable of doing. Those traditions that do not have local leadership would do well to help encourage its development so as to facilitate the civic education and those that have these in place would do well to give them greater recognition, support and skills to effectively do their job.

The Roman Catholic Church has implemented the concept of Basic Christian Communities *(Miphakati)*. Basic Christian Communities are local gatherings of Catholic Christians in their places of residence for Bible study and mutual support. One sees this as a vehicle which can be used effectively for purposes not only of pastoral issues but also community, and thus political, issues. The distinction I have made here between the pastoral and the political is really artificial because the pastoral has to do with the issues that affect the lives of the people as they relate to one another and their emotional and spiritual being and these can be (in fact are) political. The Church is the people and, as such, talking about their plight and organizing for collective action should come naturally to it. The Latin American Church has demonstrated the effectiveness of these within its context.[16]

---

[16] D.H. Levin, *Popular Voices in Latin American Catholicism,* Princeton: Princeton University Press, 1992, has also given a critique of their effectiveness as sites of political organisation.

Hymns have always been used as vehicles of imparting theology in the tradition of the Church. To this extent it would not be beyond possibility for the Church to employ this in matters of community. In fact this already happens in charismatic and youth manifestations of the Church where choruses are the order of the day and new ones are continuously produced. Stanley Hauerwas has talked about the way the church as a community of character and a character forming community can continually retell its story in response to the situation it finds itself in without losing the essence of its being.[17] In Malawian story-telling the point of the story is brought home in song which is in the form of a refrain in which everyone joins the story-teller. As a character-forming community the Church has a responsibility to call the political leaders to account of their leadership, especially since most of the leaders are members of the Church (i.e. reminding them of their story). The rest of the members would in turn see this as part of the way of life of Christians to call each other to account.

To this extent, then, the Church would be in keeping with its character to see itself as the site for civic education. If it is not doing it, it is time it too sang the people's song and danced their dance.

Yes "until the *mbumbas* learn to sing our song and dance our dance they cannot feel the village's pain" and so cannot articulate it. The *mbumba* were Kamuzu's civic educators. They sang Kamuzu songs and thus propagated the Kamuzuist political tradition. If we, in the tradition of the *mbumba* sing our songs and dance our dance, when are we going to listen to the village song? Until we learn to sing the village song and dance the village dance we cannot feel the village's pain and consequently cannot presume to be civic educators. Only then can we earn the right to use our knife.

---

[17] Stanley Hauerwas, *A Community of Character: Toward a Constructive Christian Social Ethic,* Notre Dame: University of Notre Dame, 1983 edition.

9. "Not War but Defence of the Oppressed"? Bishop Mackenzie's Skirmishes with the Yao in 1861

Jonathan Newell

In 1861 Bishop Charles Frederick Mackenzie, the first Christian missionary to attempt to establish a permanent mission in what would eventually become the independent state of Malawi, led a series of armed raids against the Yao groups in the vicinity of his settlement at Magomero. Just why he felt compelled to do this, and how he managed to justify such actions in his own mind while pursuing the vocation of a Christian missionary, is the subject of this chapter.[1]

Charles Frederick Mackenzie's brief and tragic pioneering missionary career in Malawi all began in 1857 when David Livingstone addressed the undergraduates of Oxford and Cambridge and confronted a privileged generation with what he believed to be the appalling conditions in Central Africa. His impassioned appeal led to the creation of "The Oxford, Cambridge, Dublin, and Durham Mission to Central Africa"[2] The objective of this infant missionary organisation was not only to convert the natives but also in line with all the self-confidence of the Victorian era, to virtually export the perceived advantages of British culture and social structure lock, stock and barrel to the interior of the African continent. Especially important was felt to be the need to demonstrate "the sinfulness and disastrous consequences of a

---

[1] This chapter is loosely based upon my Faith and Knowledge Seminar Paper No. 15 entitled, There are arguments in favour of our taking up arms': Bishop Mackenzie and the War against the Yao in 1861", which was originally presented on 21 January 1992. It was subsequently published in *The Society of Malawi Journal,* Vol. 45/1 (1992), pp.15-45.

[2] This rather unwieldy name was later replaced by the more familiar Universities Mission to Central Africa or UMCA.

traffic in human beings".[3] In fact, Mackenzie and his missionary party actually sailed on board a Royal Navy warship assigned to anti-slavery duty on their way to the mouth of the Zambezi river.[4]

Traditionally Mackenzie has been described as a kind of saint who could "rob you of your heart"[5] In reality, however, this is a most misleading picture of him. Mackenzie was actually chosen to lead this pioneering missionary expedition into the heart of Africa not only because of his general piety, but also because he looked every inch the confident, dominant and inspiring Victorian explorer:

> his fine manly form and presence not only indicated his great physical capacity for such a work, but caused every one who saw him to think instinctively of the homage which savage natives ever pay to personal endowments and physical powers such as his, and the great advantage that he would thus gain in his dealing with them.[6]

This was a man, therefore, who could impose himself upon others by the sheer force of presence.

The Influence of David Livingstone

A vital influence upon Mackenzie was his working relationship with David Livingstone. The Doctor had been appointed Her Majesty's Consul for East and Central Africa so that, as far as Mackenzie was concerned, he was the legally constituted secular authority for the area. Thus, where Livingstone led, the good bishop was likely to follow, even in matters of ethics and theology. In fact, before he left England, Mackenzie had expressed himself most forcefully on "the question of using arms" and maintained that it was "unlawful under

---

[3] *Report of the Oxford, Cambridge, Dublin and Durham Mission to Central Africa for 1862,* London: J.E. Adlard, 1863, p. 13.

[4] Owen Chadwick, *Mackenzie's Grave,* London: Hodder and Stoughton, 1959, pp. 9-13, 19.

[5] *Ibid.,* pp. 36-38.

[6] *Report of the Oxford, Cambridge, Dublin and Durham Mission to Central Africa for 1862,* p. 12.

any circumstances".[7] On the other hand, in February 1861 he had bought a gun and ammunition from the captain of HMS *Lyra* and charged the cost to the mission in Britain.[8] Nonetheless, on 5 July, while on board the *Pioneer* - Livingstone's vessel which was carrying the bishop and his missionary team up the Zambezi and towards Magomero in the Shire Highlands, which the famous explorer had selected as the first site for the mission - the "evening discussion [was] on forgiving enemies", and especially "what is the meaning of turn to him the other also".[9] However, the Doctor also became involved in this interchange and, when the question of what missionaries should do if attacked was raised and the bishop declared that he opposed the "taking of guns for any purpose", he was overruled by Livingstone who argued that, if the missionaries carried firearms, they would not have to use them "for they are the greatest pacificators in the world if you have peaceful intentions yourself".[10] Mackenzie found himself unable to counter the Doctor's argument with the result that the missionaries left the *Pioneer* "well armed'.[11] Perhaps symbolizing the continuing uncertainty of his own feelings concerning the matter, Mackenzie subsequently tramped through the bush towards Magomero carrying both his crosier and his gun - though significantly Livingstone took the lead.[12]

On 16 July at Mbami's village, on the way to Magomero, Livingstone released some slaves from an armed party and handed over these men to Mackenzie, who was delighted as he felt "we had at once the

---

[7] A. Anderson-Morshead, *The History of the Universities Mission to Central Africa,* London: UMCA, 1955, Vol. 1, p. 16.

[8] Mackenzie to Strong, 4 February 1861, Rhodes House Library (RHL), UMCA Al(I) A/1/65-74.

[9] Bishop Mackenzie's Journal, Vol. 2,5 July 1861, RHL, UMCA Al(I) B/3.

[10] H. Rowley, *The Story of the Universities' Mission to Central Africa,* London: Saunders, Otley and Co., 1867, 2nd edition, p. 84.

[11] Lovell Procter's Journal, 8 July 1861, RHL, UMCA Al (II) B.

[12] Mackenzie's Journal, Vol. 2, 15 July 1861.

materials of definite mission work".[13] Over the next four days as they approached Magomero, this act was repeated with the result that the bishop's flock was from its earliest days made up exclusively of liberated slaves. Meanwhile, the events of 16 July altered Mackenzie's views about the employment of armed force. "I am clear that in such cases it is right to use force, and even fire if necessary, to *rescue captives*. I should do so myself if necessary," he now declared.[14] On the other hand, he still remained totally convinced that such activities were not a fitting task for a bishop and his entourage, arguing that it was "more becoming" for guns to be wielded by others, rather than by himself or any other member of his profession. Moreover, he also expressed the hope that Livingstone would not "beat his ploughshare into a spear altogether, or whatever it ought to be".[15]

The Situation in the Shire Highlands

It would be wrong to suggest that Mackenzie's gradual acceptance of the legitimacy of armed force was purely the result of his interaction with Livingstone. The very political and social environment itself in the Shire Highlands in this period, it might be argued, virtually demanded action of some kind. As one Scottish missionary put it about twenty years later, as he confronted the harsh realities of slavery in roughly the same area: "People at home cannot, I think, feel as we feel when we stand face to face - ay, and often helpless - before such scenes."[16] Essentially, social order had all but disintegrated around Magomero and the missionaries found some of the scenes of human misery which they witnessed almost too much to bear: "All this misery is either

---

[13] Mackenzie to Bishop of Cape Town, 4 November 1861, RHL, UMCA Al(I) A/1/32-37.

[14] Rowley, *The Story of the Universities' Mission to Centra Africa,* p. 106.

[15] *Ibid*. Mackenzie was referring to Joel 3:10 which in the Authorised Version reads: "Beat your ploughshares into swords, and your pruning hooks into spears". He had clearly failed to recall the precise wording of the verse.

[16] William Robertson, *The Martyrs of Blantyre. Henry Henderson. Dr John Bowie. Robert Cleland,* London: James Nisbert and Co., 1892, p. 124.

heartbreaking or heart hardening; God help me, I sometimes fear that it is having the latter effect upon me," one of them con-fessed.[17]

In effect, what Mackenzie encountered at Magomero was something for which even Livingstone was not prepared. Since the Doctor's last visit to the area in 1859, the local political situation had deteriorated drastically. As far as the bishop could make out, the Yao were ravaging the area and enslaving the local Mang'anja.[18] Initially, Mackenzie believed that the Yao had only been in the area for about three months.[19] H. C. Scudamore, probably the most levelheaded of the bishop's party,[20] summarized the extent of information available to the bishop at about this time in a letter home:

> He found them [the Mang'anja] in a state of alarm and misery caused by the invasion of a hostile tribe which threatened to sweep over the whole country ... He learnt that this tribe had communication with the slave traders who were interested in their marauding, and bought their captives of war, and probably supplied them with arms and ammunition.[21]

Not surprisingly, therefore, as far as Mackenzie was concerned, the Yao were clearly the aggressors since they lived "on the produce of the industry of others",[22] while the Mang'anja were patently deserving of his sympathy.

In reality, however, such assumptions, based as they were upon limited information, were dangerous half-truths which would cause the missionaries to become embroiled in a political landscape they did not fully comprehend. The Yao were not simply temporarily raiding the

---

[17] Rowley to brother, 24 January 1863, RHL, UMCA Al(II) A/Rowley MS/146-147.

[18] Mackenzie to Bishop of Cape Town, 4 November 1861.

[19] Mackenzie's Journal, Vol. 2, 20 July 1861.

[20] Landeg White, *Magomero: Portrait of an African Village*, Cambridge: Cambridge University Press, 1987, p. 13.

[21] Scudamore to Edward, 2 October 1861, RHL, UMCA Al(I) A/Scudamore MS/29-38.

[22] Mackenzie to Mrs Crawley, 25 September 1861, RHL, UMCA A1(1)/B1.

environs of Magomero; rather they were being pushed south by the Ngoni and had come to stay.[23] But the situation was actually far more complicated than this simple analysis suggests. In their desperation to understand what was going on around them, Mackenzie and his companions tried to impose European ideas upon an African environment. Thus, in their opinion, inter-"tribal" conflict appeared to be rather like "the collision of different balls on a snooker table. The balls moved around into new positions, but the number and size and colour was constant".[24] In fact, however, the Mang'anja were divided into different chieftaincies and the mere appearance of the missionaries actually weakened Mang'anja unity. The Yao, meanwhile, were far from the monolithic ethnic group Scudamore and the bishop believed them to be, but rather were themselves separated into independent chieftaincies who spent probably as much time fighting each other as they did raiding the Mang'anja. Furthermore, there already was a considerable degree of "ethnic mixture" between Yao and Mang'anja in the Shire Highlands, with relationships based upon kin or ethnic group mattering less than those between patron and client.[25]

The Mission Site at Magomero

Given the nature of the turmoil in the surrounding countryside, it was always likely that the primitive mission station established at Magomero would be somewhat out of the ordinary. In speaking to local Mang'anja leaders, for example, Livingstone initially stressed that the site would be "a strong place to which women and children might flee in case of attack".[26] Essentially, therefore, Magomero was to be a quasi-military refuge for the local people. As a result, the missionaries wasted no time in seeking to improve the defensive qualities of the site, which was basically a low-lying peninsula created by a small river

---

[23] G.H. Wilson, *The History of the Universities' Mission to Central Africa*, Westminster: UMCA, 1935, p. 10.

[24] White, *Magomero: Portrait of an African Village*, p. 46.

[25] *Ibid.*, pp. 46-49.

[26] Mackenzie's Journal, Vol. Ia, 25 July 1861.

with steep banks.[27] A fence was put up, a dam considered in order to raise the level of the river and so improve the defences, the immediate vegetation was cleared and a system of "night watching established to avoid surprise".[28]

Slowly but surely the traditional work of a mission station gave way to a concentration upon defensive arrangements and military matters.[29] Moreover, even daily routines amongst the mission's very flock could take on a military appearance: "The boys are also drilled every day, they bathe at the word of command, jumping when the order is given, from a log into water **up** to their waists".[30] Not surprisingly, given the activities of the missionaries, these same boys started to fashion toy guns out of bamboo "just like English boys".[31] Frequent alarms caused by reports of approaching groups of warriors made routine spiritual work difficult and forced Mackenzie, for instance, to climb the nearest hill with his field glasses "to see what was to be seen".[32] This "strange character" of the mission at Magomero made it **hard** for the missionaries to think and act objectively, or break free from **the** para-military side of their work which took up so much of their time.[33] Indeed, Mackenzie began to think in terms of mission sites, like that at

---

[27] The site can be visited today and the steep-sided walls of the river bank still strike one as significant defensive features.

[28] Mackenzie's Journal, Vol. 2, 26 July and 3 August 1861.

[29] For example see Rowley, *The Story of the Universities' Mission,* p. 300.

[30] Mackenzie to Aunt Mary, 12 October 1861, RHL, UMCA Al (F) A/1/4-7.

[31] Horace Waller quoted in White, *Magomero: Portrait of an African Village,* p. 26. Waller was another of the mission's personnel.

[32] Waller's Journal, 30 July 1861 quoted in *Report of the Oxford, Cambridge, Dublin and Durham Mission to Central Africa for 1861,* London: Spottiswoode and Co., 1862, p. 24.

[33] R. Keable, *Darkness or light: Studies in the History of the Universities' Mission to Central Africa Illustrating the Theory and Practice of Missions,* London: UMCA, 1912, p. 109.

Magomero, as potential strong-points which would "pacify" the country by their very presence.[34]

The First Armed Expedition and Skirmish

Realistically, merely to construct a mission site at Magomero with the intention of working amongst the Mang'anja, while at the same time offering them refuge from the raiding Yao, meant that there was a very high probability Mackenzie and his colleagues would be drawn into further conflict with the Mang'anja's enemies. Livingstone made this high probability a virtual certainty by leading the first armed expedition out of Magomero on 22 July 1861. The original aim of this particular move is not entirely clear, with Mackenzie merely recording that he and his colleagues marched out of Magomero to "try to do something".[35] The result was a small-scale skirmish, after a hopeless attempt at a parley, between the Europeans and their Mang'anja "allies" and the Yao on 23 July. A local Yao village was burnt down and shots and arrows were exchanged at 50 yards; but very little was achieved other than the total alienation of the neighbouring Yao towards the mission.[36]

Though this punitive attack probably did not impress the Yao a great deal, it did have a profound impact upon Mackenzie himself. Although he tried to distance himself from direct involvement in the fighting, he was nonetheless deeply affected by what he saw that day. He was standing by the Doctor when the "order" was given to open fire and offered his own weapon to Livingstone on realizing that the latter actually had no rifle with him. In his own words the bishop explained his thinking at this moment: "I preferred not to use it [the rifle] and ...

---

[34] Mackenzie's Journal, Vol. 2, 19 September 1861.

[35] Mackenzie to Bishop of Cape Town, 4 May 1861.

[36] Photocopy of a letter by David Livingstone from Fitzwilliam Museum, Cambridge, held in Malawi Collection, University of Malawi Library, n.d. Chadwick gives the date of this encounter as 22 July (see *Mackenzie's Grave*, p. 49). However, he was probably wrong since Mackenzie's Journal, Procter's Journal and Livingstone himself all place it on 23 July.

thought it more seemly that his finger should pull the trigger and not mine".[37] Nevertheless, Mackenzie, for all his reservations, found the action secretly rather exciting. In his journal he made a sketch map of the area in which the "battle" took place, while at the same time noting how the enemy's shouts of defiance reminded him of Homeric encounters and the story of David and Goliath.[38]

Livingstone's Legacy

Livingstone left Magomero at the end of July. Before doing so, however, he warned Mackenzie not to lead another similar expedition, as he would be "oppressed with requests" if he did so.[39] Nonetheless, Livingstone does seem to have given the Mang'anja a somewhat ambiguous message concerning the events of 23 July. According to Mackenzie he told them that the mission had come to "teach them about God, and to promote peace"; however, he then went on to suggest to them that if the Yao did not learn from the experiences of the raid on their village then "we would look after them again".[40]

None too surprisingly, many writers have sought to argue that Livingstone's legacy, which he bequeathed to the bishop at Magomero, was a destructive one. Henry Rowley, another of Mackenzie's colleagues, claimed that the bishop's later armed expeditions were "the inevitable consequence of his [Livingstone's] advice and deeds".[41]

It certainly is true that the action of 23 July 1861 set the pattern for future developments, as there can be little doubt that Mackenzie's own punitive excursions, in terms of their organisation and execution,

---

[37] Mackenzie to Bishop of Cape Town, 4 November 1861.

[38] Mackenzie's Journal, Vol. 2, 23 July 1861.

[39] Rowley, *The Story of the Universities' Mission*, p. 123.

[40] Mackenzie's Journal, Vol. Ia, 25 July 1861. Chadwick questions the accuracy of the bishop's journal here (see *Mackenzie's Grave*, p. 51).

[41] H. Rowley, *Thirty Years in Central Africa*, London: Wells Gardner and Co., 1881, p. vi. See also Anderson-Morshead, *The History of the Universities' Mission*, p. 18 and H. Goodwin, *Memoir of Bishop Mackenzie*, Cambridge: Denton, Bell and Co., 1865, 2nd ed., p. 280 for similar arguments.

bear a striking similarity to the first skirmish with the Yao led by Livingstone.[42] However, we would do well not to blame Livingstone for everything. He was probably almost as "politically innocent" of the real circumstances around the mission as was Mackenzie.[43] With the good Doctor gone, there was no reason why Mackenzie might not have followed a totally different policy if he had felt the need to do so. The fact is that he did not. Indeed, by the time of Livingstone's departure it is clear that he now accepted the essential justice of taking up arms against the Yao - but, even so, he still remained uneasy about becoming directly engaged in such action himself.

Mackenzie Personally Leads a Second Expedition

As Livingstone had predicted, Mackenzie was bombarded with requests from the Mang'anja chiefs to assist them against their Yao enemies. At first the bishop would have none of this. Slowly but surely, however, his resistance was worn down by repeated petitions. Finally, in the second week of August, after hearing all that had been said about the suffering of the Mang'anja at the hands of the Yao, he became convinced in his own mind that "an ordinary body of English would be right to go, to drive these marauders and murderers out of the country" and that he and his colleagues, even though they were churchmen, would have to do this, "in the absence of any others to go and lead the Mang'anja".[44] It was this kind of reasoning that convinced Mackenzie he should act.

> There were arguments in favour of our taking up arms, the real reason of our doing so being, however, that when the chiefs ... called upon us to help ... against a powerful enemy, and we felt that the result depended under God on our going or refusing, we could not refuse.[45]

---

[42] This fact seems to have been generally overlooked by other writers.

[43] White, *Magomero: Portrait of an African Village*, p. 24.

[44] Mackenzie's Journal, Vol. 2, 9 August 1861.

[45] Mackenzie to Strong, 30 September 1861, RHL, UMCA Al(I) A/1/109-116.

Of course, there were other arguments too. A further blow struck at the Yao would, the bishop hoped, help to "pacify" the country and so facilitate the spread of Christianity in the future.[46] Furthermore, additional skirmishes could possibly, he thought, deliver a "death blow" to the slave trade in the area.[47] After all, he and his colleagues reasoned, there were examples in God's Word of expeditions launched to release captives. Did not Abraham rescue Lot and his family from captivity by a military expedition?[48]

All these deliberations ultimately resulted in a second raid. On 14 August a mixed force of missionaries and Mang'anja attacked a Yao camp after yet another futile parley. A confused skirmish ensued, one man was shot and another two villages were burnt.[49] It was in this engagement that Mackenzie crossed his own personal Rubicon and took an active part in the fighting itself; a fact which he freely admitted in his letters: "In this fight, I used my gun to the best of my skill as did all the rest".[50] But this particular encounter was a disturbing experience for the bishop. The "cold blooded cruelty" practised by his Mang'anja "allies" was a considerable shock to him, as were "the sickening sights witnessed by many" during the conflict.[51]

---

[46] ibid.

[47] Mackenzie to Bishop of Cape Town, 4 November 1861; Mackenzie to Mrs Crawley, 25 September 1861.

[48] Procter's Journal, 15 August 1861. Mackenzie had also thought about this possible biblical parallel. See Chadwick, *Mackenzie's Grave,* p. 46 and Genesis 14:14-16.

[49] Mackenzie's Journal, Vol. 2, 14 August 1861. It seems that the precise location of this encounter was a place called Sazi Hill. See C. Baker, "Magomero and the Battle of Sazi Hill, 1861", *Nyasaland Journal,* Vol. 13/2 (July 1960), pp. 88-94.

[50] Mackenzie to Bishop of Cape Town, 4 November 1861.

[51] Mackenzie to Mrs Crawley, 25 September 1861; Procter's Journal, 15 August 1861.

Debates amongst the Missionaries

The action of 14 August did not end the repeated calls for help against the Yao. During the second week of September the bishop was told that the village of Chief Nampeko, no less than 40 miles to the north of Magomero, was being ravaged by the Yao.[52] On 19 September Mackenzie led an important discussion about what should be done concerning this new information. The bishop was all for another expedition, but he was stubbornly opposed by a number of his colleagues.[53] Eventually, Mackenzie was compelled to impose his authority. "My vote decided that we should go", he laconically noted in his journal.[54]

The nature of the debate of 19 September which divided the missionaries, was central to the whole question of whether they should be fighting the Yao at all. Mackenzie basically put forward the same ideas as had been used in August to justify a para-military sortie of some kind. He maintained that "a Christian man may take up arms to defend his country and this is not war but defence of the oppressed".[55] Such theorizing did not convince all his co-workers, who expressed doubts as to whether the previous raid had really achieved anything, as well as concern that work was being neglected at Magomero, along with the anxiety that - even though they were all supposed to be preachers of peace - they were about to use guns once again.[56] The bishop remained impervious to the objections of his comrades, however, and had it not been for the fact that Nampeko was discovered to have been lying about the extent of the damage to

---

[52] Mackenzie's Journal, Vol. 2, 9 September 1861.

[53] Chadwick, *Mackenzie's Grave,* p. 60 says the meeting was "not quite unanimous", which hardly reflects the level of intensity of the disagreement which emerged.

[54] Mackenzie's Journal, Vol. 2, 19 September 1861.

[55] Ibid.

[56] Ibid. Mackenzie noted down each objection raised along with his response to it in his journal.

his village, the missionaries would almost certainly have marched out to raid the Yao to the north. This was clearly significant.

Mackenzie's views had evolved once again. Now he actually referred to the Mang'anja of Nampeko's village as "our people". In effect, what had occurred was that Mackenzie had started to see himself as a temporal potentate in the Shire Highlands. He already referred to himself as "the English chief" when in council with the Mang'anja, and even began to consider ideas for the expansion of the mission by establishing a site near Nampeko's village.[57] To all intents and purposes, therefore,-the bishop had now come to accept that armed expeditions might be launched in order, partially at least, to extend the mission's area of influence and not merely to release captives.

The Final Skirmishes

It is possible to view Mackenzie's final months at Magomero - from the end of September until his sudden death on 31 January 1862 - as a period during which he tried to extend his authority more firmly throughout the region. He appears to have been genuinely optimistic about the influence of the mission in October and November.[58] It was certainly true that the missionaries did effectively hold "the balance of power" between the competing local polities in the Shire Highlands for six months.[59] In the middle of October, however, Mackenzie received information that dead bodies, burning villages and ravaged fields filled the countryside towards Zomba, which prompted the bishop to attempt yet another armed trek against the Yao. The motive seems to have been to punish the Yao for atrocities that had already been committed, rather than simply to prevent further marauding and enslavement.[60] The resulting expedition proved to be a total fiasco, for even though the bishop marched out with over 1,000 Mang'anja

---

[57] Procter's Journal, 12 August 1861; Mackenzie's Journal, Vol. 2, 19 September 1861.
[58] Chadwick, *Mackenzie's Grave*, p. 82.
[59] White, *Magomero: Portrait of an African Village*, p. 61.
[60] Mackenzie's Journal, Vol. Ib, 13 and 16 October 1861.

"allies" - which in itself says something about the escalating scale of these actions - he failed to locate the enemy at all and merely abducted 400 Yao women and children, after setting fire to yet more huts.[61] For Mackenzie this was a bitter experience: "I do not think I ever spent a more miserable day ... finally doubting whether on the whole we had done much good by our fighting."[62]

The bishop's final punitive raid had nothing to do with the Yao at all and demonstrated still further the extent of his changing attitude towards armed intervention. An attack upon two of the mission's personnel in December by the people of an Nguru chief named Manasomba,[63] caused Mackenzie to lead a fresh expedition to recover the mission's property and to punish "the perpetrators of so treacherous an act".[64] Mackenzie sought to dispel any thought of revenge from his heart, however:

> It is true that our Lord said to his disciples they knew not what spirit they were of. But in this case [we] were not revenging ourselves. We prayed on our way that ... if the thought of private revenge entered our fancy He would drive it away.[65]

Rowley, for one, felt such action could not be condemned anymore than could the punishment of a criminal in England.[66] But this excursion merely resulted in yet another village being torched. Mackenzie firmly insisted that, "We had punished the robber," but in fact Manasomba and his people - in a considerable twist of irony - had probably originally mistaken the missionaries for slavers bent on

---

[61] Chadwick, *Mackenzie's Grave*, p. 51.

[62] Mackenzie's Journal, Vol. Ib, 17 October 1861.

[63] Procter's Journal, 5 December 1861.

[64] Scudamore to mother, 22 February 1862, RHL, UMCA AI(II) A/Scudamore MS/56-59; Mackenzie to Strong, 11 December 1861.

[65] Mackenzie to Strong, 11 December 1861. The biblical reference is to Luke 9:55.

[66] Rowley, *The Story of the Universities' Mission*, p. 252.

preying upon them.[67] Without realizing it, therefore, Mackenzie had, by his increasingly uncontrolled zeal for punitive action, attacked one of the strongest enemies of slavery in the area. It was a sad end to a courageous - if often mistaken - campaign.

Mackenzie in Retrospect

It is easy to be critical of Mackenzie. He was a prisoner of his culture and age, and therefore not surprisingly his solution to the social and political fragmentation which confronted him in the Shire Highlands was very much a Victorian one - impose law and order and right wrongs by the righteous power of the gun if necessary, thereby liberating the land for the gospel and the benefits of "civilization". Of course, he did not fully understand the dynamics of the political relationships of the area, tending to see his environment through a simplistic perspective which emphasized the horrors of slavery and the backwardness of the indigenous peoples, while overlooking the existing political and social complexity that in reality characterized the inter-ethnic contacts of the region. It is tempting to suggest that every generation of foreigners working in Africa seem to make this same mistake as they impose - frequently with insufficient thought or humility - the **prevailing** orthodoxies of their dominant cultures upon the great continent.[68]

Interestingly enough, later missionaries who laboured in generally the same area as Mackenzie did, found it possible to avoid the plunge into armed excursions. Robert Cleland of the Blantyre mission, for example,

---

[67] Mackenzie quoted in Chadwick, Mackenzie's Grave, p. 97; White, *Magomero: Portrait of an African Village*, pp. 52-54.

[68] John Stott in *The Contemporary Christian*, Leicester: Inter-Varsity Press, 1992, pp. 24-29 has suggested that Christians in the West need to practise what he calls "double lisiening"; namely the task of both responding to the Bible and being aware of modern culture. In Africa, however, there is an urgent requirement for such men and women to exercise "treble listening", or the additional necessity of "listening" to African culture, as well as to the Bible and their own social values.

was able to prevent chief Chikumbu of Mulanje from enslaving a village by a simple act of courage. Cleland, we are told:

> made his way through the fight to the chief, and quietly but firmly ... ordered him to desist. Strangely impressed, the chief submitted ... saying, "Lala [Cleland] has a brave heart, like Chilcumbu himself.[69]

Those who followed in Mackenzie's footsteps, therefore, tended to be more circumspect when it came to becoming directly embroiled in local conflicts.

However, that they came to the Shire Highlands at all was partly due to Mackenzie's own pioneering efforts. Nor should it be forgotten that many of Mackenzie's successors, regardless of their denomination, virtually ruled vast tracts of territory throughout Central Africa towards the end of the nineteenth century, as if they were the "lawgiver ... policemen ... prosecuting attorney, and ... judge" all rolled into one.[70] Mackenzie would have understood this.

Mackenzie remains a classic example of the devout and sincere Christian leader who felt compelled to use force in the service of his Lord. As such, his experience is illuminating in terms of the centuries old debate within the church as to the acceptability of Christian involvement in any form of institutionalized violence.[71] I have tried to trace the development of his ideas in this chapter, which swung from a total rejection of the legitimacy of the employment of force at all, to virtually the complete opposite -• the use of limited quasi-military raids to establish local political stability. The bishop's example demonstrates the force of extreme circumstances in radically altering a Christian's outlook on this most controversial of issues. Perhaps it

---

[69] William Robertson, *The Martyrs of Blantyre*, p. 132.

[70] Robert Rotberg, *The Rise of Nationalism in Central Africa. The Making of Malawi and Zambia 1873-1964*, Cambridge, Massachusetts: Harvard University Press, 1966, p. 10.

[71] For a recent evangelical perspective on this debate see O.R. Barclay (ed.), *Pacifism and War. When Christians Disagree*, Leicester: Inter-Varsity Press, 1984.

was always inevitable that the experience of the first Western missionaries to enter the Shire Highlands would be both "war" and "the defence of the oppressed".

It might be suggested in conclusion that the Shire Highlands in the 1860s were similar, in all their political fragmentation and sudden eruptions of violence, to some of the so-called "failed states" in contemporary Africa. Somalia, Angola, Liberia, Rwanda, Burundi and parts of Zaire all present the modern Christian worker with challenges not dissimilar to those faced by Mackenzie. If there is one significant difference between Mackenzie and twentieth century Western missionaries at this level, it is that the general tendency in more recent times has been to try and get all personnel out of a country as quickly as possible whenever violence erupts.[72] Mackenzie never considered this option, but sought to live and work - and fight - in the most difficult of circumstances, in the hope that by so doing his example would win converts and the trust of the local people; an aspiration which does appear to a certain extent to have been fulfilled.[73] He remains, therefore, for all his mistakes, a lasting example of the importance of commitment to a foreign people - "our people" he called even the Mang'anja 40 miles away - and their livelihood, no matter what the personal cost or obstacles involved.

---

[72] For example see *New Christian Herald* (Worthing), 14 December 1996, p. 1, where it was reported that 250 missionaries were "rescued" from a disintegrating Zaire. The glorification of such "rescues" probably does not encourage western missionaries to stay in the field.

[73] There is evidence that Mackenzie's example did have such an impact. See Robertson, *The Martyrs of Blantyre*, pp. 25, 62-63 and J. Cooke Yarborough, *The Diary of a Working Man in Central Africa*, London: Society for Promoting Christian Knowledge, n.d., pp. 28, 47-48. Ironically, of course, the mission was evacuated from the mainland after Mackenzie's death.

Part Three:

Humanities

10. What About Those Difficult Phases in the History of Black People?: A Christian Appraisal of the African Experience

Kings M. Phiri

Introductory Remarks

As a Christian who is also a practising historian, I share the view that there is a way in which the past can be approached from a Christian perspective.[1] The essence of this view is that the God we worship is one who intervenes in human affairs, and that although so many things might go wrong in the world there is a redemptive purpose toward which human events are ultimately directed. At the same time, I also share the view that history as it has developed since the Enlightenment is based on certain methods and objectives which logically lead to findings that sometimes run contrary to what we Christians believe about God and the way he interacts with mankind.[2]

One area of study where my Christian convictions have been forced to intersect with the meaning we attach to historical experience is that of Black History. This is a branch of historical studies which in the main deals with the past experience of dark peoples or peoples of African descent in Africa and the diaspora (i.e. the black world outside Africa); the impact they have had on other civilizations of humankind and the contribution they have made to the stock of human civilization since earliest times.[3] It is an exciting and challenging area of inquiry, but

---

[1] For a summary of the Christian view of history, see David Bebbington, *Patterns in History,* Leicester: Inter-Varsity Press, 1979, pp. 43-67.

[2] Cohn Brown, *History and Faith: A Personal Exploration,* Leicester: Inter-Versity Press, 1987, p. 74; cf some of the arguments raised in the paper by Kenneth R. Ross, "Faith in Jesus and Historical Criticism", Faith and Knowledge Seminar No. 3, Chancellor College, University of Malawi, February 1990.

[3] Frank M. Snowden, *Blacks in Antiquity: Ethiopians in the Graeco-Roman Experience,* Cambridge, Mass.: Harvard University Press, 1979; Martin Bernal,

one which raises more questions than it answers about the hand of providence in the configuration of human affairs. This is due to the fact that while it is relatively easy to marshall historical evidence of how God has guided the destinies of other races of mankind, such evidence as it relates to black people is hard to come by. The issue is one I for one have pondered, on and off, for well over twenty years now. Three experiences in particular have drawn me to it.

The first took place at the time I arrived in Madison, Wisconsin, USA, to begin my graduate studies in 1971. Some sympathetic American friends and well-wishers there, referred me to a Faith Baptist Church in a suburb called Middleton. I thus found myself joining an ultra-white, middle class Christian congregation and the people who recommended it to me at first appeared right about its commitment to sound biblical teaching. Before my first semester or American University term was over, however, I detected a definite American middle class bias especially when it came to prayer time. The prayers stressed the fact that God had blessed America and the American people. God was thanked for making America and Americans so privileged when compared to Third World countries and their wretched peoples. Americans thus had so many things to thank God for, and to gauge that fact they only had to turn to what television and newspapers had to say about starving masses in Haiti, India, Bangladesh and Africa. And indeed, much of what television and newspapers said about these other countries and therefore black people, was negative. Africans in particular, were simply portrayed as a hopeless failure in the ongoing story of mankind. They certainly had not and could not establish a claim to the humanistic salvation which mankind was trying to work out for itself. As a black man from Africa in the midst of an extremely affluent or successful white community that mounted the attack, I was at that time not able to dismiss so easily this line of thinking about black people and their place in the development of Christian civilization.

Black Athena: The Afro-Asiatic Roots of Classical Civilisation, New Brunswick: Rutgers University Press, 1987.

The second experience was a crisis which we had in the Inter-Varsity Christian Fellowship chapter of which I had become a member. The crisis was precipitated by black American members who unilaterally pulled out of the main group and started meeting in a relatively small sub-fellowship of their own. Worse still, they appealed to those of us who were from Africa to join them, in the interest of black solidarity. I must admit that I was then extremely naive about the nature and depth of grievances which young black Americans held against their society. My reading about black issues prior to my going to the USA had not quite prepared me for the real thing. At the time of the crisis under review, my black American brothers were greatly influenced by the publication of James Cone's handbook on *Black Theology and Black Power*.[4] Coming out at the height of the black revolution which changed the politics and socio-cultural texture of the big American cities in particular, the book taught them that white middle class theologians had perverted Christianity by sidestepping the Christ of the Bible and substituting in his place one who could co-exist with the materialism and racialism that had become endemic to white middle class culture. The Christ of the Bible, it argued, was a man of the oppressed and exploited - a co-struggler with them.

In trying to make themselves heard and understood, the black apostates argued that it had become necessary for them to go it alone, because their white "kid-brothers" were fond of praising God for what He had done for America while they wanted to be free to reflect even upon those things for which God would punish America. They drew attention to such American "crimes" as the war in Vietnam which was then still raging, the neglect of blacks in the ghettoes, the tolerance of racist malpractices, etc. Above all, they argued that their overall experiences as black people were so different from those of their white counterparts that they could find no logic in trying to view reality through the same lens as that used by whites. Indeed, in a later publication, their guru, James Cone, was to declare that his theology "will not be the same as that of my colleagues at Union Theological

---

[4] New York: Seabury Press, 1969.

Seminary, because our experience is different."[5] These were exciting revelations to me at the time and I must again admit that it was not easy for me to dismiss their implications with impunity.

Thirdly, back in Malawi in the mid-seventies, I was fortuitously appointed by my head of department to be the tutor in charge of Black History, by which we in Africa mean the History of Africa and Peoples of African Descent Abroad. Since then, I have done my best to read whatever volumes our library has on the subject, to consult a number of journals on it, and even to publish one or two articles on what have been topics of greatest interest to me. What has struck me about most of the works I have read, however, is that they have in the main been documentations of failure on the part of black people. More specifically, black people are portrayed as having failed to make a meaningful contribution to human civilization or progress. This has on many occasions tempted me to ask myself whether such failure, if conceded, had a moral dimension as well. My answer to this question will be found in the third section of this chapter.

Profile of Black Suffering

The almost total way in which the history of black people has been dominated by suffering and misery makes it almost unique among the histories of humankind. In his twelve volume work, Arnold Toynbee, an Oxford philosopher of history, for example, concluded that the historical experience of most civilizations can be compared to a seesaw type of movement "either away from God or to God".[6] In other words, one could detect in the overall histories of most of the civilizations he studied epochs during which the hand of God was apparent or clearly manifest, as well as others during which the good was almost completely overshadowed by the bad. Perhaps because the experience of black people did not quite fit his model, Toynbee had virtually nothing to say about their history. He should perhaps be

---

[5] James H. Cone, *God of the Oppressed,* New York: Seabury Press, 1975, p. 3.

[6] Arnold J. Toynbee, *A Study of History,* 12 Volumes, Oxford University Press, 1934-52.

excused on the grounds that he wrote his work at a time when little reliable research had been done on the history of black people in both Africa and the diaspora. Contrary to what one would expect, however, the dramatic expansion of research and writing on the history of black people over the past thirty years - itself a response to the movement for African independence - has done little to change the view that the dominant experience of black people has been that of suffering and failure. A major exception to this has been the writings of the late Senegalese scientist and historian, Cheikh Anta Diop. In two of his books best known to the English-speaking world,[7] Diop has, with dogmatic insistence, sought to challenge widely acknowledged assumptions about the negligible role black people are said to have played in the making of human civilization and suggested a more sympathetic way of viewing the African past. His however has been very much a lonely voice in the wilderness. In other words, we for the most part have to deal with works that present a relatively malign view of the black man's past. We will now proceed to look at some of the themes in the treatment of which such a view would not be slow to emerge.

No historical theme has been as closely identified with black suffering and overall underdevelopment as that of slavery and the slave trade as they flourished in Africa and the New World from the 16th to the 19th century. It was common practice then to buy, sell and yoke black people like beasts of burden. Those who were enslaved in this way within Africa had to face the challenge of survival under inhospitable circumstances. They were in many cases forced to do onerous work with blunt implements, to eat food from the floor like dogs, and to take their drink from broken or dirty gourds. Their counterparts who were taken to plantations of the New World had to face the terror of the "middle passage" as the voyage by ship across the Atlantic was called. The mortality rate due to epidemics and lack of fresh air and food was sometimes as high as 25%. Once in the New World, the

---

[7] Cheikh Ants Diop, *The African Origins of Civilisation: Myth or Reality*, Westport: Lawrence Hill and Company, 1974; Cheikh Anta Diop, *Pre-colonial Black Africa*, Westport: Lawrence Hill and Company, 1987.

slaves that made it were in for regimented toil and strict control. The treatment they received was that of non-humans. They could not be taught to read and write, own property, hold unsupervised meetings, argue with white people, etc. The forms of punishment inflicted on those of them who did not comply with any of these stipulations and requirements were often unusually cruel.[8]

Indeed this traffic in black human merchandise was a dark page in the history of not just black people but that of humankind as a whole. While it lasted, it was a challenge to the Christian conscience of many people especially in the nations of Europe which played a part in the trade in question.

In the New World, the abolition of the slave trade and slavery from the 1860s onwards was followed by the institution of yet another gimmick for dehumanizing black people in the form of racial segregation. As it developed in the U.S.A from the 1880s to 1948, for example, racial segregation was characterized by white mob violence against blacks; the wholesale exclusion of blacks from essential means of production and skilled jobs; as well as from participation in mainstream politics and access to quality educational and health services.[9] Under the circumstances, blacks came to be reduced into a demoralized, childish and irresponsible lot.

Similarly, in Africa the abolition of the slave trade and slavery was followed by the "scourge" of colonialism. The old balance-sheet approach to what colonialism might have meant to Africa and Africans has now been discredited for ever. In its place has risen the voice of the new school, according to which colonialism as it was established and consolidated over much of Africa from the end of the 19th century to World War II brought untold misery to African peoples. In some

---

[8] V. Rubin and T. Arthur (eds.), *Comparative Perspectives on Slavery in the New World and Plantation Societies,* New York: Academy of Sciences, University Press, 1977; P.E. Lovejoy, *Transformation in African Slavery,* Cambridge University Press, 1983.

[9] A.H. Taylor, *Travel and Triumph: Black Lee and Culture in the South Since the Civil* War, London: Greenwood Press, 1976.

parts of the continent, for example, Africans ended up losing their best lands to incoming colonial settlers; in others they were subjected to compulsory labour; while in yet others they were drawn into patterns of outward labour migration that brought great suffering to their families and resulted in the introduction of new killer diseases. As if this was not enough, in places where Africans and Europeans were likely to be in close touch with one another, a lot of restrictive and discriminatory legislation was also enacted. This was particularly applicable to schools, hospitals and recreational centres. To Africans, then, colonialism - whether it was British, French, Portuguese or Belgian - was synonymous with oppression, exploitation and poverty.[10]

The extent to which violence has tended to dominate contemporary aspects of black history needs little emphasizing. It is a theme which can be elaborated with the help of many examples drawn from the diaspora as well as Africa.

Several black American writers whose childhood and youth was lived in the urban ghetto environment for example, have sensitively documented the high rates of violence and crime which characterize the black experience in the big American cities. They depict an environment which is infested by street gangs and warfare, armed robberies, drug trafficking, loose morals, etc.[11] In that kind of environment, life for many young blacks has tended to be fast, short and brutish.

Indeed at the height of the black consciousness movement in the USA in the 1960s, urban black communities were torn by so much strife and violence, as militant black youth rioted, looted and burned, to the

---

[10] Walter Rodney, *How Europe Underdeveloped Africa,* Dar-es-Salaam: Tanzania Publishing House, 1972; J. Suret-Canale, *French Colonialism in Tropical Africa, 1900-1945,* London: Oxford University Press, 1971.

[11] Malcolm X and Alex Haley, *The Autobiography of Malcolm X,* New York: Ballantine Books, 1964; Claude Brown, *Manchild in the Promised Land: A Modern Classic of the Black Experience,* New York: Macmillan, 1965; Sylvester Monroe and Peter Goldman, *Black and Poor: A True Story of Courage and Survival,* New York: Ballantine Books, 1988.

peril of the communities concerned. In the process, homes, schools and shops were vandalized or destroyed and neighbourhood streets reduced to a battleground between rampaging youth and law enforcement agents.[12]

There have been more recent examples of violence in the black American community. The one which readily comes to mind is that of the Los Angeles riots of May 1992, during which blacks in the south-central part of the metropolis looted, burned and killed, in protest against the discriminatory treatment they had been receiving at the hands of the predominantly Korean business/landlord class. The riots left mile after mile of destruction and resulted in loss of property valued at over $2 billion.[13] Many white American observers saw the riots concerned as clear evidence of innate black criminality. It was hard for them to swallow the alternative view, according to which the riots should have been seen as a sad commentary on the fact that America is in essence made up of two societies which are separate and unequal, one black and the other white.

Equally depressing has been the violence which has bedevilled several post-independence African nations, as well as those that have only recently undergone the transition from minority to majority rule. The list is long and includes Sierra Leone, Liberia and Nigeria in West Africa; Sudan, Ethiopia and Somalia in north-east Africa; Uganda, Burundi and Rwanda in east-central Africa; and Angola, Mozambique and South Africa in southern Africa. I will here cite Nigeria, Uganda, Burundi-Rwanda and South Africa as case studies.

Within seven years of her attainment of independence, Nigeria, Africa's most populous nation, was turned into a glaring victim of Africa's worst wasting disease, tribalism. The world stood a stunned observer as several constitutionally elected leaders were executed during the military coup d'état of 1966. This was followed by bitter

---

[12] V.H. Bernstein, "Why Negroes are Still Angry", in M. Drinuner (ed.), *Black History*, New York: Doubleday and Company, 1968, pp. 514-530.

[13] Tom Morganthau et al., "Beyond Black and White: Rethinking Race and Crime in America", *Newsweek*, 18 May 1992, pp. 12-21.

inter-ethnic tension and conflict especially between the Hausa of the north and the Igbo of the east. As violence bred violence and events drifted towards war during the second half of 1966 and early part of 1967, a vast pool of refugees was created out of threatened Igbo fleeing the north for the east and Hausa trying to escape in the reverse direction.[14] The war between the north backed by the Federal Government and the east, which opted for secession from the federal government, thus became inevitable.

Indeed, while it lasted from 1967 to 1969, the Nigerian Civil War was a human tragedy of gargantuan proportions, especially with regard to the mass suffering of the Igbo people but also on account of the atrocities perpetrated on both sides of the fighting. Neither soldiers nor civilians were spared the brutal effects of the war. The worst took place in Biafra as federal government troops advanced on a broad front during the second phase of the war and the amount of territory under the secessionist government shrank. Biafra then became the sum-total of all evils associated with war: high concentrations of refugees, acute shortages of food, and festering diseases of all sorts.

Uganda, on the other hand, was a prey to another kind of tragedy that has become almost endemic to several parts of black Africa - that of political intolerance and fascist dictatorship. Once described as a "jewel in the British imperial crown", Uganda had only eight years of shaky civilian rule following her attainment of independence in 1962. In January 1971, General Idi Amin Dada and his military colleagues overthrew the government of Milton Obote, and in the process ushered in what has come to be known world-wide as "the tragedy of Uganda". This essentially refers to the killing and looting of innocent civilians because the regime in power suspected them of dissident leanings. Ugandans suffered unmitigated atrocities of that nature between 1972 and 1985, and the scars of it all are there to see for all observers visiting Uganda today.

---

[14] For a simple but able summary of those events, see Patrick O'Malley, "No Such Country': Footnotes on the Nigerian Civil War", History Seminar Paper, Chancellor College, University of Malawi, 1983/84.

It is now estimated that Idi Amin during the eight years of his maverick rule was directly or indirectly responsible for killing not less than 100,000 Ugandans. In reactions to the insecurity which prevailed, hundreds upon hundreds of intellectuals, planners and skilled manpower who had once made Uganda the envy of other African countries fled the country in search of havens elsewhere. What is rarely realized is that Amin's atrocities were more than dwarfed by those perpetrated during the Second Obote Regime (1980-85). In its abortive mopping-up campaign against those who did not want Obote to be returned to power, Obote's army is said to have been responsible for the death of another half a million Ugandans. In the process, production in many parts of the countryside was either disrupted or brought to a standstill.[15]

In recent times, the world has been scandalized by the resurgence of ethnic clashes between the Tutsi and Hutu in the tiny east-central African states of Burundi and Rwanda in the borderlands between the bigger states of Uganda, Tanzania and Zaire (now Democratic Republic of Congo). The differences between these two ethnic groups comprising these countries, as has been repeatedly demonstrated, are historical: they are rooted in the competition which in pre colonial times characterized relations between militant and transhumant pastoralists (Tutsi), on the one hand and, peaceful, sedentary agriculturalists (Hutu). Their recent violent outbursts began in 1990, as a struggle for control of government by Hutu and Tutsi representatives backed by their respective supporters.

In Burundi the crisis came to a head in October 1993, when the then democratically elected President, Melchoir Ndadaye, from the majority Hutu, was assassinated by Tutsi rebels in the army, after having been in power for only five months. The assassination sparked widespread violence as the Hutu went on a country-wide rampage during which many Tutsi in positions of authority and their families,

---

[15] Dan Mudoola, "Post-Colonial Politics in Uganda: An Interpretation", *Mowazo,* Vol. 6/2 (1985), pp. 19-29; *Newsweek,* 6 November 1986, p. 24.

were hacked to death. The resulting blood bath is estimated to have left over 150,000 people dead.[16]

Rwanda was then well on its way to ethnic disintegration. The intensification of the crisis there, began early in 1993 when over 350,000 people, mostly of Hutu origins, were displaced from the north-western and northeastern parts of the country, as the Tutsi-based Rwandan Patriotic Front (FPR) intensified its armed struggle against the Hutu-dominated government of General Juvenal Habyarimana. The crisis peaked in April 1994 with the shooting down at Kigali airport of the plane bearing President Habyarimana and his advisors, returning from a conference in Arusha, Tanzania.[17] That presidential assassination sparked widespread Hutu-Tutsi clashes and killings which lasted for four months. In the process, about half a million people perished and over one million fled the country and became refugees in neighbouring Tanzania and Zaire.

We must also mention the violence which characterized the last decade of the struggle against Apartheid in South Africa, from 1984 to 1994, as much of it was incomprehensible and appeared irrational to many international observers at the time. It was black violence directed as much against agencies of the Apartheid state as against black peoples themselves, i.e. those who were perceived to be working in collaboration with the state, as well as those who were deemed to be carrying out the struggle the wrong way.

The violence in question began in 1984 when the African National Congress (ANC), as the main liberation movement, declared its intensification of armed struggle against the Apartheid state and called on blacks throughout South Africa to join hands with it. The response to the appeal was violence on an unprecedented scale. Strategic security installations were sabotaged, security agents assaulted by hit-and-run armed gangs, houses and businesses of perceived collaborators were petrol-bombed and a number of collaborators

---

[16] *The Standard of Kenya,* No. 24590, Nairobi, 30 October 1993, p. 7.
[17] *New African,* No. 343, July 1996, p. 11.

were publicly "necklaced" i.e. set alight by having burning tyres thrown round their necks and clothes.[18]

With the passage of time, the violence was compounded by the differences which emerged between the ANC, with imprisoned Nelson Mandela as leader, and the Zulu-based Inkatha Freedom Party led by Chief Gasha Buthelezi. This was a factor which led to running battles between followers of the two parties especially in the province of Kwazulu-Natal and on the Rand.[19] Between 1988 and 1993, for example, faction-fighting between supporters of the ANC and Inkatha Freedom Party in the Kwazulu-Natal province alone, resulted in the deaths of over 7,000 people. On the Rand, fights between Inkatha-based Zulu and ANC-affiliated Xhosa mine workers became the order of the day. They claimed 3,402 lives in 1992 alone.

Ironically schools were a major victim of the black perpetrated violence which then engulfed South Africa. For example, four cases of disruptive violence caused to school life on the Rand were reported on 8 February 1992. In one of them, a white male teacher was stabbed and clubbed, doused with petrol and set alight. In a second incident, a white female teacher was grabbed by the hair, punched in the face and stabbed in the hip. In a third, a black teacher was shot dead on her way to school. In a fourth incident, a black headmistress was beaten up and left with two broken ribs.[20]

Like their counterparts in the diaspora then, Africans have really had it rough even in the post-independence era that began with so much promise and euphoria in the early sixties. They have continued to be victims of their own tribal antipathies, regimes that are alien to democratic traditions, declining food production capacities, low commodity prices dictated by the international economic order, etc. This leads us to the question of whether as Christians we should entertain a similarly bleak view of their prospects in life.

---

[18] "Black Rage Explodes in South Africa", *Moto Magazine,* No. 38, September 1985, pp. 15-17.
[19] *The Guardian,* Vol. $14^7/_2 3$, 6 December 1992, p. 10.
[20] *Sunday Times,* Cape Town, 9 February 1992, p. 3.

Material Deprivation and Openness to the Gospel

While the black or African experience has been a relatively pathetic one from a techno-materialist perspective and from that of social engineering, there has been quite a lot happening in Africa and other parts of the black world to encourage interested Christians. One of these is that for quite some time now the church in Africa has been registering one of the highest growth rates. Over 45% of Africa's population is now Christian, nominally at least.[21] And when Billy Graham organised his crusade for evangelizing the world in Amsterdam, Holland, in 1986, Africa sent more delegates than any other continent. Clearly, then, Africa is the continent of the future as far as Christianity is concerned, and we ought to be encouraged by this. It is one evidence to support the view that God's Spirit has been on the move here.

This may be a cruel thing to say. It also seems to me that Africa's material poverty may be the source of its spiritual wealth. The continent's dependence on humanitarian charity from the West, though embarrassing to some of us, is an established fact, although the diagnosis of what leads to its perpetuation is still a matter of debate among economists and political scientists. But, is poverty of some sort not one of the means by which we are drawn nearer to the Kingdom of God? Consider what one of the beatitudes says: "Blessed are the poor (i.e. who realize that they lack something) for theirs is the kingdom of God" (Matthew 5:3). Then of course there is the other popular saying of our Lord to the same effect: "It is easier for a camel to pass through the eye of a needle, than for a rich man to enter the Kingdom of Heaven."

To be poor and degraded must undoubtedly have its own temptations, but it need not always have undesirable consequences. As Brother Andrew *once* put it, it is when we are divested of material possessions

---

[21] David Barrett (ed.), *World Christian Encyclopedia,* Nairobi et al.: Oxford University Press, 1982, p. 782; David B. Barrett and Todd M. Johnson, "Annual Statistical Table on Global Mission: 1998', *International Bulletin,* Vol. 22/1 (January 1998), p. 27.

that we are in the best position to trust God for all our needs.[22] Thus, it may well be that poverty and suffering have been the best school through which our people have been taught to depend on God for their needs. The fruits of this disposition have been encouraging from a spiritual point of view. Let me qualify what I have in mind here.

When I last visited Tanzania in 1984, the people there were in great distress economically. The currency had virtually collapsed, the shops were empty, and the black market economy had established itself against all official efforts to curb it. Compared to what I saw when I visited the country in 1973, there were signs of retrogression everywhere. I was led to conclude that something is drastically wrong with the way we manage our affairs in Africa. This would have demoralized me quite a bit, had it not been for the experience of attending a church service that was packed to capacity. So, people could still praise God in spite of their socio-economic deprivations!! Not surprisingly, in 1992 I chanced to speak to a widely travelled evangelist who had recently been to Tanzania.[23] He was of the opinion that looking at the whole of Christian Africa, Tanzania is now leading as a country where people are most responsive to the Gospel.

Even here in Malawi, the openness of the poorer sections of the population to the gospel has been astonishing. Rev. Reinhard Bonnke, for example, was in Blantyre in 1986 on his "Save Africa Crusade". The enthusiasm with which the low-income masses patronized his huge meetings was a contrast to the cool and calculated response of those who are materially well off. In typical middle class fashion, the latter gained notoriety then for debating the merits and demerits of what the renowned international evangelist from Germany had to offer to Malawi. One does not have to glorify the poor, of course. Suffice it to say that African's material poverty should be appreciated in relation to the view that material and spiritual well-being can run counter to each other.

---

[22] Brother Andrew, *God's Smuggler,* London: Hodder and Stoughton, 1968, pp. 65-82.

[23] Stephen Mungoma of Africa Enterprise, a Ugandan based in Nairobi.

Other Signs of Hope

I think we should also take courage from the moral strategies black people in Africa and the diaspora have been increasingly adopting in coping with the difficult challenges that they have to face from time to time. This can be illustrated with their struggle for civil rights in the diaspora, the way they have been trying to cope with the problems of conflict and refugees in Africa and their current application of democratic solutions to problems of governance on the African continent.

The Civil Rights Movement in the USA in the 1950s and 1960s, for instance, was a moral crusade through which American blacks were able to make an enormous contribution to the worldwide struggle for justice and human dignity. Through it and its activities, as well as the inspired speeches of Martin Luther King Jr, the Movement's leader, blacks were able to raise the moral conscience of American society and indeed of Western society as a whole.[24] Thus, it is not surprising that despite dissenting, militant black voices here and there, the civil rights era is viewed by many as a golden age in the annals of black American history.

In Africa, the problem of civil strife and the masses of refugees to which it has sometimes given rise, has also been an opportunity for the best in the African personality to emerge. In the late 1980s, for example, there were over 5 million people on the continent who had been displaced from their countries by fighting and political persecution. Wherever they took refuge, they were totally dependent on the charity of host communities and governments as well as agencies of the United Nations. The heartening fact for observers lay in the ease with which such refugees were accommodated, looked after, and in some cases even absorbed by the host communities.

---

[24] P.P. Cooke, *The Civil Rights and the United State,* Washington: Meridian House Foundation, 1966; H. Walton, *The Political Philosophy of Martin Luther King Jr,* Westport: Greenwood Press, 1971.

Malawi stands out as a good example here. Between 1985 and 1990, she was subjected to an influx of over 1 million refugees from the war between FRELIMO and RENAMO in neighbouring Mozambique.[25] In at least one district, Nsanje, the refugees, who totalled 276,556, clearly outnumbered the indigenous inhabitants who should consequently have felt threatened and resentful. This, however, did not happen. Despite being a land-hungry and poorly endowed people in several respects, Malawians rose to the challenge that the Mozambican refugee crisis posed and were able to share with the refugees, the little they had in the way of shelter, food, land and medical facilities.[26] The sacrifices they made in the name of black brotherhood and good neighbourliness could not have been easily rivalled anywhere in the world.

Equally inspiring has been Black Africa's recent search for democratic ways of restructuring the political order on the continent. This movement has attracted a good deal of international attention and goodwill, for it represents a marked departure in African affairs from the 1960s and 1970s when military coup d'états were the most fashionable ways of tackling problems of governance. Free and fair elections based on "one person one vote" are currently the order of the day.[27] They have already been successfully staged, among other countries, in Senegal, Mali, Cote d'Ivoire, Ghana, Cameroon, Gabon, Kenya, Tanzania, Malawi, Zambia, Mozambique, South Africa and

---

[25] W. Finnegan, *A Complicated War: The Harrowing of Mozambique,* Berkeley: University of California Press, 1992, pp. 206-228.

[26] Violet M. Bonga, The Experience of the Mozambican Refugees in Malawi", a CONGOMA-sEonsored research report, Blantyre, April 1992.

[27] P.A. Nyong'o (ed.), *Popular Struggles for Democracy in Africa,* Tokyo: United Nations Press, 1987; John A. Wiseman (ed.), *Democracy and Political Change in Sub-Saharan Africa,* London: Routledge, 1995. For the case of Malawi see, Matembo S. Nzunda and Kenneth R. Ross (eds.), *Church, Law and Political Transition in Malawi, 1992-94,* Gweru: Mambo, 1995; *Kings* M. Phiri and Kenneth R. Ross (eds.), *Democratization in Malawi: A Stocktaking,* Blantyre: CLAIM, 1998.

Namibia. The democratic culture with which they are associated is already giving the continent a new lease of life, politically.

Summing Up

I would like to begin this closing section of the chapter by quoting my favourite verse of the Scriptures, 2 Corinthians 12:9 "My grace is sufficient for you, even when you are weak". This verse reminds us that God has been and is near to his people even in their time of weakness or helplessness. This would be my message to black people who may have lost sight of God's face in the midst of their tribulations, historical or contemporary.

While most of the calamities afflicting black people have been manmade, the solution to them has come from God. This was the case, for example, with slavery and the slave trade - a theme with which we began the substantive part of this chapter. In both Africa and the New World, these were brought to an end through pressure from God's People, whether they were identified as concerned Christians, abolitionists or humanitarians. Prompted by the spirit of Christ such people joined hands in the 19th Century to fight the slave trade and its evils. In other words, we can see here that in his own time and way, God intervened to bring this dark chapter in the history of black people to an end.

The same could be said about God's intervention on behalf of black victims of racial oppression and exploitation in the New World and Africa. This may be stated as an act of faith, we need not bother much about that at this point. Blacks gained their rights in the U.S.A and have been able to do so in South Africa because God has willed it. It was the genius of Martin Luther King Jr that at the height of racial discrimination and struggle for black civil rights in the U.S.A in the 1950s, he assured his followers not to doubt Gods love and mercy for them. He pointed out to them that through their suffering God was quietly working out his will for America.[28] Indeed, it did not take long

---

[28] Walton, *The Political Philosophy of Martin Luther King Jr.*

thereafter for Americans as a nation to realize that they had to work harder towards securing justice for all their citizens.

A parallel example of God's providential intervention in human history comes from the collapse of the seemingly impregnable walls of communism in Russia and Eastern Europe in the course of 1989 and 1990. It was an event which left many people the world over, gasping in astonishment. The impossible had happened! To a committed Christian, however, that should have come as no surprise because the speed and surprise with which our God is able to act in history, is but a manifestation of His omnipotence.[29]

As a historian who is also a Christian, I admit the tragedies which have marked the black experience in the past but also profess a hope in a brighter future for our people both in Africa and the diaspora. The basis of that hope lies in what God can do for us through Christ and in spite of the limitations of our past and present circumstances. It is this very same hope which makes it possible for us Christians to breathe an air of freedom even when so many things appear to be going wrong around us.

---

[29] Christopher Wright, "Responding to the God of History", *Themelios,* Vol. 15/3 (1990), pp. 7576.

11. Paradigm Shift in Scientific Advance: A Model for Christian Conversion in the Modern World?[1]

Kenneth R. Ross

Introduction

Since the Enlightenment of the eighteenth century an intellectual climate has developed in the Western world which is inimical to Christian belief. Anti-supernaturalism and historical relativism have so shaped the thinking of 'the modern world' that the claims of historic Christianity can scarcely be taken seriously. A plausibility structure has been developed in which, e.g., the Christian claim that Jesus rose from the dead is manifestly inadmissible.[2] It may be acknowledged that the disciples had experiences which led them to the belief that Jesus had risen from the dead, and that such a belief may remain inspiring today as a private religious conviction of those who choose to accept it. Post-modernity, indeed, is quite hospitable to such a construction. What cannot be accepted is the claim of historic Christianity that the resurrection provides the indispensable clue for a proper interpretation of the nature of the universe and the purpose of human life. In the public realm of commonly accepted scientific facts, on the basis of which all important collective decisions are taken, there can be no place for a risen Jesus Christ. When, through education, people are introduced to this modern view of the world they generally either set aside their religious beliefs as irrelevant, or retain a religious dimension but keep it strictly separate from the business of life in the 'real world'.

---

[1] This chapter was published in an earlier version in the *Scottish Bulletin of Evangelical Theology*, Vol. 11/1(1993), pp. 1-16 and is included in the present volume with the Editor's permission.

[2] See, e.g. Peter L. Berger, *The Heretical Imperative: Contemporary Possibilities of Religious Affirmation,* London: Collins, 1980, pp. 1-30.

Neither position can do justice to the comprehensive claims of biblical Christianity. The New Testament calls for a conversion through which Christ becomes the controlling centre for all our thinking and the basic interpretative clue for our whole understanding of life. For those conditioned by modernity, this constitutes a revolution of the most radical order. This chapter is an attempt to consider how such a revolution may occur. The approach taken is to examine the character of the major intellectual revolutions which have occurred in scientific history and to consider how these may suggest a pattern for the change of mind demanded by Christian conversion under the conditions imposed by modernity. In particular, since Christian conversion is often regarded as a lapse into irrationality, I will attempt to locate the rational ground within modern conditions for such a change of mind. This is by no means intended to suggest that conversion is entirely and exclusively an intellectual matter. Other aspects of the human psyche have their legitimate place. However, it is particularly necessary today to demonstrate that Christian conversion does not require the surrender of intellectual integrity and that there is a firm rational basis within modern conditions for the change of mind demanded by the Christian message. Lest we imagine that this is exclusively a Western or European kind of discourse, it is worth noting that modernity is a very significant player in African cultural and intellectual life.[3] In as much as modernity is a global phenomenon, the issues raised in this chapter are of relevance to all who have been exposed to Western-style education.

Paradigm Shift in Scientific Revolutions

At the outset it has been freely admitted that a radical alteration in our whole perception of reality is required in the transition from a modern world-view to a Christian one. We may begin our study by noting that such revolutionary change is not unknown, or even unusual, in intellectual progress. In his *The Structure of Scientific*

---

[3] For a historical introduction, see Jean and John Comaroff, *Of Revelation and Revolution: Christianity, Colonialism and Consciousness in South Africa*, Vol. I, Chicago and London: University of Chicago Press, 1991.

Revolutions, Thomas S. Kuhn has argued persuasively that any decisive scientific advance is characterized not by the steady accumulation of knowledge, but rather by the sudden emergence of a completely new perception of reality. Scientists normally work within well-established paradigms - models from which spring particular coherent traditions of scientific research - so that normal science consists in "extending the knowledge of those facts that the paradigm displays as particularly revealing, by increasing the extent of the match between those facts and the paradigm's predictions, and by further articulation of the paradigm itself".[4] What normal science does not do is to challenge or overthrow the commonly accepted paradigm. However, such revolutionary development does occur at the truly momentous occasions in scientific advance when a paradigm shift takes place. The progression involved in this kind of reconstruction is described by T. F. Torrance:

> Certainly the recognition of what is new requires as a base of operations a conceptual framework to help us distinguish it from what we already know, but what is new can be identified properly and grasped only as we are able to break free from an antecedent framework and if we are able to assimilate what we are able to grasp of it out of itself through a reconstruction of that framework. Such is the heuristic function to which a scientist hopes to put his formalization, but a transformation of the formal framework on which we rely in scientific reasoning, an adaptation of it in the very act of applying it to something new, so that it will enable us to strengthen our grasp of it, is a feat of an educated and disciplined intelligence of considerable intuitive power: yet that is precisely what happens in the moments of great creative advance in science.[5]

---

[4] Thomas S. Kuhn, *The Structure of Scientific Revolutions,* 2nd ed., Chicago: Chicago University Press, 1970, pp. 10, 24.

[5] Thomas F. Torrance, *Transformation and Convergence in the Frame of Knowledge: Explorations in the Interrelations of Scientific and Theological Enterprise,* Belfast: Christian Journals, 1984, p. 146.

I hope to show that this kind of paradigm shift offers a suggestive model for consideration of Christian conversion in its intellectual aspect.

From an exhaustive historical study of such scientific revolutions, Kuhn concludes that what occurs on such occasions is, first, the awareness of anomaly. So long as the commonly accepted paradigm is unchallenged, scientific observers experience only the anticipated and the usual, even under circumstances where anomaly will later be observed. However, when a researcher, who is often either very young or very new to the field, persistently draws attention to something wrong in the paradigm itself, then the revolution is underway. That awareness of anomaly opens a period in which conceptual categories are adjusted until the initially anomalous has become the anticipated. At this point the discovery has been completed.[6] Such a discovery, since it cannot be accommodated within the existing paradigm, leads to a crisis, and eventually to the construction and acceptance of a new paradigm.

This reorientation of science by paradigm change is described by Herbert Butterfield as "handling the same bundle of data as before but placing them in a new system of relations to one another by giving them a different framework", or more colloquially, as "picking up the other end of the stick".[7] Butterfield notes that "change is brought about, not by new observations or additional evidence in the first instance, but by transpositions that were taking place inside the minds of the scientists themselves".[8] The result of such paradigm shifts as, e.g. those associated with Copernicus or Newton or Einstein, is very far reaching: "when paradigms change, the world itself changes with them".[9] It is not a matter of gradual adjustment. Rather an entirely new perception of the world is quite suddenly put in place.

---

[6] Kuhn, *Scientific Revolutions,* p. 64.

[7] Herbert Butterfield, *The Origins of Modern Science 1300-1800,* London: G. Bell and Sons, 1949, RP . 1, 7.

[8] *Ibid.,* p. 1.

[9] Kuhn, *Scientific Revolutions,* p. 111.

The kinship of scientific paradigm shift to the intellectual revolution of Christian conversion may be illustrated by noticing a personal involvement in one of the classic scientific revolutions: the development and acceptance of quantum theory in physics in the early twentieth century. In the months before Heisenberg's paper on matrix mechanics pointed the way to a new quantum theory, Wolfgang Pauli wrote to a friend: "At the moment physics is again terribly confused. In any case it is too difficult for me, and I wish I had been a movie comedian or something of the sort and had never heard of physics." Less than five months later the 'conversion' had occurred and we find Pauli writing: "Heisenberg's type of mechanics has again given me hope and joy in life. To be sure it does not supply the solution to the riddle, but I believe it is again possible to march forward."[10] This case illustrates how personal, and indeed how costly, is the engagement and commitment required of a scientist in the process of paradigm shift. The conversion experience is extremely demanding and the new paradigm is usually fiercely resisted when first advanced. Often it is only the next generation which is able to accept the new paradigm and work on the new basis.

Christian Conversion as Paradigm Shift

The argument of this chapter is that it is a 'paradigm shift' of the sort described by Kuhn which occurs in the process of Christian conversion. No suspension of proper scientific procedure is involved. On the contrary, what is required is the application of the kind of intense scientific inquiry which is characteristic of the great discoveries in the history of knowledge. We begin with the anomaly, in this case the resurrection of Jesus, which does not fit the currently prevailing paradigm. Then as our inquiry inexorably convinces us of the validity of the resurrection, our acceptance of **the** anomaly throws the current paradigm into crisis. The crisis is resolved **only** with the emergence of

---

[10] R. Kroning, "The Turning Point", in M. Fierz and V.F. Weisskopf (eds.), *Theoretical Physics* in *the Twentieth Century: A Memorial Volume to Wolfgang Pauli,* New York, 1960, pp. 22, 25-6, cited by Kuhn, *Scientific Revolutions,* pp. 83-84.

a wholly new paradigm in which the whole of reality is viewed in the light of the resurrection.

As a matter of history, it was a paradigm shift of this sort that occurred under the impact of the gospel in the early centuries of the Christian era. As Torrance has commented, the incarnation and resurrection of Jesus Christ "forced themselves upon the minds of Christians from their own empirical and theoretical ground *in sharp antithesis* to what they had believed about God and *in genuine conflict* with the framework of secular thought or the world-view of their age". The great constitutive events of the Christian faith "forced themselves upon the mind of the Church against the grain of people's convictions, as ultimate events bearing their own intrinsic but shattering claims in the self-evidencing reality and transcendent rationality of God himself, and they took root within the Church only through a seismic restructuring of religious and intellectual belief".[11] Torrance notes that the same kind of conversion occurred, e.g., in modern physics in the transition from Newtonian principles to those of relativity and quantum theory. An ultimate reality forces itself upon our attention and, since it cannot be fitted into the formal framework of hitherto acquired knowledge, presents us with a dilemma: *either* to reject what is disclosed as absurd *or* to commit ourselves to a radical restructuring of our whole conceptual system. As we become engaged with the intrinsic claims of the subject matter, these finally assume a compelling quality which drives us to take the second alternative, no matter how costly or disturbing that may be.

In the case of the apostolic witness to the resurrection as an historical event in space and time, modern Westerners find that they cannot accommodate it within their existing conceptual framework. This may lead them to reject it but there is an alternative: to rise to the challenge of rethinking our whole understanding of reality in the light of the resurrection of Jesus. This involves a reconstruction of our understanding of God. All dualistic thinking about the relation

---

[11] Thomas F. *Torrance, Space, Time and Resurrection,* Edinburgh: Handsel Press, 1976, p. 17.

between God and the world is overthrown, for since God has entered the creation he must be understood as a living God whose very being and life are accessible to human knowing and participating. It involves a reassessment of our understanding of Jesus. The resurrection marks him apart from all other leaders and teachers, vindicates his divine claims and demands of us our ultimate loyalty and obedience. It involves a re-evaluation of the material creation and of God's commitment to it. Space and time are not closed but open to God who by his dynamic action establishes their identity. It involves a revolution in our understanding of death. As C. S. Lewis graphically put it, "He has met, fought and beaten the King of Death. Everything is different because he has done so. This is the beginning of the new creation. A new chapter in cosmic history has begun."[12] In fact, as we unfold the intrinsic intelligibility of the event of the resurrection, our whole conception of reality is steadily reconstructed. The anomaly throws the existing paradigm into crisis and the result is a paradigm shift which produces a wholly new view of the world.

The Question of Rationality

The question remains, however, of the relation between the old paradigm and the new and how we may make the transition from the one to the other. Is it a 'brainwashing' exercise in which we abandon all our previous knowledge and are indoctrinated into the new system? Or is there some rational continuity in the conversion process? To return to Kuhn, his thesis has been criticized on the grounds that it posits a total discontinuity between the old paradigm and the new at a time of scientific 'revolution so that there is no point of contact or comparison between them.[13] This, it is said, suggests that there is a lack of rationality in the progress from one to the other - it is a 'leap in the dark', conditioned chiefly by social pressure. Interestingly, a similar criticism is often made of the intellectual aspect

---

[12] C.S. Lewis, cited by Michael Green, *The Empty Cross of Jesus,* London: Hodder and Stoughton, 1984, p. 132.

[13] See, *e.g.,* John Polkinghome, *One World: The Interaction of Science and Theology,* London: SPCK, 1986, pp. 13-14.

of Christian conversion. Lesslie Newbigin addressed himself to it in his recent consideration of Kuhn's thesis:

> While there is radical discontinuity in the sense that the new theory is not reached by any process of reasoning from the old, there is also a continuity in the sense that the old can be rationally understood from the point of view of the new. In Einstein's physics, Newtonian laws are still valid for large bodies in slow motion. Newtonian physics are still valid for mechanics. Thus to recognise a radical discontinuity between the old and the new is not to surrender to irrationality. Seen from one side there is only a chasm: seen from the other there is a bridge. By analogy ... the new understanding of the converted person might make it possible ... to find a place for the truth that was embodied in the former vision and yet at the same time offer a wider and more inclusive rationality than the old one could.[14]

Likewise Torrance emphasizes that, while the Christian message demands a very radical reconstruction of our whole conceptuality, it does not involve any surrender to irrationality. Rather there is sufficient continuity for us to see at work "the relation between the created rationalities and the transcendent rationality of God in which the latter is recognized not as an intrusion into the former but rather as their affirming and establishing on their true and ultimate ground".[15]

Considerations of this order lead Newbigin to the important conclusion that,

> From within the plausibility structure that is shaped by the Bible, it is perfectly possible to acknowledge and cherish the insights of our culture. There is an asymmetry in this relationship, as between the paradigms of science, but not a total discontinuity. From one side the other looks quite irrational but from the other side there is a rationality that embraces both.[16]

---

[14] Lesslie Newbigin, *Foolishness to the Greeks: The Gospel and Western Culture,* London: SPCK, 1986, pp. 52-53.

[15] Thomas F. Torrance, *Space, Time and Incarnation,* London: Oxford University Press, 1969, pp. 85-86.

[16] Newbigin, *Foolishness to the Greeks,* p. 63.

This means that in the process of conversion there is no requirement for Christians to abandon the whole of their previous understanding. Rather it is taken up and embraced within a wider rationality so that they are still able to relate meaningfully to their previous interests, though their total frame of reference has been infinitely expanded. What we know with our modern mind is not abandoned but rather embraced and given a wider frame of reference in which its true bearing and proportion is brought to light.

This may readily be understood against the background of the emergence of a growing appreciation of the ontological stratification of the universe and the corresponding multi-levelled character of knowledge. The collapse, following the work of Einstein, of the idea of the universe as a closed mechanistic system has led to a deepening awareness of the infinite range or depth of objectivity and intelligibility in the universe and of the need for open systems and open structures of knowledge to comprehend it. No sys-tern can be complete or comprehensive on its own. In mathematics the incompleteness theorem of Kurt Godel demonstrated that no logical system can be complete without some reference outside the system to something beyond it. Applied beyond mathematics the Godelian theorems have had the effect of giving firm shape and justification to the multi-levelled structure of knowing.[17] The universe is conceived as comprising a sequence of rising levels, each higher one controlling the boundaries of the one below it and embodying the joint meaning of the particulars situated on the lower level. As we move through progressively higher levels of knowledge each one can embrace all that has been found on the lower levels, yet at the same time transcend them.

It is as we move up this hierarchy of levels of reality, from the more tangible to the intangible, that we penetrate to matters that are increasingly real and full of meaning. As Michael Polanyi illustrates the point, interpreting a grandfather clock or a Shakespeare sonnet in

---

[17] See Michael Polanyi, *Personal Knowledge: Towards a Post-Critical Philosophy,* London: Rout-ledge and Regan Paul, 1958, pp. 190ff., 259ff.

terms of physics and chemistry may produce an analysis that is valid as far as it goes but which at the same time calls for interpretation on a higher level.[18] In Christian conversion we begin to come to terms with these higher levels of reality. This does not involve abandoning or making a break with the structures of understanding developed at the lower levels. Rather these are incorporated and given their proper place and proportion within a truer grasp of reality in all its depth and range. Within this structure there is a line of rational continuity which runs through and sustains our transition from one paradigm to another in the process of Christian conversion.

The Question of Circularity

The idea of executing a paradigm shift by rethinking our conceptuality on the basis of the incarnation/resurrection has aroused objections on the grounds that it involves an essentially circular procedure, i.e. we interpret the incarnation/resurrection within a framework of thought of which it itself is a constitutive determinant. Therefore we are not standing outside the object of our enquiry and examining it in the light of external criteria. Such an objection may carry weight where the object in question is patient of examination by cross-reference. However, it is not valid here since in the case of the incarnation/resurrection we are dealing with *ultimate* realities for which, in the nature of the case, there is no higher or wider system of reference within which they may be proved. As Michael Polanyi points out: "Any enquiry into our ultimate beliefs can be consistent only if it presupposes its own conclusions. It must be intentionally circular."[19] There is no way of escaping a complete circularity of the conceptual system but this does not foreclose the possibility of rational analysis and assessment. As Torrance indicates:

> The system must be one which is internally consistent and which rests upon the grounds posited by its constitutive axioms, without any alien additions, so that the conclusions we reach are found to be anticipated in the basic presuppositions. Such a system,

---

[18] *Ibid.*, p: 382.
[19] *Ibid.*, p. 299.

of course, even if entirely consistent within itself, could conceivably be false, and must therefore be open to reasonable doubt: but that means that the system stands or falls with respect to its power as a whole to command our acceptance.[20]

If we are dealing with a paradigm shift then such a procedure is not unreasonable, given that the axioms of the new paradigm can, in the nature of the case, be examined not by reference to any higher or wider system but only in terms of their own intrinsic intelligibility and compelling reality. There is no vicious circle here.

In fact, all branches of scientific study depend on at least a provisional acceptance of the axioms of the system. In physics, for example, we have to presuppose that there is order in the universe. It is an axiom which must be assumed and, finally, our acceptance or rejection of that ultimate truth depends on the power of the system as a whole to command our acceptance. The paradigm shift of conversion to Christianity involves the provisional acceptance of certain key axioms of the Christian world view but there is nothing irrational or unscientific about venturing to test out these axioms by seeking an apprehension of the system as a whole.

The Question of Subjectivism

A further criticism of the demands of Christian conversion is the allegation that they involve an inescapable and insidious element of subjectivity, in that they speak of realities which can be accepted only by faith. This carries weight where the ideal of knowledge is one which envisages a series of objective facts existing in absolute distinction from the investigator. However, in the face of the progress of twentieth century science, the ideal of pure objectivity has proved to be a mirage, and the inquiring, experimenting, theorizing, *subject* has come to be seen as intrinsically necessary to the development of scientific understanding. It is in the interplay between the objective reality and the subjective investigator that the real substance of scientific advance is to be found.

---

[20] Torrance, *Space, Time and Resurrection*, p. 15.

The work of Michael Polanyi has been particularly influential in drawing attention to the role of intuition, conjecture and the creative power of the imagination in scientific advance. He has sought to undermine the rigid objectivism of the positivist approach through a demonstration of the crucial role in scientific work of the 'tacit dimension': the intuitive apprehension of a structure in reality which lies behind all our scientific investigation and guides the integrative activity by which we make sense of what we perceive. It is upon this informal and implicit 'personal coefficient' that even the most completely formalized logical operations ultimately depend for their meaning and truth. Torrance points out:

> This is why Polanyi calls for a rejection of the objectivist notion of truth: complete depersonalization leaves no room for the informal acts of commitment to ontological reality upon which the assertion of factual truth depends, or for the fact that such a commitment necessarily implies certain basic beliefs concerning the nature of reality with a claim to their universal validity, since it is only in the light of those beliefs that he interprets empirical facts and observations.[21]

The importance of the role of the subject becomes clear if we look at the actual practice of science. At the frontiers of research, scientists have to make difficult decisions whether or not to commit themselves to a new line of inquiry. They have to decide which problems are worth investigating and which are not. They have to make value judgements in the light of a vision of scientific activity. Then they are sustained in their mental struggle by a passionate concern to solve the problem they have decided to investigate. The purpose and values of the knowing subject have a vital role to play in the disclosure of knowledge. In a word, it is by faith that we gain understanding.

This does not mean a retreat into a subjective conception of truth. Polanyi is very careful to guard against the danger of subjectivism and argues that his concept of the personal transcends the division between subjective and objective: "In so far as the personal submits to

---

[21] Torrance, *Transformation and Convergence,* p. 200.

requirements acknowledged by itself as independent of itself, it is not subjective; but in so far as it is an action guided by individual passions, it is not objective either."[22] In fact, however, this is the way towards a proper objective grounding of knowledge:

> It is in tacit knowing that we have to do with the ontological reference of knowledge, in virtue of which we establish empirical contact with reality in its coherence and rationality, and therefore with that aspect of knowing in which its content is grounded evidentially and objectively, although informally, upon the structure of experience or reality.[23]

There is an irreducible fiduciary component in all our knowing which is emphatically non-subjectivist, in that it arises strictly from the compelling claims of the basic reality to which the inquirer has been exposed. Polanyi suggest that Augustine's axiom *nisi credideritis, non intelligitis* ('unless you believe, you do not understand') is universally applicable:

> We must recognize belief once more as the source of all knowledge. Tacit assent and intellectual passions, the sharing of an idiom and of a cultural heritage, affiliation to a like-minded community: such are the impulses which shape our vision of the nature of things on which we rely for our mastery of things. No intelligence, however critical or original, can operate outside such a fiduciary framework.[24]

This is not to surrender to mere subjectivism. In a competent fiduciary act the agent "does not do as he pleases, but compels himself forcibly to act as he believes he must. He can do no more, and he would evade his calling by doing less."[25] Interestingly, Polanyi evokes Luther's "Here I stand. I can do no other" as the model for the position occupied by all scientific pioneers in their fiduciary commitment to the truth which

---

[22] Polanyi, *Personal Knowledge*, p. 300.

[23] Torrance, *Transformation and Convergence*, p. 158.

[24] Polanyi, *Personal Knowledge*, p. 266. Cf. Polanyi, *The Tacit Dimension*, London: Routledge and Kegan Paul, 1967, pp. 13-14, 33.

[25] Polanyi, *Personal Knowledge*, p. 315.

has become disclosed to them.[26] Far from being alien, personal belief and commitment are fundamental to scientific progress. As Polanyi puts it, "Originality in science is the gift of a lonely belief in a line of experiments or speculations which at the time no one else considered to be profitable. Good scientists spend all their time betting their lives, bit by bit, on one personal belief after another."[27]

The crucial role of faith in the gaining of understanding is all the more pronounced in regard to knowledge of God, who is the ultimate ground and source of all intelligibility and truth. As we move up the stratified levels of reality within the universe, the role of the fiduciary component in the acquisition of knowledge becomes progressively more critical. Hence it is not surprising to find that at the highest level of knowledge, when we come to the transcendent reality of God, the exercise of faith is found to be particularly important. The 'personal coefficient' is central. It is only in the context of whole-life commitment that progress in true understanding is likely to occur.

The Christian theologians of the patristic era were aware of this when they insisted that proper understanding of God not could be gained without godliness *(eusebeia)*, i.e. the embodiment of faith in a corresponding way of life and worship in the reverent service of God. The Reformers stressed on a particular aspect of this - that in order to gain an accurate understanding of God, repentance *(metanoia)* is required, i.e. a commitment to changing one's mind and to changing one's life in accordance with the results of one's investigations. Here again, the demands of Christian conversion are little different in principle from those of scientific progress of any kind. True scientists are not totally detached and unmoved observers. Rather they are committed as persons to work and are ready to change their minds and change their lives in the light of its results. Likewise in Christian conversion it is only as we get inside the way of life which corresponds to the divine revelation in Christ that we can attain the disposition of

---

[26] *ibid.*, p. 308.
[27] Polanyi, *Scientific Thought and Social Reality*, 1974, p. 51, cited by Torrance, *Transformation and Convergence*, p. 195.

mind which is able to make progress in understanding it and to develop the appropriate modes of thought and speech which it requires. No advance in understanding may be attained without the exercise of personal faith and commitment. As in other fields, faith may be exercised in Christian conversion that is firmly grounded objectively and altogether removed from any mere subjectivism.

The Question of External Corroboration

Kuhn has pointed out the importance of external corroboration in the acceptance of a new theory.[28] In the case of Christian conversion, corroborating evidence is not lacking. The outstanding developments have been in modern physics, where the scientific revolutions of the twentieth century have produced a new understanding of the universe which is vastly more compatible with Christian belief. The idea of the universe as a closed continuum of cause and effect and the sharp contrast between 'real, mathematical time and space' and the 'apparent and relative time and space' of our ordinary experience, which have governed so much modern thinking and under which the Christian faith is practically unacceptable, have now been rendered obsolete. Einstein's relativity theory has demonstrated that neither space nor time can be regarded as absolute. The old deterministic system under which everything was rigidly understood in terms of cause and effect has proved inadequate to explain such established facts as the electro-magnetic field.

Meanwhile, quantum theory has shown that there is an unavoidable factor of uncertainty in all scientific calculations. The result has been the emergence of a much more open and dynamic view of the world in which aspects of reality are understood not by reference to any uniformity of causal patterns but in terms of their proper ontological intelligibility. In this way the fatal gap between empirical and theoretical concepts is transcended, and being is found to be essentially open, requiring open concepts and open structures of thought for its understanding. In this new intellectual climate Christian

---

[28] Kuhn, *Scientific Revolutions,* p. 155.

belief in creation, incarnation and resurrection has the opportunity to be presented in terms of its own intrinsic significance and without being squeezed into any alien framework of thought. This is a dramatic turn-around. As T.F. Torrance comments:

> Nothing like this has ever appeared before in the whole history of science, philosophy and culture, except in the theology of the pre-Augustinian Greek Fathers, who had to carry through the same kind of revolution in the basis of their culture as modern science is carrying out today. For the first time, then, in the history of thought, Christian theology finds itself in the throes of a new scientific culture which is not antithetical to it, but which operates with a non-dualist outlook upon the universe which is not inconsistent with the Christian faith, even at the crucial points of creation and incarnation.[29]

Modern science, far from undermining Christian faith as is often popularly supposed, in fact offers considerable 'corroborating evidence' to anyone involved in the process of Christian conversion. A further, and corresponding, area of corroboration lies in the extraordinary social and political changes of recent times. Polanyi and other philosophers of science argued from the 1950s that the open structures of the new science, and the open universe which they disclose, must lead to the collapse of totalitarian regimes and the spread of the open society. The events of 1989-1991 in Eastern Europe have dramatically vindicated their judgement. The argument is that Marxism is a socio-political counterpart to a positivist and materialist notion of science, seeking to structure society in a way which corresponds to a closed, deterministic understanding of the universe. When transcendent realities and obligations are denied then the state invariably becomes the inheritor of all ultimate devotion. Recent developments in Eastern Europe have demonstrated the bankruptcy of such a system, and the rediscovery of spiritual values currently taking place in that part of the world acts as powerful corroborating evidence in the case of Christian conversion. None of this is intended

---

[29] Thomas F. Torrance, *Theology in Reconciliation,* London: Geoffrey Chapman, 1975, p. 270.

to suggest that the intellectual transition from a 'modern' to a 'Christian' view of the world is self-evident or without serious obstacles. However, if external corroboration has a valuable role to play we should notice that it is not lacking either in the discoveries of modern science or on the stage of world history.

Conclusion

There can be no minimizing the radical nature of the intellectual revolution demanded under conditions of modernity by the process of Christian conversion. However, this in itself should not daunt us since 'paradigm shift' is common and indeed crucial in intellectual progress. In light of the multilevelled character of knowledge, we may embrace within our new Christ-centred view of reality all the rational knowledge which has been disclosed to us by modern science. The difference is that it is all given its proper place and proportion in a comprehensive perception of reality which does justice to the full range and depth of the universe. Such a reconstruction can take place only on the basis of an acceptance of the incarnation and resurrection but, in the case of such ultimate realities, a circular procedure is necessary and the new system stands or falls by its ability as a whole to command our acceptance. Faith is indispensable in the development of the new understanding but the commitment of the personal subject is recognized to be crucial in all spheres of knowledge. Moreover, there is striking external corroboration available to anyone making the transition to Christian faith. It is never going to be possible to become a Christian strictly through a process of logical deduction but there are firm rational grounds accessible to us which offer a basis for Christian belief. The model for a change of mind suggested by the great scientific revolutions may illuminate the nature of the intellectual revolution demanded in Christian conversion. It shows that there is, at the end of the twentieth century, a path to Christian belief which is intellectually coherent and convincing.

12. Christianity and the Visual Arts in Malawi

Martin Ott

A Burdened Legacy

Art is not something that really bothers Christians in Africa. Sometimes when a certain painting or carving is displayed or removed, some parishioners share a few words of questioning. But normally African Christians seem to be concerned about other problems, like the ever lacking funds for the church or the moral behaviour of the community members. Listening to Bible readings and to the sermons on Sundays one has to admit that not very much is said about art. No, art is not an issue, and if it would be, it would only be for those intellectuals who could afford it.

The title of this book suggests that faith is at the frontiers of knowledge. For many African Christians art is at the frontiers of faith. Taking this into consideration, it seems more than a daring statement to say that the Christian aesthetic experience is a source of insights that could enhance human knowledge. If this is accepted, who can profit from it?

Even within the boundaries of Christianity, the relationship between Christianity and art is not an easy one. Many laments and complaints are brought forward. Christians all over the world feel that their own affinity to art is not reflected in the pastoral, spiritual or liturgical life of the church. Any attempt to bring together both domains is subjected to suspicion from both sides.

Furthermore, it seems that neither the theologians nor the artists like each other. Theologians look at art as something mostly luxurious, provisional and unimportant for eternal salvation. Artists, on the other hand, appreciate religious themes as a source of inspiration, but will do everything to keep away from church officials. Too deep is their fear that Christian faith, theology and church politics would become a limiting and suppressing factor in their work. Such fear is not unreasonable. Especially in the last century the relationship between faith and art underwent a deeply shattering experience. During the 19th century Christianity lost its touch with contemporary and innovative art. On the other hand, art and artists were emancipated from a pure Christian canon of themes and motifs. The famous creed *L'art pour l'art* can also be applied to the newly gained artistic self-understanding: no longer to be a servant of theology and church (and any other social or political group). This historical development had liberating effects for both sides. The Church could liberate itself from a strong linkage with Western culture that endangered the Christian faith. This assessment is applicable in different ways for the Catholic and the Protestant attitudes towards culture. The arts could rejoice in the fruits of secularized Christian values like freedom and tolerance, which have become socially effective, at first outside the church and due to the achievements of the Enlightenment.

As we approach the relationship between Christianity and faith in a non-Western context, one might hope to leave behind the burden of Western history. Alas, even in Africa we feel its presence. Christianity is a historical religion, it was not invented in Sub-Saharan Africa during the last hundred years. Whether we like it or not, with the coming of the European missionaries, African Christianity inherited some of the 'old' problems of Western Christians in the field of art and faith. One consequence of this legacy is the fact that Christian art is not a high ranking topic on the agenda of theology and the Church in Africa.

Nevertheless, the encounter of Christianity with a new culture and the possible perspectives of a successful inculturation could cause hope for the establishment of a contextualized and innovative Christian art. Looking at Malawi, where Christianity settled more than 100 years ago, I have tried to assess how far this process has gone. I want to investigate if and how far a local Christian art has developed and how it has been welcomed in the pastoral reality of the churches and in the piety of local Christians. The considerations of this chapter are limited to visual arts, leaving aside other domains such as music, drama, dance, poetry and literature. I have attempted to shed light on fields that remained unresearched in a former study of this subject in Malawi.[1]

For many, art is seen as an eye-opener for realities not yet perceived by humankind, a signpost for future developments. It is hoped that art and artists would be more sensitive to the *zeitgeist* and the activity of the Holy Spirit. In such a conception, art really would appear with an aura of newness and thus would contribute to knowledge at the frontiers of faith. Maybe this is due to an archaic association that connects the artist with the role of the prophet in society. This is exactly what we want to keep in mind when we place the "results" of Christian art next to other domains of knowledge-gathering in Malawi.

Why Visual Arts in the Christian Experience of Life?

Before looking at the Malawian situation, I offer a brief overview of some major reasons why visual expression is an essential component of Christian experience. During its 2000 years of history the church experienced some turbulent phases where the use of images in liturgy and worship, were very much in the forefront of discussion. The most famous phases were the iconoclastic controversy in the 8th and 9th centuries and the Puritan Reformation of the 17th century. Today there is a strong mainline conviction in favour of the use of images. Contributions from different areas, like anthropology, biblical studies, philosophy and systematic theology complement each other and form a strong demand for the integration of visual arts in the Christian faith. For this discussion in an African context it might be interesting to note that the objections against the integration of visual arts in theology are brought forward by the same authors or theological schools who disparage African religions as pure "paganism".

The Christian faith tries to relate the whole person to God. To believe is not just an intellectual, or emotional act. In the process of bringing the personal life under the guidance of God, all the human senses

---

[1] *Martin Ott, Dialog der Bilder. Die Begegnung von Evangelium und Kultur in afrikanischer Kunst,* Freiburg: Herder, 1995 (English translation td be published in 1998 in the Kachere Series).

have their unique function. We are well aware that hearing is an essential activity in faith ("faith is from hearing", Rom 10:17) but seeing is equally part of our "being in the world" and therefore should be integrated into Christian life. To achieve that, a culture of seeing has to be created ("we have seen the truth"). The Christian understanding of the incarnate Christ as the "visible image of the unseen God" (Col 1:15) allows us to transcend any visual form, towards the Invisible. Aloys Grillmeier states:

> In the same way as in Jesus' life his body was the form of the presence of God, so within the church the visible picture may become the witness for the invisibility of God. Christian art participates in God's revelation in time and space. The incarnate God enters history without losing his transcendency. The 'image' becomes an illustration and elucidation of the 'Word'.[2]

Thus, *seeing* anticipates the final reality of the kingdom of God where we will see "face to face" (1 Cor 13:12). The connection of hearing and seeing corresponds to the 'already' and 'not yet' of the coming of the Kingdom of God. Thus, in Jesus Christ there is the possibility of transcending every image within creation to the invisible mystery of God. The Risen Christ encourages his disciples to express their new understanding of the coming kingdom with all their creativity.

In this process Christians find a deep source of inspiration in their surrounding cultures. It may not be accidental that the logo on the cover of *The Catechism of the Catholic Church* (African edition) shows a shepherd resting under a tree.[3] This pagan motif was borrowed by the early Christians in the 2nd century from Roman culture. They filled it with new meaning and used it as a symbol for the rest and happiness that the soul of the departed will find in eternal life. Thus we find it on a Christian tombstone in the catacombs of Domitilla in Rome. These

---

[2] Aloys Grillmeier, "Die Herrlichkeit Gottes auf dem Antlitz Jesu Christi. Zur Bild-Theologie der Vaterzeit", in Aloys Grillmeier, *Mit ihm und in ihm. Christologische Forschungen und Perspektiven,* Freiburg/Basel/Wien: Herder, 1975, p. 36f.

[3] Cf. the logo on the cover of *The Catechism of the Catholic Church, Nairobi:* Paulines Publ., 1994.

early Christians could use this symbol without fear of being syncretistic or pagan, because they had a deep understanding of the Roman culture including its use of pictures and the significance of their motifs. This approach of the early Christians may be exemplary in the development of Christian art in Africa.

Christian Art in Malawi today

State of affairs

When the first Christian missionaries arrived in Malawi they did not come with the Bible only, but with visual expressions of their religion. Before talking about indigenous Christian art, we have to realize that the problem is deep and complicated. Christianity introduced a new world of images before any consciously Christian art was attempted. This applies to every Christian denomination regardless of its theological attitude towards images. Even Protestants who are focused on the Bible and the preaching of the Word of God, introduced the Christian faith in a visualized form. As far as art is concerned, the best examples are the stained glass windows of the church of St Michaels and All Angels, Blantyre, the church in Livingstonia and St Peter's Anglican Cathedral at Likoma. But also the "roman" collars of their ministers, the vestments of the women's groups, the liturgical colours and symbols or just the aesthetic shape of the newly built churches. These all mould the forms in which Christian worship takes up its inevitable visuality. Catholics play an exciting role in that process because their worship is more liturgy orientated and their theology less resistant to the use of visual arts. As times goes by we find mass vestments, statutes of saints, sacred tools for liturgical use like chalices, monstrances, statutes of Our Lady, tabernacles, stations of the cross etc.

All these items offered a visual realization of the immigrating religion. In some sacristies and storerooms of parishes today, the remnants of these imported pious articles can still be admired. The first generations of missionaries can be said to have set the standard in the field of a visualized Christianity. The way the churches were built, the pictures used for catechetics and pious activity (medallions with motifs of Our Lady, Sacred heart of Jesus, Guardian Angel), stations of the cross, Statues of Our Lady and St Joseph, and the crosses displayed in the churches and outstations, formed a kind of canon for a Christian picture world. An outstanding example is the Catholic church in Phalombe, which is the exact replica of the Catholic church in Vaals, Netherlands. Thus the missionaries did not only introduce 'copies' of European Christian art, but they failed to give the Christian art in Malawi a local identity, rooted in the visual traditions of the Malawian culture. Of course they acted in the mainstream of cultural alienation that went along with colonization. Has there ever been research into what it really means for a new nation and its identity when the biggest town does not have a local name, but is named after the birthplace of a *mzungu*?

The domination of the founder generation of missionaries covers both the fields of theology and spirituality, and the field of Christian art. Little wonder that today the Christian art brought by them is still dominant in official church use. We can confirm this when we look in the songbook used in the Catholic church in Malawi. The *Buku la Nyimbo ndi Mapemphero*[4] collects samples of that type of Christian art: a portrait of Jesus, the Redeemer of the Sacred Heart (p. v), the Holy Family (p. 146), St Joseph with Infant Jesus (p. 181), Infant Jesus with Sacred Heart (p. 279), and Risen Christ appearing before Mary Magdalene (p. 285). The pictures are reproductions of common samples of religious artwork common in the early decades of this century in Europe. The style is moulded by a naive realism where the three figures of the Holy Family, guardian angels and other biblical figures are designed according to the imagination of the faithful of that period. Their faces are sweet and soft, the infant Jesus is a soft boy, as an adult he has a beard. All figures are *azungu* - white people. Special emphasis is given to the holy family and to the guardian angels. Also the stations of the cross are copies of those one would find in Europe today. The people gathered whom Jesus meets on the way to the Cross, are *all* Europeans. Even recent samples of Church art in

---

[4] *Baku la Nyimbo ndi Mapemphero,* newly revised and completed edition, Lilongwe, 1989.

Malawi reflect the cultural and geographic background of expatriate missionaries. The newly built St Montfort church in Balaka is a good example of this. Although the Montfort missionary M. Leidi, the painter of the altar, somehow tries to integrate Malawian life into biblical scenes, the faces of the Malawians and of Jesus are like the people in Bergamo, northern Italy, where the painter originates from. The church paintings in Balaka are a good example of a rootlessness 'between' the missionary and the Malawian culture.

Attempts at indigenous Christian art

In order to offer a classification of art in this context, I refer to a short definition given by L. Meurer: "African Christian art should be Christian, African and of aesthetic merit. "[5] In this chapter I have limited myself to the relationship between the Christian faith and its Malawian context, neglecting the discussion of the aesthetic aspect of Meurer's classification.

If one accepts the general historical remark that Christian art mostly developed from the existing art in its cultural context, then it is necessary to assess what kind of starting point the Malawian culture provides as far as visual arts are concerned.

In the year 1991 Kay Chiromo, the then Head of the Department of Fine and Performing Arts at Chancellor College in Zomba, published the video tape "Visual Art in Malawi".[6] Chiromo collated 12 areas of Malawian visual arts, some of more historic importance, others of actual importance. In some detail he mentions: the Akafula rock paintings, the Chewa mask-production (both carved masks and manufactured animal structures), beadwork of the Ngoni, artistic activities linked to Yao initiation ceremonies (Jando), airport art (mostly wood carving), ceramics, pottery, mat and basket weaving,

---

[5] L. Meurer, "Christliche Kunst fur Afrika", in *Katholische Missionen,* Vol. 98/4 (1979), *p.* 118. For further explanation on the meaning of these three criteria see *Ott, Dialog der Bilder,* p. 63ff.

[6] Kay Chiromo, *Visual Art in Malawi,* Video Tape, Department of Fine Arts, Chancellor College, Zomba, 1991.

cotton spinning and textile design, contemporary art (sculpture and painting), and Christian religious art. Fr Claude Boucher, a White Father missionary based in Mua, counts six areas of traditional activities in the field of Malawian visual arts: paintings, pottery, iron work, bead work, wood carving, and sculpture.[7] In Chichewa there is no word for art in general. Steve Chimombo forms the neologism *ulimbaso* in order to systemize and to integrate art activities under one heading.[8]

Art is always concrete and it is described with the word for a specific activity. Not all of these activities are directly connected with their use in traditional religions. Mostly the masks of the *gule wamkulu*, their colours and material (wood) have an important religious function. Compared with other African countries, Malawi has no comprehensive tradition of visual art. How did Christians react to this visual heritage of Malawi? There is only one art centre in the country that tries to bridge the present with history and build up a contextualized Christian art that converses with the artistic and cultural heritage of the country. I refer, of course, to the KuNgoni Art Craft Centre in Mua, half way between Balaka and Salima. Apart from a few artists who occasionally painted church walls or carved crosses, stations of the cross, small panels and the Poor Clares in Lilongwe who design mass vestments, I am not aware of any centre or individuals involved in the development of Christian art in Malawi.

The KuNgoni Art Craft Centre, directed by Fr Claude Boucher, does not encompass all fields of Malawian artistic activity. It is mainly focused on carving and painting. Many of the carvings try to relate to themes of Malawi's political, social and religious history, focusing on the history of the Chewa, the Ngoni and the Yao. These include themes such as creation myths, rain rituals, mask dances *(gule wamkulu,*

---

[7] Claude Boucher, "The Artistic Heritage of Malawi", unpublished typescript, 1989, 8 pp.

[8] Steve Chimombo, *Malawian Oral Literature: The Aesthetics of Indigenous Arts,* Centre for Social Research and Department of English, Chancellor College, Zomba, 1988, pp. 61-79.

ngoma dance), rites of passage (birth, initiation, marriage, death, accession of chief and elders) healing ceremonies, witchcraft and witchcraft cleansing. I have taken the example of two works which focus on the idea of inculturation, i.e. the dialogue between culture and faith.[9] Out of the large number of church decorations[10] I have selected the painting "Parable of the Dragnet" in Milala, diocese of Zomba, and the panel "Chauta" in the parish church of Mua, diocese of Dedza.

Parable of the Dragnet: Milala

In 1982, artists painted a huge church fresco for the first time, with the general theme of inculturation. It is an 8x3m picture in the church of Milala, an outstation of Lingoni parish. The parable of the dragnet, Matthew 13:47-50, is set in a landscape near Lake Chilwa where Milala is located, on the western shore. In the background we recognize Mount Mchisi which stands out in that part of Lake Chilwa. In the foreground we see Jesus and his apostles as fishermen sitting on the shore. Their faces and clothes identify them as Malawians. We also see local fish from that side, like chambo, magazin, mulamba, utaka, samwamowa and sapuwa.

What is so typical about that painting? First, the artist located a biblical scene in a Malawian landscape. The message is, what happened long ago happens here and now. Here as well as there, he selects his disciples, he narrates the parable of the good and the bad fish. This is something that the fishermen of Milala can well understand.

Milala, is an outstation of Lingoni and may be visited once a month by a priest who comes to say mass and preach the gospel. The painting in the small church remains in Milala all the time. It is the permanent visible symbol of the gospel that occurs in their neighbourhood and in

---

[9] Aylward Shorter, *Toward a Theology of Inculturation,* New York: Orbis, 1988, p. 11.

[10] The centre contributed to the decoration of about 100 churches in Malawi, and about 20 churches outside the country in Kenya, Zambia, Mozambique, South Africa, Italy, Germany, Austria, and Canada.

the life experience of the people. Thus, the painting in Milala can be connected with the tradition of the *biblia pauperum* ("Bible of the Poor") in the medieval churches of Europe, where the reliefs in the *thympanon* and the stained glass windows played the same role.

For the people in Milala the introduction of this form of visual art was something new. Never before had they seen a painting on the wall with figures that are so realistic that you can even identify the faces of some local people. The reactions of people seeing the painting for the first time seems naive: "How is it possible that the water sticks to the wall and does not drop?" A new way of perceiving reality had just entered that small village in the eastern border of Malawi.

This pedagogic effect on the people challenges them to see things in a new way. The picture on the wall is not the reality, but the message it portrays, is nevertheless meaningful to them. It is the introduction of the *symbolic* use of pictures, and furthermore, the *symbolic use of images* in Christian faith, that has entered Milala. The pictures arc not what they show, but they visualize and revive a reality that is beyond their visible image and yet a reality that is evoked by their visibility. This is the way in which the church adapted the use of images during its history, either for instructive, affirmative or liturgical use.

Chauta: Mua

Our second example is taken from the parish church in Mua, the home of the KuNgoni Art Craft Centre. In 1991 the whole church was renovated and the artists planned an extensive decoration of the church including altar, lectern, baptismal font, statues of Our Lady and St Joseph, station of the cross, and tabernacle. On the altar wall **a large mural,** integrating a wooden cross of the Risen Christ and a carved tabernacle, portrays the theme of "Old and New Creation". A vast rainbow connects a panel with themes of the Malawian creation myth from Kaphirintiwa mountain ("Old Creation") with the figure of the Risen Christ ("New Creation"). Above the altar, just under the roof, the artists placed a round wooden panel called "Chauta", about 1.50m high.

On the panel we see a mask that is meant to represent Chauta ("the great Rainbow"), the High God of the Chewa. His mask is in the foreground of a vast sun that is decorated in the form of banana leaves. Around the central mask of Chauta other masks are placed like Malya, Simoni or Tsempho. These are characters from the *gule wamkulu,* the traditional dance of the secret Chewa society. The panel is carved in such a way that the arms of Chauta embrace the other masks and find their prolongation in the rainbow which is painted at the altar wall. The whole setup of altar paintings and carvings wants to stress Chauta as the giver of rain; the one who enables the ancestral community (the *gule wamkulu* spirits) to give fertility. He gave life at times of creation, he continues to give life with the help of the community of the living dead and he finally, guarantees the new life through and in the resurrection of his Son Jesus Christ.

In the decoration of the Mua church we can identify several aspects in the process of establishing a local and inculturated Christian art in Malawi. First of all, the main theme of the church offers an excellent opportunity to begin a vivid dialogue with the local history and religion. Under the heading "Old Creation", each theology of inculturation refers to the starting points of the existing religion. Here in Mua, a few miles north of the mission there is the rain shrine of Mankhamba, the central sanctuary of the Karonga chiefs.[11] Thus, at the altar wall we find a small picture of a shrine hut, similar to the one erected during the rain rituals in Mankhamba. At this place the chiefs and priests on behalf of the people of that area, ask for rain, i.e. for fertility for the land, for the animals, and for people. The artists decorated the church in such a way that in front of the wall-picture a carved tabernacle was placed. For the observer the shrine hut and the tabernacle become one. Looking at the whole ensemble, it is neither shocking nor surprising that the two main symbols of the old and of

---

[11] Ian Linden, "Mwali' and the Luba Origin of the Chewa. Some tentative suggestions", in *Society of Malawi Journal,* Vol. 25/1 (1972), p. 11-19; Ian Linden, "Chisumphi Theology in the Religion of Central Malawi", in Matthew Schoffeleers (ed.), *Guardians of the Land: Essays on Central African Territorial Cults,* Gwelo: Mambo, 1979, pp. 187-207.

the new religion intermingle and somehow merge. The place of the tabernacle-hut is located in the centre of the rainbow. On one side we find a panel portraying the events of Kaphirintiwa mountain, the mythical story of the rain ritual practices in Mankhamba; the other end connects with the statue of the Risen Christ. Bridging the "old" creation on Kaphirinthiwa with the "new" creation on Golgotha, the rainbow leads the eye of the observer towards the centre to the symbols of the ritual the Christians celebrate, the change from the old to the new; the Eucharist and participation in the life and death of Christ who has become the "bread of the world", the new life, the warrant of eternal fertility.

Summarizing the essentials of this kind of inculturated Christian art, we can appraise that the key features of Malawian traditional religion and the main themes of the Christian faith have been visualized at the same time and in the same place. Through the composition and the arrangement of the artists a dialogue between African Traditional Religion and the Christian faith has been evoked. This way of dialogue in pictures is genuine and unique. Could this dialogue be copied or transferred to a literary form? Judging by the fact that these works are not just art objects but liturgical tools, the intended dialogue is not an intellectual one but is one that takes place in the realm of sacred liturgy and worship. Thus, objects of inculturated African Christian art help to establish a dialogue between religions in the heart of their own identity. Taking this into consideration we understand that the symbolic character of Christian art can assume a quasi-sacramental function within worship. In a unique way these samples of African art can demonstrate how the integrative power of the incarnated Christ is able to transform the myths, rituals and persons of the "Old Creation" Malawi in the "New Creation" of the coming kingdom of God. Those who see and understand, will undergo a rite of passage. They will change their old ways of looking at African Traditional Religion and the Christian faith. Thus African Christian art here is inculturated, innovative, educational and liturgical at the same time.

The Crucial Question of Reception

The question of how useful and important African Christian art is, depends on how it is received in the congregation of the faithful. Apparently Africans do not have much interest in "dead" artefacts i.e. those which are out of use. This applies equally to objects of liturgical art. Whereas altars, crosses, banners and churches are beautifully decorated during the services and thus create a festive atmosphere, the same decorations remain unattended after the service, in a corner of the church. Moreover, it seems that much more effort is put into the decoration of human beings (vestments, flowers in the hair, festive dresses, etc) than of "dead" artworks. Christian Art has to be art in use. This attitude reflects the anthropocentric, social and ritualistic worldview of Africans and it is a good prevention against all kinds of aestheticism where artworks are deprived of any social and human use. At the same time this opens the door for the use of Christian art especially in the liturgy, where the traditional connection between art and ritual can be taken up. In that context an observation of J. Healey and D. Sybertz in Tanzania is very interesting: "The local Tanzanian people seem to accept Jesus Christ being portrayed as an African in plays much more readily than in art, drawings and pictures."[12]

The question of reception of art has to be dealt with in two sections. Firstly, to understand why most of the Malawian Christians stick to the inherited European art; and secondly, how they react to the new indigenous art under the programme of inculturation. O. Wermter, a Catholic missionary in Zimbabwe, describes an interesting experience. One day he asked his parishioners which type of statue would appeal most to them when ordering a new statue of Our Lady. They choose a 16th century Madonna by the German painter Matthias Grünewald, and not a sample of an African Mary by the famous Serima artists of their own country and in their own vicinity.[13] "The very energetic

---

[12] Cf. Joseph Healey and Donald Sybertz, *Towards an African Narrative Theology of Inculturation,* Nairobi: Paulines Publ., 1996, p. 102, footnote 57.

[13] Cf. A.B. Plangger, and M. Diethelm (eds.), *Serima: Towards an African Expression of Christian Belief. EM Versuch in afrikanisch-christlicher Kunst,* (German-English), Gwelo: Mambo, 1974.

daughter of a German farmer, with red hair and a very white complexion, had to be the model!"[14]

Wermter summarizes: "The problem of Christian art in Zimbabwe remains largely one of reception."[15] The Zimbabwean experience could have been a Malawian one as well. The reluctance of African or Malawian Christians to let go of the pictures of their founder generation, has primarily to do with the inner connection of these pictures with the spirituality and Christian impact of the early missionaries. Just as Malawians received the gospel, the truth about God and his Son Jesus Christ, they received 'true' images which helped to express and to support their new found Christian faith. Perhaps the general custom of Africans to honour their ancestors supports this faithfulness in the tradition of their European Christian ancestors.

However, the religious art brought in by the missionaries came from a continent and from an era where Christianity had lost contact with the modern world and modern art, and had tried to save "Christendom" in an antimodernistic way. The religious art used in that time was backward, out of date and reflected an ecclesiastical concept that separated the church from society and culture by imprisoning itself in a cultural ghetto. Now, more than 50 years later, the Western understanding, use and reception of Christian art has changed. But these changes were not part of the missionary impact.

If it comes to modern Christian art, especially under the idea of inculturation, Malawian experiences confirm the general assessment of the acceptance of modern art in African societies. J. Miller notes that African artists were outsiders in their own societies and their art was mainly appreciated by Europeans and expatriates.[16] We find a similar reaction when it comes to African Christian art.

---

[14] O. Wermter, "Zimbabwean Art in Christian Symbolism", in *AFER*, Vol. 31 (1989), p. 164.

[15] Ibid., p. 163.

[16] Judith Miller, *Art in East Africa: A Guide to Contemporary Art,* London: Frederick Muller and Nairobi: Africa Book Service, 1975, p. 13.

> The whole contemporary movement of an African Christian art is the result of an initiative taken by European missionary clergy and religious, and [...] it corresponds to the philosophical and moral ideals of foreign ecclesiastics. As such, African Christian art today is almost wholly an "appendix" to European Christian art. There is no real dialogue with the language of African cultural traditions. African Christian art does not emerge spontaneously from the consciousness of the local community of faith. It is mainly the product of a sincere, but eclectic, missionary exercise, which finds no echo in the hearts of ordinary African Christians.[17]

How can we analyze this state of affairs? Let's look closer at the process of reception of this new Christian art in the Malawian church. We have already mentioned the reaction of the Christian community in Milala near Lake Chilwa. How could they appreciate, or even claim something that they see only for the first time? However, is this a reason to refrain from confronting people with this new world of Christian iconography and the symbolic use of pictures that is connected with it? Even in the remotest villages of Malawi the "new" world is about to approach. The communication era with its representatives of television and the internet may not yet have reached Milala, but this is merely a question of time. The people have already been confronted with new media of visual communications. Why should Christian motifs not be the first to be introduced into the new era? Thus, as long as communication systems in the rural areas are so limited, one must not underestimate the effects of a permanent visual catechism on a church wall. African Christian art has been rightly compared with the biblical picture stories in medieval cathedrals, which served as the *biblia pauperum* and were an illustrated and permanent visualization of scenes from the gospel and church history.

In some churches pictures of a black Christ had to be removed because of the fact that Jesus was portrayed as a Malawian. The Africanization or Malawianization of biblical figures is a major break with former

---

[17] Aylward Shorter, "The Function and Future of African Christian Art", in Aylward Shorter, *Christianity and the African Imagination: After the African Synod. Resources for Inculturation,* Nairobi: Paulines Publ., 1996, p. 67.

visual habits. For many it is not acceptable to portray the Infant Jesus as a Malawian child nor Mary as a Malawian mother.[18] Hence, some of these paintings or carvings had to be removed or changed in order to comply with the expectations of the local community. The conflicts rising from the challenge of African Christian art can be outspoken with the example of the statue of the Risen Christ carved in the early 1970s by Lenardi Chikasassa (nicknamed 'Akamitondo' which means mortar carver), a Moslem artist.

Today the statue can be seen displayed on the front wall of the parish church in Mua. When the statue was to be displayed in the church in 1972, the Bishop of Dedza, Cornelius Chitsulo, was reluctant to bless the work. According to him the statue offended the convention in three ways: first, Christ was a Malawian; second, the figure was made of wood, a material that was always connected with *gule wamkulu;* third, it showed the Risen Christ and not the crucified Christ. Bishop Chitsulo was supported by Father Siwinda, a Malawian White Father who was also born in Mua. Father Siwinda was against all carvings because they were "the work of *gule wamkulu* and therefore from evil". Bishop Patrick Kalilombe, like Bishop Chitsulo born in Mua, finally convinced his confrere to bless the crucifix. The reactions of the people involved are somehow representative of the attitude of African Christians towards African Christian art and are therefore interesting to evaluate. This is done with respect to the actors involved, concentrating on the theological convictions that became obvious in that conflict.

The first argument of the Bishop concerned "Jesus being a Malawian". He would have shared the arguments that a young Ugandan priest, Paul Kalanda, brought forward in 1960 when he publicly protested against certain works of African Christian art of the time, that showed Christ "with a short face, flat nose, thick lips, and crisped hair".[19]

---

[18] Several of the statues of Mary portray her as pregnant and happily drawing attention to her pregnancy. This causes offence to many Malawians because "Malawian women do not do this".

[19] Paul Kalanda, "Christ in African Art", in *AFER,* Vol. 2/4 (1960), pp. 324-326; reprint in T. Olcure, P. van Thiel, et al., *32 Articles Evaluating Inculturation of*

Kalanda argued that according to the tradition and the iconographic praxis of the church, Jesus "was a white man, with a long face and long hair; his lineaments were Jewish". Kalanda summarizes his criticisms as follows:

> Changing the traditional image of Jesus Christ now, would not only be confusing to our Christians, but could also render them suspicious. To show them a black Christ-picture, though similar to them in features, would make our Christians wonder: whether Christ is like a 'chameleon', which changes its colour with the surroundings. They might even begin to doubt the veracity and historical genuineness of the Gospels. Indeed, to paint Jesus Christ as black and to give him African features robs him of his race and personality. It is, therefore, misleading, against history and the approved tradition of the Church.[20]

The concerns of Kalanda and Bishop Chitsulo were twofold: First, a theological concern that a black Jesus would not be in line with the Catholic tradition; second, pastoral concern that the faithful might become confused and doubtful about the truth of the gospel that was passed on to them. It is more than understandable that a Catholic pastor brings forward these arguments reflecting two essential and unimpeachable facts of his pastoral concern. Thirty years later, Paul Kalanda having since studied anthropology at Oxford and been consecrated as Bishop, was asked to comment on his opinions towards African Christian art.

> The new insights and the knowledge of inculturation in the church today, have helped me to see better than I did thirty years ago. I have come to know that the image of the Incarnate Christ, the God-man, the risen Jesus Christ, is not limited to any colour or racial features. [...] If I had time to write another article on the same subject now, I would not insist on historical realism in Christian art, but more on the symbolic function of art for the

---

Christianity in Africa (Spearhead No. 112-114), Eldoret, 1990, pp. 213-215, at p. 213.

[20] *Ibid.*, p. 215.

promotion of Christianity. I think that is what is meant by inculturating Christianity, making it an effective expression of the Church and its message in particular African and other cultures of the world.[21]

Kalanda's 'conversion' helps us to give an answer to the second concern of Bishop Chitsulo, where he saw the use of wood directly connected with its significance in *gule wamkulu,* so that such a chosen starting-point of Christian art would not bring forward the development of African Christianity, but bring it backward towards 'paganism'. Indeed, the fear of the Bishop is serious. Without a change in the attitude towards the visualization of religious objects of worship the visual representation of *gule wamkulu* masks in churches would irritate the faithful. Hence, the keyword in Bishop Kalanda's statement is "symbolism". In African Traditional Religions (e.g. in the *gule wamkulu* of the Chewa secret societies) the masks do not only represent the world of the ancestors. It is believed that the ancestors actually become present during the ritual use of the mask. How deep the spiritualized concept of a man-created mask or figure is still rooted in the Malawian culture is proved by the statement of a potter woman from Kamzati village in Ntcheu district. Asked why she does only produce low price objects like pots and jars, and not human figures which were more appreciated and bought by customers, the lady responded: "How can I fire [she means 'bake'] a human figure? This is inhuman."[22] In the Christian use of images, on the other hand, the represented object is a pure image or symbol. When referring to traditional motifs, themes, colours, forms, proportions, etc in Christian art, these have to undergo a certain process of secularization. By accepting this it is possible to integrate visual traditions from African traditional Religions in samples of Christian art; masks of the *gule wamkulu* in churches can symbolize the history that God had with the Malawian people before the arrival of the missionaries. It was through

---

[21] P. Kalanda, "A New View on 'Christ in African Art", in Olcure, Thiel et al., 32 *Articles,* p. 217

[22] Cf. the interview in Chiromo, *Visual Art in Malawi.*

them that he provided ethical orientation and rain, i.e. fertility and life for his people.

This is the way we can interpret the panel "Chauta" in the parish church in Mua. The *gule wamkulu* masks there do not have "life" of their own, they are aligned to Chauta, the High God who alone, according to the Christian faith, can grant "power". With a symbolic attitude towards pictures, even the High God Chauta, now identified with the father of Jesus Christ, can be represented in the form of a mask. Never in Malawian or African traditions was the High God represented in visual form; but in the same way that Christian iconography dares to confront the faithful with the motif of the reconciling father in the parable of the prodigal son, Christian art is free to symbolize God in the form of a mask, knowing that this does not affect his sovereignty and mysterious invisibility. But we can see that the introduction of an inculturated Christian art necessitates a continuous and accompanying pastoral care and aesthetic education for the faithful. Or in theological terms, the images need the explanatory assistance of the Word. This Christian art education would include a dialogue with the surviving cultural traditions, the importance of visual art in the church history, the main motifs and themes of Christian art and the biblical 'background' stories to pictures. Through the accompanying Word, misunderstandings like the one Bishop Chitsulo had concerning Christian tradition only knowing representations of a crucified Christ, could easily be avoided.

A Plea for African Christian Art in Malawi

Is it responsible to encourage artistic activity in one of the world's poorest countries where people do not have enough money to buy the necessary things for everyday life? Similar issues have been raised elsewhere. Is it possible to write poems and to pray to God after Auschwitz? J.B. Metz gave an answer: Yes, it is possible, because poems were written and prayers were said in Auschwitz. Despite the poverty in Malawi we should remember that the kingdom of God is not only a kingdom of justice and peace, but also a kingdom of beauty and magnificence, of splendour and glory. For Christians in Malawi the task of establishing the kingdom of God is not only the struggle for social justice, political freedom and poverty alleviation.

Why then Christian art in Malawi? Malawians have continued to be creative and to produce artworks throughout their history. It is also human to develop artistic and aesthetic capacities. With the coming of the Christian faith the artistic legacy of Malawi has not come to an end. All the human capacities of creativity and of visual artistry want to be integrated into a Christian personality. The kingdom of God wants to be established in all its fullness, freedom and beauty. Moreover, as we have demonstrated, Christian art is capable of touching the human reception of symbols, and thus evokes a process of dialogue, conversion and symbolic experience that is deeper than a mere intellectual approach. It reflects the fact that the Christian faith wants to embrace all aspects of the human consciousness and to root the liberating faith in Jesus Christ, the Incarnate Son of God, in the deepest depths of the human soul.

Christian worship, being ritual and aesthetic, helps us to identify the crucial starting points with African traditional religions. It does not follow aesthetic rules if we believe that only the richest and the best is good enough for the Lord. This was exactly why Jesus did not hinder the woman from anointing his feet with precious and expensive ointment (Luke 7:3650). This applied to the sanctuary and the ark in the Jewish temple in Jerusalem (Exodus 35:30-35); it applies in other ways for the wide variety of artworks that have been created during Christian history in order to honour God. Africa and Malawi are invited to offer their best creative gifts and to join the line of worshippers. Of course we have to remember that in Christian fellowship, art is never an end in itself. A prayerful atmosphere is more important than any sophisticated liturgy that would include highly developed music, dance or visual arts. "A simple people's folk art - even children's drawing or dance - the best they are capable of, coming from their innermost selves, can be art truly worthy of worship.[23]

---

[23] L.J. Luzbetak, *The Church and Cultures: New Perspectives in Missiological Anthropology,* 7th ed., Marylcnoll: Orbis, 1996, p. 382.

The examples I have given in this chapter represent only one facet of Christian art in Malawi. New themes, new ways of visualizing the experience of Christian faith are still to come. During its history the church has often been a patron of art, even when artists provoked the establishment with their new insights. To invite more and further Christian art necessitates an acceptance that artists sometimes refuse to be integrated into the ecclesiastical mainstream and that tensions between them and the established churches will be a 'normal' feature. By providing orders and facilities for display, the churches could give a sign of reestablishing their role as patrons of art and of accepting its prophetic role.

Can art be an expression of faith at the frontiers of knowledge in Malawi? As far as the development of Christian art in Malawi is concerned, we are at the beginning of a long journey. Each journey starts with an initial step. This has begun in Malawi. It is up to each Christian and each Christian denomination to ensure that religion and art meet once again in Malawi.

13. Christianity: Liberative or Oppressive to African Women?

Isabel Apawo Phiri

Introduction

From the outset I want to make it clear that I am writing this chapter as a woman of faith, committed to God and the institution of the Church. My intention is to raise issues in African Christianity so that it becomes a liberative force for all that dwell in the continent of Africa, an African Christianity that speaks against oppression of women and men as they build the kingdom of God together here on earth while waiting for the second coming of Jesus Christ. When women are writing theology from a woman's perspective, it is said that anger is one of the motivations for theologizing. It is anger against patriarchy for denying women their humanity. I am not angry at any one individual or the institution of the church even though I do not accept some of the ways the church has interpreted the Bible with regard to women members of the church. I promote a spirit of dialogue on issues of disagreement between men and women in church and society. Genuine dialogue takes place between people who are liberated by Jesus and are free to express their opinions without fear of one party dominating the other. Fear and domination are the elements of oppression. The main questions that this chapter raises are: does Christianity as it is practised in Malawi bring liberation or oppression to the Malawian woman? In what ways is a Malawian woman liberated by Christianity or oppressed by it?

Different theologies of Africa - African Christian theology, African theology, African liberation theology, Black theology, Reconstruction theology, African women theology - are classified as liberation theologies. In this context it is liberation from western classical theology. The underlying principle here is that all theology must be done in a particular context. If theology is done in Malawi within a western classical framework, it becomes oppressive to the Malawian

Christian. Christianity is not adhered to in a cultural vacuum. As stated by John Mbiti:

> The question of relating the Gospel to culture comes up automatically when the Gospel is proclaimed in any given place and time. Culture is the voice which responds to the Gospel, the voice which welcomes or rejects the Gospel, the voice which interprets the Gospel, the voice which propagates the Gospel and the voice which celebrates the Gospel.[1]

Therefore, when Christianity was born in Palestine it was within a Jewish culture. The founder of this faith did not intend to keep it within Jewish culture because he left instructions that the Gospel must be spread to the end of the world.[2] Thus, within a short time it was received in the Hellenistic culture. Since then it has influenced and it has itself been influenced by many cultures. By the time Christianity reached Malawi, it came via Europe and therefore with some elements of European interpretation. Decisions on what is acceptable for a Malawian Christian or what is not, were not only based on what the Bible says, other factors also came into play. What does the mother missionary institution say? What are the missionaries who are still in Malawi saying? Depending on the issue, what does the Malawi culture say?

An example here is the issue of the ordination of women to ministry. For a long time the decision has been denied in the mission churches in Malawi because the mother churches were not doing it. However when changes began to take place in the mother churches, the arguments started shifting. In the case of the Anglican church in Malawi, Reverend Canon R.S. Hunter argued against the ordination of women on the basis of maintaining what was the tradition of the very

---

[1] John Mbiti, "The Gospel and African Culture: Use and Unuse of Proverbs in African Theology", paper presented at the Missiological Consultation on African Proverbs and Christianity, Maputo, Mozambique, 27-31 March 1995, pp. 1-2.
[2] Acts 1:8.

first Anglican missions. The possibility of maintaining unity with the Roman Catholic church suddenly becomes important. He argues:

> I should like both of the dioceses in this country to declare an intention not to debate in Synod any motions which damage the common tradition which we hold with the Roman Catholic Church. This would extend beyond the question of the ordination of women. This would not imply an immediate further revision of the settlement of religion made at the Reformation. The settlement is already embodied in the book of Common Prayer. The intention would be to protect the common tradition which has united us with Catholic Christians since the Reformation and which we in this country received from the UMCA.[3]

This is an example where European missionaries influence the identity of the church in Malawi. On the other hand there is a counter voice coming from a Malawian woman who is a representative of the Mothers' Union in the same Anglican church. She argues for the ordination of women on the basis of one of the Malawian cultures where Christianity has come to make a home. She reminds the church that some of the Anglicans are Chewa. Chewa tradition allows women to take up positions of religious as well as secular leadership. She goes on to argue that:

> We have noted with great concern that reasons given so far for rejecting the ordination of women to the priesthood are based on the cultural practices of the Jews as reported in the Old Testament and Paul's letters to various groups which embraced his teachings on Jesus' life and ministry ... In our case here in Malawi, our ancestors had totally opposite perceptions about women from the one the Jews had. European missionaries found that in African

---

[3] See the letter of the Reverend Canon R.S. Hunter to the Bishop of Lake Malawi 1993 on the issue of the ordination of women in the Anglican church, in Kenneth R. Ross (ed.), *Christianity in Malawi: A Source Book*, Gweru: Mambo, 1996, p. 113.

tradition, women were regarded as the very keepers of life (Makewana).[4]

In this case, who decides as to what is liberating or oppressive to Malawian Christian women? As the final decision showed, it is those who have administrative and economic power in the church who determine the form of Christianity that is practised in Malawi. Perhaps turning to the teachings and practices of the founder of the faith can empower the Malawian woman who does not want to be discouraged by the decision makers in the institution of the church.

Christianity and Liberation

When Jesus Christ (the founder of the Christian faith) started his ministry, it was very clear in his mind that he brought a message Of liberation for all humanity. He said:

> The Spirit of the Lord is on me, because he has anointed me to preach the good news to the poor. He has sent me to proclaim freedom for the prisoners, recovery of sight for the blind, to release the oppressed, to proclaim the year of the Lord's favour.[5]

When Peter was summarizing the mission of Jesus when he was in Cornelius's house (a centurion in what was known as the Italian Regiment), he commented on

> how God anointed Jesus of Nazareth with the Holy Spirit and with power, and how he went around doing good and healing all who were under the power of the devil because God was with him.[6]

The message and mission of Jesus shows that his aim was to engage people in their own liberation from sin, ignorance, poverty, social injustice and any other forms of oppression. This message was transformative unlike the beliefs and practices of the time. It is charismatic in that it recognizes the power that was received through

---

[4] E.C. Kishindo, "Statement of the Mothers' Union 1994", in Ross (ed.), *Christianity in Malawi*, pp. 114-115.

[5] Luke 4718-19.

[6] Acts 10:38.

the Holy Spirit. It is contextual in that it locates itself within the context of the society in which it found itself. More than that, it is prophetic in that it was in agreement with the radicalism of the prophets who challenged social injustice.

If the message of the founder was that simple - liberation for all - how come women in the universal Church of Jesus Christ are complaining that they are not enjoying the full liberation that Jesus brought? Where is the problem and who is causing it?

In order to answer the above questions, I will approach them from four angles by examining: a) the relationship between Jesus and women in the gospels; b) the church and women; c) the liberation movements of women and church women; and d) the church in Malawi and women.

a) *The relationship between Jesus and women in the gospels*

The gospels present a positive relationship between Jesus and women. The position that Jesus took should be understood in the context of his time. Jesus was a Jew living in first century Palestine. Jewish culture was patriarchal like most of the cultures of the world today. Elisabeth Fiorenza has done a good background study of the status of women around Jesus' time.[7] However to get a better picture we must go further and look at women from the Jewish Scriptures. Betty J. Ekeya has summarized for us the ancient position of women in the Jewish culture in the following way:

a) Women were put in the same inferior state as slaves and gentiles. The rabbi's daily prayer reflected this. "O Lord God, master of the universe, I thank and praise you that you did not create me a woman, a slave or a gentile."

b) Women had no legal status. They could not own property or inherit their husband's property.

---

[7] See Elisabeth Schussler Fiorenza, *In Memory of Her: A Feminist Theological Reconstruction of Christian Origins.* London: SCM, 1983.

c) There was no certainty that woman was made in God's image. She was regarded as man's tempter, the cause of man's sinning.

d) Women were not allowed to study the Law of God (of Moses). Death was to be preferred by a Rabbi than to teach the Torah to one's daughter.

e) Woman's place was in the home. As wife and mother she had to produce sons for her husband. Failure to do so was regarded as wholly her fault.

f) A woman could be divorced for any fault the husband saw in her. She could not remarry if her ex-husband refused to give her a certificate of divorce.

g) Marriages were arranged for the girls by their fathers or male guardians. It was a disgrace for a man to fail to arrange marriages for his daughters.

h) The plight of widows was especially sad. There was no protection for them.

i) Widows, if young, had to be inherited by the next of kin of their husbands for the purpose of producing offspring for the deceased husbands (Deut. 25:5-10).

j) Women had to be heavily veiled in public and none could address, or be addressed in public by a man, especially a rabbi.

k) The uncleanness laws prohibiting women from joining in worship. They were doubly unclean after producing a daughter.

l) Women could be and were accused of adultery and if found guilty, were stoned to death in the market place. The men involved were not killed.[8]

Phyllis Trible has argued that when we are reading the Bible we should know that there are counter voices within the Bible itself.[9] Although

---

[8] Betty J. Ekeya, "Woman's Place in Creation", in Mercy Amba Oduyoye and Musimbi R. Kanyoro (eds.), *Talitha Qumi! Proceedings of the Convocation of African Women Theologians 1989*, Ibadan: Daystar, 1990, pp. 100-101.

the parameters are set by patriarchy, one sees a change in favour of women. It should also be acknowledged here that such counter voices of the above position of women in Jewish culture are few and far between. In the same culture there were some women who held positions of honour. For example Mirriam the prophetess;[10] Deborah, a prophetess and a Judge who was also known as mother of the nation, had the same honour as Samuel.[11] Huldah the prophetess ministered during the same period as Jeremiah and Zephania.[12] In the time of Jesus there was the prophetess Anna who was a coworker with Simeon. When both of them saw baby Jesus they recognised the vision of God for the liberation of humanity.[13]

In the gospels Jesus transformed and liberated the lives of both men and women. In my judgment his interaction with and liberation of women was above the expectation of the rabbis of his time.[14] He broke the barriers of culture by: teaching theology to Mary;[15] holding a theological discussion with a Samaritan woman;[16] being anointed by a woman whom the male writers of commentaries have called a prostitute;[17] touching a woman with an issue of blood;[18] releasing a woman caught in adultery who was about to be stoned;[19] including

---

[9] See Phyllis Trible, *God and Rhetoric of Sexuality*, Philadelphia: Fortress, 1978, pp. 8-9.

[10] Exodus 15:20.

[11] Judges 4:4-5.

[12] 2 Kings 22:14.

[13] Luke 2:25-38.

[14] See Isabel Apawo Phiri, "Women in the Gospel of Luke: an African Woman's Perspective", in *Journal of Constructive Theology*, Vol. 3/1 (1997).

[15] Luke 10:38-42.

[16] John 4:4-42.

[17] Luke 7:36-50 and Mark 14:3-9. In the case of the second passage Jesus said that what this woman did should be told wherever the Gospel is preached in memory of her. Unfortunately this has been ignored by the Church worldwide.

[18] Luke 8:43-49.

[19] John 8:2-12.

women in his travelling team.[20] Such concerns confirmed his message where he said: "I have come that they may have life and have it to the full."[21] This full life is for both men and women.

Women too responded with courage to the way he treated them. When everybody had deserted Jesus at the cross, a group of women risked their lives by staying up to the very end of his life.[22] They showed courage and love for Jesus by going to the tomb to anoint his body at the earliest opportunity when it was still dangerous to do so. Mary Magdalene's persistence was rewarded because she become the first person to see Jesus after resurrection. She was entrusted with a message to pass on to the rest of the disciples even though Jesus knew that the testimony of a woman would not be taken seriously.[23] "His commission that day made them (women) apostles - sent ones. For two thousand years this fact has been totally ignored."[24]

The questions which I am mostly asked are: Why did God send a man to save the world and not a woman? Or: Why did Jesus choose only men among his disciples? In addition, western women theologians are also asking, can a male Saviour save women? I will return to these questions in another section.

b) *The church, theology and women*

The images and positions of women in the early church seems to be more positive than in Jewish culture and religion. I want to propose that this was because of the emphasis on the power of the Holy Spirit as the one guiding the early church. In the book of Acts, women and men are included in the group of one hundred and twenty disciples of Jesus that received the Holy Spirit and power to work for God. Following the advice of Elisabeth Schussler Fiorenza in reconstructing

---

[20] Luke 8:1-3.

[21] John 10:10b.

[22] Mark 15:40-41.

[23] John 10-19.

[24] *Umtata Women's Theology Group Bible Studies Booklet No. 4,* South Africa, 1990, p. 5.

the history of the early church, we must take into account that the language of the period (as well as of the present) was androcentric. She therefore argues that where women are not mentioned specifically, it should be assumed that they were included unless when it is specifically said that the passage is referring to men only.[25] Thus, she views women as missionaries, apostles and co-workers in the early Christian church, and Paul mentions them as such.

With the spread of Christianity to a wider area, its adherents were mostly influenced by a Greco-Roman (Hellenistic) culture. In this culture women enjoyed a much freer lifestyle compared to Jewish culture. The women were not restricted to a home life. They worked in trades, dined with their husbands, attended shows, games, parties, and even political gatherings, and were notorious for receiving preachers of strange cults into their homes.[26]

The book of Romans mentions a number of women of whom Phoebe, Prisca (Pricilla in other passages) and Junia are said to be the outstanding ones. Phoebe is introduced by Paul as a minister or a leader of a church at Cenchrae, a sea port of Corinth. Although many commentators have downplayed her role by reducing it to a deaconess, Fiorenza has argued convincingly that she was a leader of a local community. Her ministry was not limited to serving other women but the whole church in Cenchrae.

Prisca and her husband Aquila were co-workers as travelling missionaries. In the New Testament the names of Prisca and Aquila are mentioned six times, in four of which Prisca's name comes first. This indicates that she was a prominent Christian woman in her own right. She was a charismatic preacher and teacher through whom the great Apollos received his accurate teaching about faith in Jesus Christ.[27]

---

[25] Elisabeth Schussler Fiorenza "Missionaries, Apostles, Co-workers: Romans 16 and the Reconstruction of Women's Early Christian History", in Ann Loades (ed.), *Feminist Theology: A Reader,* London: SPCK, 1990, pp. 59-60.

[26] *Ibid.,* p. 71.

[27] Romans 18:26.

Another couple who were co-workers in missionary work were Andronicus and Junia.[28] Paul gives them the title of apostles like himself because they also suffered imprisonment for their work and they worked equally hard for God. For a long time commentators argued that Junia was a male name

because they could not handle the idea of Paul calling a woman an apostle. To this Fiorenza has said that:

> In recent years however, it is more and more recognised that this androcentric theological assumption cannot be maintained exegetically, since we have no evidence whatsoever for a male name Junias. But plenty of evidence for the occurrence of the female name Junia in antiquity."[29]

These women stand out not as wives of missionaries but because of their great commitment to God. Their ministry was not limited to other women or children but to the whole church of Jesus Christ. There were many women who worked hard in the service of the Lord Jesus Christ but we do not hear about them because their paths did not cross with Paul's. Paul did not mention them because he did not know them.

The controversial verses

I have often been asked in theological colleges and churches about the interpretation of 1 Timothy 2:11-15; Ephesians 5:21-25; 1 Corinthians 11:3; 14:34-36; 1 Peter 3:1-7. For this we need to remind ourselves about interpretation of passages in the Bible. I want to submit that a passage must be interpreted in the context of other passages in the Bible on the same theme. If the interpretation does not harmonise with other scriptures on the same subject, then the interpretation is wrong.[30] In the light of this understanding I will deal with the issue of women being silent in the churches as found both in I Corinthians

---

[28] Romans 16:7.

[29] Fiorenza, "Missionaries, Apostles, Co-workers", p. 68.

[30] Kenneth E. Hagin, *The Woman Question,* Tulsa: Faith Library Publications, 1983, p. 32.

14:34-36 and 1 Timothy 2:11-12. In A. S. Worrell's translation of the New Testament, he has pointed out that it is important to understand that in the original Greek language there is one word for man and none for husband. There is also a Greek word for woman *(gyne)* and none for wife. He argues that in the context of the passages quoted above, the context of the passage requires that the translation should have been "let the wives keep silent in the assemblies; for it is not permitted for them to speak, but let them be in subjection, as also says the law. And if they wish to learn anything, let them ask their husbands at home; for it is a shame for a wife to speak in an assembly." Worrell applies the same translation to 1 Timothy 2:11-12. Hagin has concluded then that "(1) Paul is not talking about all women but wives. (2) He is talking about *learning something and asking questions*".[31]

The background of the passage is also important here. The passages assume that the wives did not have much knowledge about things of God. The husbands were the ones who had the knowledge. Therefore instead of interrupting the services in order to ask questions, they were to ask such questions at home so that there should be order in the service. Since then the position of women has changed. While it is true that in the Malawi context the illiteracy rate is higher among women than men, there are women who have a sound knowledge of the things of God. They have studied theology and there are also others who have not but are sure of their call by God to preach. Should such women still remain silent in the church in Malawi? If a husband is not knowledgeable in the things of God, should the wife remain ignorant and wait for the time when her husband will become knowledgeable? If we answer these questions in the affirmative, what we are saying is that the salvation of the wife depends on the knowledge and salvation of her husband. This is far from the message that was brought by Jesus Christ. He came that all may be saved directly.

---

[31] *Ibid.,* p. 29.

In other passages, like 1 Corinthians 11:5, Paul is talking about women prophesying and praying in public. In Full Gospel circles, prophesying may include preaching, praying and teaching under the revelation or inspiration of the Holy Spirit. This passage shows that women can prophesy and pray in public while in the same letter, in chapter 14, Paul is telling them to be quiet! As shown already, both the Old and the New Testament have examples of women who prophesied under the power of the Holy Spirit. In fact, on the day of Pentecost, Peter quoted Joel as having said "In the last days, God says, I will pour out my Spirit on all people. Your sons and daughters will prophesy". It is on the basis of this that women missionaries were sent to other lands to share the gospel. What I do not understand is why our churches in Malawi are quick to accept the ministry of a foreign woman (especially European and American) but use the negative passages of Paul out of context to bar Malawian women from full participation in the leadership of the church. I also do not understand why women may be allowed to preach in church once a year but not every day. Why are women allowed to teach Sunday School or preach in the women's guild? In those churches that ordain women, why are women allowed to preach and yet may not have a congregation of their own or where they have a congregation they can not baptize, conduct a funeral or a marriage ceremony? Why double standards? What is the biblical basis for such inconsistency?

Paul commended highly the ministry of women such as Pricilla and **Junia.** Therefore where he said women (wives) should learn in silence, one needs to take the context of the message seriously in our interpretation so that we do not make a universal law for all ages and for all women. This applies also to the issue of women covering their heads in church. In Paul's argument, women are to cover their heads not for God but as a sign that they were under the authority of their husbands. Therefore this was mainly an issue of relationship between husband and wife as dictated by the culture of the day. It was also a custom of the time that women should have long hair and men should have short hair. Imposing such rules on the Malawi Christian women is to labour the issue. One needs to ask the same question: Does any Malawi culture require that all women should cover their heads as a sign that they respect their husbands? Secondly, for a Malawian Christian woman to grow her hair long, she needs to plait it. If one is legalistic about the women issue, then the women would be in conflict with 1 Timothy 9-10 and 1 Peter 3:1-5. I believe what is being said here is that there is need to strike a balance. One needs to spend more time as a Christian in fellowship with God so that one's anointing can affect all areas of one's life.

It is unfortunate that as the church got more settled by the end of the first century, the involvement of women in leadership' positions was reduced. Examples of stories like that of Thecla from Iconium in modern Turkey show that women had to choose celibacy in order to be accepted to preach or play a prominent role in the church.[32]

When Thecla got converted through the ministry of Paul, she rejected marriage to the dismay of interested parties and relatives. Paul gave her the commission to become an evangelist. Virginity became highly spoken of to give the impression that a virgin was an honorary man. It was during that period that Mary the mother of Jesus got exalted to the virgin Mary and become very important in the church. Monasteries for both men and women were opened. Some of the monasteries were headed or founded by prominent women.

For the rest of the women, their images and positions were very low. This was made worse by the theological analysis of the positions of women's spirituality by the church fathers such as St Augustine and Aquinas. Women were said to bear the image of God in a secondary nature. The only time a woman was considered to reflect the image of God to the full was when she was with her husband.[33]

The contribution of Luther to the Reformation of Christianity in the sixteenth century had far reaching consequences for women in the church. The virgin Mary's position was reduced to that of an ordinary

---

[32] Karen Armstrong, "The Acts of Paul and Thecla", in Loades (ed.), *Feminist Theology*, pp. 59-60.

[33] Genevieve Lloyd, "Augustine and Aguinas", in Loades (ed.), *Feminist Theology*, p. 92.

woman by the Protestant churches. Marriage was encouraged for clergy and laity alike. But the role of women is focused on the home - marriage and motherhood.[34] Luther's views have been modified to various degrees to worsen or improve the position of women in the home and in the society by twentieth century theologians like Karl Barth.

Not all churches were guided by the reflections of some conservative theologians on images and positions of women in the church. With the birth of Holiness and Pentecostal movements came also a new liberation for women in participation in the church. The involvement of women in the early stages of the Holiness Movement[35] of the nineteenth century compares well with Fiorenza's analysis of Romans 16. Women who were set free from the oppression of patriarchy claimed their liberation under the guidance of the Holy Spirit.

c) Liberation movements and church women

It was in the nineteenth century that women in society came to realize that they were being excluded from issues that affect their very existence. Women started coming together in the United States and later in Europe through conversations to discuss their images and positions and decided to demand the right to vote and work for equal pay among many other things. Although it took a while, their voices were heard and their demands met.

In the church too, women slowly started to re-read the Bible with new eyes. Those who studied theology began to question the theoretical framework used in the interpretation of the Bible on issues that affect women.[36] In is in the 20th century, especially from the 1960 that more

---

[34] Mary Wiesner "Luther and Women: The Death of the Two Marys", in Loades (ed.), *Feminist Theology*, p. 124.

[35] See Klaus Fiedler, *The Story of Faith Missions,* Oxford: Regnum Books, 1994, p. 295.

[36] See Elisabeth Cady Staton, *The Woman's Bible,* Seatle Coalition Task Force on Women and Religion, 1974, 2nd edition.

literature has been generated by women on their position in the church.

For western women theologians, they have re-examined the doctrines of the church and raised questions that affect them as they seek their liberation in Jesus Christ and fight the oppression imposed on them by an androcentric theology.[37] By studying Biblical languages and the histories and cultures in which the Bible is situated, women theologians have affirmed the importance of inclusive images of humanity in Christian theology. The issue of whether a male Jesus can save or liberate women became pertinent for western women theologians.[38] Ruether revisits the arguments of Aristotle and the early fathers of Christianity who argued that it was necessary that Christ be born male because maleness alone "is the normative or generic sex of the human species". In other words, conservative theology has argued that it is only the male humanity that represents the fullness of human nature. In this regard it is said it was necessary that Christ be born male in order to reflect the true humanity and it is only males who can stand in the place of Jesus in the church. Taking the argument further, Mary Daly has argued what this means is that if God is male, the male is God.[39]

Such interpretation puts both men and women in bondage because in the case of women, when they think of images of God and Christ they feel excluded while for men they feel pressurized to act like God.[40] Jesus' earthly ministry did not support an interpretation of exclusion. He went out of his way to break barriers created by culture in order to uplift the oppressed. The glorified Christ too was not bound by race,

---

[37] See Elisabeth Cady Staton, *The Woman's Bible,* Seatle Coalition Task Force on Women and Religion, 1974, 2nd edition.

[38] See Rosemary Radford Ruether, "The Liberation of Christology from Patriarchy", in Loades (ed.), *Feminist Theology,* pp. 139-147.

[39] Mary Daly, *Beyond God the Father,* Boston: Beacon Press, 1973, p. 78.

[40] Carolyn Osiek, "Changing Images of God and Christ", *in Journal of Constructive Theology,* Vol. 3/2, (December 1997), p. 11.

class or gender and it is to such that women appeal to as their liberator from all that oppresses.

d) African women and Jesus

In Allan Ngumuya's song *"Jesu mwamuna wa mtanda"* (Jesus the man of the cross), two images of Jesus come out.[41] The first one is the maleness of Jesus and the second is the suffering Jesus. I do not know whether the composer used *"mwamuna" (man)* to emphasize the courage demonstrated by Jesus in bearing suffering on the cross or that he had to be a man to bear that kind of suffering. The suffering of Jesus has been emphasized a lot by African theologians as a mark of Jesus that Africans identify with. For example, in Gabriel Setilione's poem "the Frontier" he says it is when Jesus is on the cross, being beaten by the sun, and sweating that the South African recognizes Jesus as one of their own. Considering the context of suffering experienced by black South Africans, that image is acceptable. However when no other positive images are drawn, ending at associating oneself with the suffering of Jesus becomes a problem.

African women theologians are now refusing to remain with the image of a suffering Christ as their liberator. Mercy Oduyoye has argued that African culture encourages a picture of a mother who is always sacrificing for the sake of husband or children. She may suffer abuse in her home but does not talk about it for the sake of preserving the good image of the family. In the traditional set up, when there is lack of food, she works hard to get food for the family but she is the last one to eat. She is the first one to get up in the morning and the last one to go to bed. In fact during the traditional initiation for marriage, Malawian women are warned not to allow their husbands to wake up before them. If this is not followed, the husband will drain all the wife's energy for the day. The call to African women is to arise and love themselves as they love others. Christ the liberator does not call African women to remain at the cross and suffer with him. They are called to climb the cross and be lifted up to view the world with Jesus.

---

[41] Allan Ngumuya is a very popular Malawian Gospel singer.

Jesus' suffering was for a purpose - to bring deliverance. It was a plan of victory. He did all the suffering that there is. The part of the follower of Jesus is to maintain the victory that has already been won.

As the body of Christ, men and women must work together to realize the victory plan of Jesus and eradicate suffering of one at the hand of the other. For example the World Council of Churches established the Decade of the Churches in Solidarity with Women (1988-1998).[42] 1998 is a year of reporting as to what the churches have done to further the goals of the decade in question. What will be the report of the church in Malawi? Mercy Oduyoye has said that

> In Africa, as in other areas of the world, the churches often wait for a political crisis to make statements, civil war to work on reconciliation, natural disasters to provide humanitarian aid. The church in Africa tends to be a "rear-action" church, rarely visible on the front lines and often delayed in arriving on the scene afterwards to pick up the pieces.[43]

Are we in Malawi waiting for a crisis in order for the church to respond to the cries of the female congregation? Why are we not allowing both men and women to enjoy the liberation which Christ brought? Why are we opening doors for the devil to come and bring bondage when Christianity is a message of liberation?

Jesus Brought Liberation for Women in Malawi

a) Pastor Rachel Masimo called to preach the Gospel

To conclude on a positive note, let me tell you the story of the first Malawian Woman to be ordained to the position of a pastor in a big church. Pastor Rachel Masimo was ordained in the Assemblies of God Church, Lilongwe on 12 July 1994. Although she was the first in this

---

[42] See Isabel Apawo Phiri, *Women Presbyterianism and Patriarchy: Religious Experience of Chewa Women in Central Malawi*, Blantyre: CLAIM, 1997, p. 127.
[43] Mercy Amba Oduyoye, *Daughters of Anowa: African Women and Patriarchy*, Matyknoll: Orbis, 1995, p. 184.

position in the whole country, her ordination went without pomp in the media.

Since 1974 she felt the call of God upon her life. She then worked with New Life for All as an evangelist reaching out to people all over Malawi for liberation in Jesus Christ. She joined the Assemblies of God Church in 1980 and went to the church's college to study for a Diploma in Theology. By the grace of God she graduated with a degree in theology in 1991 obtained from a correspondence programme with ICI University. As part of her training she established a congregation in Area 47, Lilongwe where she experienced the guiding hand of God despite other trials she went through.

Her ordination become possible because of church leadership that recognised the call of God on women. Despite opposition, under the leadership of Pastor Chakwera the church searched the scriptures and sought the guidance of the Holy Spirit on the issue and agreed to start ordaining women. In so doing the church has made it possible for women who have been called to respond positively to the call of God. Anointed women of God like Mayi Opal have had a chance to go to the same church college to study theology and continue with their evangelistic ministries.

While the intention to ordain Pastor Masimo was in line with the Assemblies of God Church's understanding of liberation by Christ, there were other leaders who felt uncomfortable with a woman leading a congregation. After much discussion, she was made National Director of children's ministry. Pastor Masimo is from Chikwawa. This is a good example of saying yes to women's call to ministry but putting them in bondage because of church tradition.

Rosemary Radford Ruether has pointed out that most churches who have ordained women seem not to create enough space for them to operate effectively.[44] She argues that there is need to redefine our understanding of the ordained ministry so that we do not make the ordination of women a token the church does not know what to do

---

[44] See Ruether, *Sexism and God-Talk*.

with. The encouraging part is that the church has opened doors for women and it will be interesting to see what kind of positions will be given to those women who are studying with a view to being ordained in the Assemblies of God Church.

b) *Mayi Chimpondeni, founder of Namatapa Miracle Centre*

Mayi Chimpondeni was a member of the Seventh Day Adventist Church. At one time she became very sick. She sought medical help but was getting worse by the day. One day a group of women went to pray for her to be healed. She had no faith in divine healing, but the women persisted in coming to pray for her. On one such occasion she suddenly become blind and her ears popped open. That was the time she heard God calling her to work for him. The women who were present with her prayed even more and she regained her sight. From, that time she was healed and spent a lot of time alone in prayer. It was through these long prayer periods that she got instructions as to how to pray for other people in need.

In 1992 she asked her former church to release her so that she can pray for people at home. Since then the number of people that she ministers to have grown a great deal. The Seventh Day Adventist Church does not look kindly on her ministry. In fact, anyone who is discovered to have attended her services is threatened with excommunication from the mother church. But people from all denominations you can think of go to her home for prayers. By the end of 1995 she had opened twelve branches of her church in the Southern Region. The church is called Namatapa Miracle Centre. Of special interest is the fact that all the pastors heading the branches of her church are male.

Mayi Chimpondeni is married but had no children of her own when I met her in 1995. She comes from Mulanje. Her church can be classified as a charismatic church that reaches out to both men and women from all classes.[45] Prophecies and healings from all diseases are her special gifts.

c) Mayi Nyajere from Chilobwe Healing Centre.

Mayi Nyajere has a background in the Church of Central Africa Presbyterian. Her call to ministry also came after a long illness. She has had dreams and visions of interaction with Jesus Christ and angels. She also received a special call to work for God in the ministry of healing, preaching and prophecy. She describes her call and mission in the following way:

> At 9.00 am God spoke to me and said "I am Jehovah. I want you to be a minister. The lame will be healed the blind will see and the prisoners will be set free" I know that I am doing God's work. God, Jesus, the Holy Spirit, and angels are with me from the day I started. They encourage me to persevere like the prophets in the Bible. They remind me to rely on God alone.[46]

Mayi Nyajere is from Rumphi and is married to Mr Nkhonjera. She has a family and the main centre is behind her house. Like the case of Mayi Chi-mpondeni, she is able to attend to people at home and do house work as well. She has also established branches which have pastors.

d) Bishop Mchika, Blessed Hope Church and Ministries

Bishop Yami Mchika is co-founder of the Blessed Hope Church with Pastor Lumwira. Bishop Mchika is the director of the church and ministry. Her responsibilities include controlling the finances of the church, paying pastors, grounding new converts in the word of God and in good business. Her special calling as she sees it is evangelism and ministry to blind people. She is also responsible for the training of pastors.

---

[45] I am in the process of writing a book about the ministry of the women mentioned in this section.

[46] Interview with Mayi Nyajere by Grace Namalanga in December 1995 at the Chilobwe Healing Centre.

Pastor Lumwira's job is field director. He visits the churches regularly and also helps with administration. His special title is an apostle who ministers to prisoners because that is where he received his call to work for God.

Bishop Yami Mchika gave her life to the Lord in 1976. She comes from a Providence Industrial Mission background in Chiradzulu. She received her call through New Life for All ministry. She started as an open air evangelist preaching at bus stations and wherever she could find people. She was given the title of Bishop by people when the saw her enthusiasm for the things of God. People say she preaches "like a man" whenever she conducts funeral services for people who do not belong to any church. For her what is important is not the person who has died but a chance to witness to the people who have gathered and win them for Jesus.

Bishop Mchika is from Chiradzulu, and married with a family. e) Mayi Gonthi, Revival Ministries.

Mayi Gonthi is the founder of Revival Ministries which is sometimes thought to have been founded by Pastor K. Mbewe. The members of the church mention Mayi Gonthi as the founder. She has a CCAP background. A primary school teacher by profession, she is married with children.

Mayi Gonthi received her call during a Sunday service at another church. She felt the touch of God upon her life and after the service she continued in prayer for three days without food or sleep. After that she had a burning desire to do door to door evangelism which she fulfilled. As she touched the lives of many people with a message of liberation from sin, the people started coming to her for more teaching. In order not to be in conflict with her CCAP church she had her meetings on Sunday afternoons. Through outreach programmes she has established branches in different parts of Southern Africa. Mayi Gonthi sees her calling mainly as an evangelist and teacher.

Conclusion

It can therefore be said that while Christ has brought liberation for the Malawian women, the institution of the church can and/or has resisted the move of the Holy Spirit that inspired Peter to say:

> In the last days, God says,
> I will pour out my Spirit on all people.
> Your sons and daughters will prophesy,
> Your young men will see visions,
> Your old men will dream dreams.
> Even on my servants, both men and women,
> I will pour out my Spirit in those days,
> and they will prophesy.[47]

Nevertheless, if the women are being called by God to minister, a way forward will be found and no-one can stop it. All those who are opposing women's ministry will find that they are persecuting Jesus (like the case of Paul in Acts 9). If God had not called them, all those people who claim to be saved or healed through a woman's ministry will go to hell.

---

[47] Acts 2:17.

14. Christian Missions and Western Colonialism: Soulmates or Antagonists?[1]

Klaus Fiedler

Assumptions Galore!

When the colonial period was coming to an end for most of the countries of Africa in the 1960s, some wise men in Europe were convinced - and even published books on the subject - that with the end of colonial rule, Christianity, too, would come to an end. The argument was so simple that readers believed it: Christianity is very alien to Africa, those (comparatively few) Africans who did become Christians did so because they were forced (by circumstances or more directly) to accept the religion of their masters. With the decline of colonialism, collaboration would not yield any benefits any more, so Christianity would lose its appeal and would decline. Islam, being a genuinely "non-white" religion, would then take over.

Being so devoid of any factual content, the argument is worth quoting for the fun of it (and because many people believed it and even German television gave the author repeated opportunity to spread his wisdom):

> At the same time the Christian mission in Africa lost its appeal. During the colonial period acceptance of Christianity might have brought some advantages - the convert would have been the partner of the powerful. But to confess Christianity at the end of the colonial era would make no sense, would be ruinous.[2]

---

[1] *Recently published as Klaus Fiedler, "Christian Missions and Western Colonialism: Soulmates or Antagonists?" in Klaus Fiedler, *Conflicted Power in Malawian Christianity. Essays Missionary and Evangelical from Malawi*, Mzuzu: Mzuni Press, 2016, pp. 142-159.

[2] Gerhard Konzelmann, *Die islamische Herausforderung*, Hamburg, 1980. See chapter "Afrika, der islamische Kontinent [Africa, the Islamic Continent]". The quote is from p. 285. Translation mine. To support his argument for the

Konzelmann assumes that the only success Christianity had in Africa, it had because it was part and parcel of the colonial machinery of oppression, and in such an oppressive situation, there are always a few collaborators. African Christianity is nothing genuine, because, being alien to Africa, it simply can not be genuine.

Here Konzelmann and many others follow the Marxist concept that there is nothing spiritual in religion, that it is just a reaction to material deprivation. And as soon as communism/socialism will do away with material deprivation (and that will be very soon!), religion will just wither away since there will be no need for it. In the same way, if Christianity is seen as nothing but an aspect of colonialism, then there will be no need (and no use) for it any more as soon as colonialism withers away. But while colonialism did wither away, in most countries barely putting up a fight, Christianity did not wither away as promised, indeed, after independence Christian growth rates increased considerably, while the predicted growth of Islam did not take place at all. Today Africa is a predominantly Christian continent, and Africa south of the Sahara even more so.

At a time when colonialism was declining, but socialism/communism was not yet obviously following the same course,[3] Walter Rodney put similar arguments to better use. In his book *How Europe Underdeveloped Africa*,[4] which during my days as a student at Daressalam University sold like hot cakes there,[5] he does take note of some the differences between the missionaries and the colonial powers. But they all grabbed alike "their" sections of Africa: Karl Peters

---

inevitable rise of Islam to become the religion of Africa, he quotes a French missionary who in the 1920s (!) described the spread of Islam in the early years of this century, when Islam *did* spread in East Africa.

[3] "A glance at the remarkable advance of Socialism over the last fifty-odd years will show that the apologists for capitalism are spokesmen of a social system that is rapidly expiring" (Walter Rodney, *How Europe Underdeveloped Africa*, London/Daressalam, 1972, p. 18).

[4] London/Daressalam, 1972.

[5] That was before socialism had fully mined the economy, so that people could still buy books.

(Mkono wa Damu), Livingstone, Stanley, Harry Johnston, de Brazza, General Gordon.[6]

> The Christian missionaries were as much part of the colonizing forces as were the explorers, traders and soldiers. There may be room for arguing whether in a given colony the missionaries brought the other colonialist forces or vice versa, but there is no doubting the fact that missionaries were agents of colonialism in the practical sense whether or not they saw themselves in that light. The imperialist adventurer, Sir Henry Johnston disliked missionaries, but he conceded that 'each mission station is an exercise in colonisation'.[7]

In Rodney's concept of African realities, the missionaries, by being more human by degrees (and therefore even fighting some gross abuses of colonialism), had the important task of keeping the engine of colonialism from overheating and thereby destroying itself. But their very difference made them part of the system: Oil is very different from an engine, but oil and engine belong to the same system. Try to drive a car without oil, or try to drive oil without an engine, and you will see that they need each other to achieve anything at all in the way of transport.

> The church's role was primarily to preserve the social relations of colonialism, as an extension of the role it played in preserving the social relations of capitalism in Europe. Therefore the Christian church stressed humility, docility and acceptance ... churches could be relied upon to preach turning the other cheek in the face of exploitation, and they drove home the message that everything would be right in the next world.[8]

Rodney concedes that in serving colonialism the church performed a few progressive tasks, like the fight against the killing of twins,[9] and he is also willing to accept that not all missionaries *saw* themselves as the

---

[6] Rodney, *How Europe Underdeveloped Africa*, pp. 154f.

[7] *Ibid.*, p. 277.

[8] *Ibid.*, p. 278.

[9] *Ibid.*

agents of colonialism that they were. But these small differences do not account in any way for the survival of Christianity after the fall of colonialism. For this a new interpretation is necessary. Yes, the missions were part and parcel of colonialism, and that they have not died with colonialism is due to the fact that in the 1960s colonialism did not really die, but just transformed itself from (political) colonialism to (economic) neocolonialism. And the engine of neocolonialism needs spiritual lubrication as much as the exploitative machine of colonialism had needed it before. This is clearly shown by the fact that the educated elites of the Livingstonia type ("black Scotsmen")[10] were not really the leaders into independence but the nucleus of the capitalist elites that would become the bridgeheads of the metropolises in the periphery, thus perpetuating the colonial exploitation with more sophisticated (neocolonial) methods.[11]

To round off the picture, a few glimpses from Cameroon (or, to be more precise, from a German's interpretation of events that happened in Cameroon). These glimpses refer to the missionary work of the church into which I was born and of which I am still a pastor, the German Baptist Convention and its missionary efforts in Cameroon.[12] The Baptists were there before any colonialist took any sustained note of the area. Günther, the author of a "non-imperialist mission history"[13] states that "the Baptist missionary movement for Cameroon (the missionaries and the mission society) integrated itself without resistance into the colonial state", and humbly offered its services to educate the Africans to become "obedient subjects" and "useful

---

[10] *Ibid.*, p. 272.

[11] In this concept of history it is assumed that the capitalist world, centred in the "metropolises" of Europe and America, relies on local elites in the exploited countries for continuing the colonial exploitation in a more indirect and more efficient (neocolonial) way.

[12] Jurgen Günther, *Mission im kolonialen Kontext. Beitriige zur Geschichte der Mission der dew-schen Baptisten in Kamerun 1891 - 1914,* Initiative Schalom, 1991, 148 pp. [MA Hamburg 19851.

[13] *Ibid., p. 3.*

workers".[14] He accuses the German missionaries especially of teaching German in their schools, the language of colonialism. In order to keep his concepts clear, he sometimes bends the facts. A vivid example is this: After describing the "progressive" ideas of Eduard Scheve, the founder of the German Baptist Mission in Cameroon, he concludes:

> This programme, sounding similar to present missionary concepts, can not have been meant to be serious, because right from the beginning Scheve and others shared the ideological concept of the superiority of Europeans over Africans.[15]

Some Facts that Need Interpretation

I love wild statements and beautiful assumptions because they make such fascinating reading. But I think I have presented a sufficient florilegium of these. We know by now that missionaries really were the soulmates of the colonialists. Some missionaries were happy to be just that, and those who refused to be soulmates were soulmates nevertheless.

As a missionary or ex-missionary I may be forgiven for not accepting every statement about the likes of us which I find in scholarly books, and as a historian I can not just answer wild statements from the other side by shouting equally wild statements from "our" side. Is it not true that the missionaries put an end to the slave trade? Did Livingstone not discover Africa? And did the missionaries not bring civilization, progress, good agriculture and real faith into the darkness of heathen Africa? And did not the missionaries fight for Africa's independence?[16] People like these can not have been soulmates of colonialism!

---

[14] *Ibid.*, p. 83.

[15] *Ibid.*, p. 49. Günther *assumes* what concepts Scheve shared. It is a fact that several Cameroonians lived for years with the Scheve family to get their education in Berlin. But maybe the Scheve family did not mean that seriously either.

[16] Catholic missionaries for example, paid the only fine Julius Nyerere was ever convicted to pay in his struggle for the independence of Tanzania.

Leaving aside slogans, accusations and glorifications, there are three basic facts about the relationship between colonialism and missions which can not be disputed, but which nevertheless need interpretation.

Missions are older than colonialism

Christianity was ever a missionary religion. The oldest church in Africa, Alexandria, is just 30 years younger than Christianity,[17] and Christian missionaries had reached Ethiopia in the 4th century, the Visigoths, remote ancestors of my own tribe,[18] in the same century and China in the 7th.[19]

For those African areas which European Christian missionaries reached via the ocean, some "complicity" between missionaries and colonialists can be assumed because they used the same transport, but even in more recent missionary history, they did reach a number of areas before any colonialist cast a coveting eye on them. Take for example Mary[20] and Robert Moffat, working for five decades among the Southern Tswana in Kuruman. Two notable examples on a larger scale are the kingdoms of Imerina (Madagascar) and Buganda (Uganda) which both became Christian kingdoms before colonial rule after going through a period in which the church was severely

---

[17] This was the first congregation of what is now the Coptic Church of Egypt, and African theologians decisively influenced the course of Christian history.

[18] Ulfilas, son of a Greek mother (a captive of war) and a Gothic father, translated the Bible into the first of the many Gennanic languages. A beautiful copy of the Bible he translated was kept for centuries in the monastery of Werden, Ruhr, 25 km south west of Waime-Eickel, where I was born. During the 30 Years War the Swedes stole it, now it is kept in Uppsala. Maybe it was good that they stole it, they may have looked after it better than the Germans might have done.

[19] We only know the Chinese name of the first missionary: A-lo-pen. He came overland from the Church of the East ("Nestorians").

[20] For her life see: Mora Dickson, *Beloved Partner: Mary Moffat of Kuruman*, Gaborone/Kuruman: Botswana Book Centre/Kuruman Moffat Mission Trust (POB 34 Kuruman, South Africa), 1989 [1974; 1976].

persecuted and which then ended in a "Christian revolution"[21] Malawi offers further examples: One can rightly accuse the early missionaries at Magomero (1861),[22] Cape MacLear (1875) and Blantyre (1876) of meddling in politics, but only imagination can make them colonialists.

During the colonial period the relationship between the missions and the colonial government was characterized by cooperation and conflict

Here again Malawi offers many examples. When the European powers had decided to start the scramble for Africa at the Berlin Conference in 1884/5, the Blantyre missionaries accepted the fact and tried their best to make sure that Britain would get Southern Malawi, not Portugal, to whom Britain had already "ceded" the territory.[23] On the other hand Scott, being among other things the editor of the first newspaper in this area, felt free to criticize whatever he (and the mission) held to be incompatible with Christian principles and good governance in the running of the Protectorate by the British.[24] There were many missionaries who behaved in the same way.

After the end of colonialism, neither mission nor church died

In spite of all ideological expectations and pious [socialist] predictions, the church had come to stay in Africa. After independence its growth

---

[21] Madagascar: John Baur, *2000 Years of Christianity in Africa,* Nairobi: Paulines, 1994, pp. 497499; Buganda: John V. Taylor, *The Growth of the Church in Buganda. An Attempt at Understanding,* London: SCM, 1958, pp. 19-60.

[22] There the UMCA missionaries under Bishop Mackenzie, engaged in aggressive warfare in order to help the oppressed Mang'anja against the Yao, who were assumed to be oppressing them. Jonathan Q. Newell, "Not War but Defence of the Oppressed"? Bishop Mackenzie's Skirmishes with the Yao in 1861", see chapter 9 in this hook.

[23] Andrew C. Ross, *Blantyre Mission and the Making of Modern Malawi,* Blantyre: CLAIM, 1996, pp. 75, 87, 95.

[24] See Kenneth R. Ross, "Vernacular Translation in Christian Mission: The Case of David Clement Scott and the Blantyre Mission 1888-1898", in K.R. Ross, *Gospel Ferment in Malawi,* Gweru: Mambo, 1995, pp. 107-125 [120].

accelerated considerably.[25] In the 1950s, Africa was 20% Christian, in 1965 about 32%, in 1970 about 36%, and today about 48%.[26]

Not only the church is still with us in Africa, even the missions are still around and thriving. Whereas in the period immediately following independence sometimes the cry was heard: "Missionary go home!", today many church leaders do not face the problem of how to get rid of the missionaries, but of how to get enough of them.

After independence the missionaries of the "classical missions" did change their position in the church, many of them becoming "fraternal workers" and keeping a lower profile. But at the same time, when the classical missions were retrenching their forces, many new missions came into various countries of Africa and were very much welcomed (not necessarily by the leaders and missionaries of the main line denominations, but definitely by the people).[27]

Conflicts of Soulmates or Cooperation of Antagonists?

This, I hope, makes it clear that missionaries and colonialists can not have been soulmates, at least not in the long run. But maybe in the short run, during the colonial episode in African history? Some more scrutiny is needed here before a verdict can be reached.

Missionary opponents of colonialism

Here Malawi is somewhat unusual since it can be proud of two missionaries who not only criticized abuses of colonialism, but who

---

[25] Figures are based on the data in David Barrett, *World Christian Encyclopedia: A Comparative Survey of Churches and Religions in the Modern World AD 1900-2000,* Nairobi/Oxford/New York, 1982.

[26] During the same period the Muslim percentage rose from about 37 to 41%.

[27] A typical example for such a mission was the Southern Baptist Missionary Board, from which the Baptist Convention of Malawi originates. Hany Longwe, MA student with the University of Malawi, is writing his thesis on its history.

totally opposed colonialism on principle, Joseph Booth[28] and John Chilembwe.[29] Joseph Booth published in 1897 a book with the title "Africa for the African".[30] In this book he calls the scramble for Africa

> a second magnificently unscrupulous proposal [after the slave trade] of the European to harness and exploit his African neighbor. The former clumsy proposal to annex and transplant the African's person was costly, cumbersome and infamous; the present proposal to purloin the land under his feet and adroitly to utilize the African as an instrument to disclose, develop and deposit its resources for the European's benefit, is the self-same in spirit, but more ingeniously dressed, further reaching in its effects, and far less likely to be challenged. It is a proposal to deprive 200 million of people of their birthright; to seize upon their property and permanently drain the wealth of Africa and the African's labor into European charnels.[31]

This concept Joseph Booth translated into political action when in 1899 he demanded, in the (in-)famous petition to Queen Victoria (Defender of the Christian Faith), that Malawi, after a period of "not exceeding 21 years" be restored "with its entire revenues to Native ownership and Government".[32]

---

[28] Harry Langworthy, *"Africa for the African". The Life of Joseph Booth*, Blantyre: CLAIM, 1996; Klaus Fiedler, "Joseph Booth and the Writing of Malawian History: An Attempt at Interpretation", *Religion in Malawi*, No. 7, 1997, pp. 30-38.

[29] The best source for John Chilembwe is still George Shepperson and Thomas Price, *Independent African: John Chilembwe and the Origins, Setting and Significance of the Nyasaland Native Rising of 1915*, Edinburgh: The University Press, 1958. The 1987 paperback edition is still available.

[30] Baltimore 1897, two editions. Republished in a scholarly edition by Laura Peri)' as: Joseph Booth, *Africa for the African*, Blantyre: CLAIM, 1998.

[31] Joseph Booth, *Africa for the African*, Baltimore, 2nd ed., 1897, p. 4.

[32] The petition was published, with adverse comment, by the Central African Times. After its publication Booth fled the territory, only to be allowed back after pledging in future to abstain from politics. For the text see: Kenneth R.

The other radical missionary opponent of colonialism in Malawi was John Chilembwe, a missionary of the American National Baptist Convention, Inc. In 1900 he started missionary work in Mbornbwe, more commonly known today as Providence Industrial Mission.[33] In 1915 he led the famous Chilembwe Rising.

Booth and Chilembwe (the first to have been baptized by Booth) shared their fundamental opposition to colonialism. They differed, though, in the means to be employed. Booth was a pacifist, so he would have rejected the idea of an armed uprising, had he known anything about it,[34] whereas Chilembwe saw the judicious use of arms as compatible with his Christian faith.

Both Booth and Chilembwe do not yield much in answering the question if missionaries and colonialists were soulmates or antagonists. Yes, they were antagonists, but they were exceptional in missionary circles of their days.

Missionaries and settlers

There is a Kikuyu proverb: "Guthiri mubey na muthungu" (There is no difference between a missionary and a settler).[35] I assume that this proverb, as so many others, expresses some truth, though not necessarily *the* truth. Was there a difference in Malawi? Settlers and missionaries often belonged to the same churches, visited each other,

---

Ross (ed.), *Christianity in Malawi: A Source Book,* Gweru: Mambo, 1996, pp. 192f.

[33] The official name of the church is African Baptist Assembly, before Kamuzu demanded a change it was National Baptist Assembly of Africa, Nyasaland, Inc. See Patrick Makondesa, "The Life and Ministry of Rev and Mrs Muocha of Providence Industrial Mission", BEd., University of Malawi, 1996, p. 1.

[34] Booth and his wife were deported from Basutoland and South Africa to England for complicity in a revolt they did not even know had happened. When Booth heard about it much later, he disapproved (Langworthy, *The Life of Joseph Booth,* p. 481).

[35] Quoted in: F.B. Welboum, *East African Rebels: A Study of some Independent Churches,* London, 1961, p. 111.

had tea together, and both were landowners and employers. Nevertheless a difference is very vividly described by Lewis Mataka Bandawe in his autobiography.

> Every European, with the exception of the missionaries and the Mandala people, had a *chikoti* - a whip made of hippo's hide - which he used on his domestic servants or labourers. The planters used the *chikoti* constantly on their labourers; it was used for any minor offence.[36]

The *machila* carriers had a song which ran like this:

> Leader: "Chikoti chiwawa." Chorus: "Chiwawanji" General chorus: "Chiwawanji, chiwawanji, chiwawa-a-a."

Missionaries were also sometimes carried in a *machila,* but would the carriers sing that song for them?

There are other observations along similar lines: The Catholic missionaries in Malawi strongly opposed the taxation system which forced the "natives" to "work" for the settlers (as if they would not work on their own land) and they tried to provide alternative employment. Nkhoma Mission had a similar attitude,[37] whereas Livingstonia tried as hard as it could to supply the settlers with skilled labour.[38]

"How good that we did not get implicated in the Chilembwe Rising"

When the Commission of Inquiry sat after the rising, Dr Alexander Hetherwick was summoned to give evidence and was given a hostile

---

[36] Lewis Mataka Bandawe, *Memoirs of a Malawian,* Blantyre: CLAIM, 1971, p. 71.

[37] Martin Pauw, *Mission and Church in Malawi: The History of the 1Vkhoma Synod of the Church of Central Africa, Presbyterian 1889-1962,* Lusaka, 1980, p. 190.

[38] Even here the question must be rightly asked if this was collaboration, subservience to the needs of colonialism, or if the mission pursued its own aims, namely giving the people as qualified an education as possible.

reception in questioning. He pointed out bad European behaviour in not replying to greetings by people of "lower rank".

> I have seen many Europeans absolutely ignore a boy's salutation. The smallest drummer boy in the British army if he salutes Lord Kitchener receives a salute in return. There will be no difficulty if the European makes acknowledgment: it indicates that two gentlemen have met and not only one.[39]

Here, as elsewhere, the missionaries achieved improvements in colonial behaviour, but they did not challenge the colonial system as such.

Occasionally missionaries would also put the colonial system to their own use. When Joseph Booth (then in Cape Town) had sent Elliot Katnwana as a Watchtower missionary to Malawi and when he had become successful, baptizing nearly 10,000 people, they forgot all about religious freedom and asked the *boma* to do something about it, and the *bona* was happy to oblige.[40] So he was banned,[41] not as a religious competitor, but as politically subversive. But I guess the Livingstonia missionaries felt this to be a happy coincidence.

In the Commission of Inquiry after the Chilembwe Rising, the missionaries were not only keen to represent African interests, they were also keen to prove that they had no responsibility for it. They managed to do this, but the fact remains that about 70 men found guilty of participating in the uprising, were "products" of the Presbyterian missions' educational system, including the second in

---

[39] Malawi National Archives COM-6 2/1/1. For more on the context see Kenneth R. Ross, *Here Comes Your King! Christ Church and Nation in Malawi*, Blantyre: CLAIM, 1998, pp.79-84.

[40] See: J.C. Chalcanza, "From Preacher to Prophet: Elliot Kenan Kamwana and the Watch Tower Movement in Malawi, 1908-1956", in *Voices of Preachers in Protest*, Blantyre: CLAIM, 1998.

[41] In present day oral history of both Bamulonda and Jehovah's Witnesses, there are interesting and widely varying interpretations attached to this event.

command Gray Kufa.[42] And the fact also remains that no "products" of the Catholic system of education were involved.[43]

Both the Presbyterians and the Catholics cooperated obviously with the colonial system. The Presbyterians, in spite of their abhorrence of armed resistance against colonial rule seem to have produced, in their educational system, people who thought otherwise.

Education or education for work?

What else is education for but for working? We all have to earn our living, and, that is the idea, education is to help us with that. But when (German) colonial rule came to what is now Tanzania, the above quote was at the centre of a major controversy. The colonialists were convinced that Africans were lazy (by nature and by predilection), but they needed them desperately as workers in their houses and on their farms. Most German colonialists did not think highly of missionaries, but felt that they should be useful fools: Not just to preach to the natives, but "to teach them to work". But then, what need would there be for the missions' schools? They were useless, only making the natives proud. The missionaries protested. They protested against the notion that Africans were lazy: "They are not lazy, they are industrious and work hard, but they want to work on their own land." And being convinced that this was exactly the place where Africans should work, they strongly opposed migrant labour.

The German missionaries in Tanzania in those days did not question the right of Germany to rule the country.[44] But by providing education,

---

[42] Shepperson and Price, *Independent African*, pp. 363-80.

[43] The Catholics at that time were happy to build the church in the context of village life and not to challenge the colonial authorities. See Ian Linden, *Catholics, Peasants and Chewa Resistance in Nyasaland 1889-1939,* London: Heinemann, 1974. On the Montfort missionaries and the Chilembwe Rising see: Hubert Reijnaerts, Ann Nielsen, Matthew Schoffeleers, *Montfortians in Malawi. Their Spirituality and Pastoral Approach,* Blantyre: CLAIM, 1997, pp. 138-145.

limited though it was, they gave the people a tool with which to assert their own identity.

A hotly debated issue among German missionaries of the 1930s was the teaching of English. Many, actually the majority of the Lutheran and Moravian missionaries, were convinced that African education ideally should be in the tribal language, and with the number of speakers being limited, Swahili would be considered. The most important reason given was that Africans should not be culturally alienated. But Africans were very keen to learn the language which would open the world for them (and which, incidentally, was the language of their colonial oppressors - or at least that's what we read in many books today). A considerable minority of the Lutheran and Moravian missionaries accepted that point and demanded that English be taught in their central schools, and they all -finally won.[45]

But how can this be judged? Where the missionaries insisted on the only use of "native" languages, they are being accused of holding the people back. Where they emphasized the use of English, the missionaries are accused of cultural imperialism and of making "Black Scotsmen". It must have been very difficult to do the right thing! I take it that the demand for learning a "colonial" language was then and is now a genuine expression of African culture, since it opens the door to the wider world'.[46]

---

[44] One missionary, the Moravian Traugott Bachmann, who was very critical of colonial abuses while in Tanzania (until 1916), *later came* to the conviction that even good colonialism was fundamentally wrong (Traugott Bachmann, *kh gab manchen Anstoss,* Konstanz: CVA, 21964, pp. 1180. So far as I know, this is the only Moravian or Lutheran missionary in Tanzania before 1940, who had such ideas.

[45] Dealt with in detail in Klaus Fiedler, *Christianity and African Culture: Conservative German Protestant Missionaries in Tanzania, 1900-1940,* Leiden/New York/Koln: Brill. 1996, pp. 125-128, 143-148.

[46] African culture should not be defined as that which has historic roots in Africa but as that which *is relevant* for Africans. If the *historic* definition would be applied to the West, European culture would not contain reading or writing, not even the zero (and imagine today's computers without it!).

If one accuses the missionaries of being unwittingly allies of colonialism, here is a chance to accuse them of being unwitting anticolonialists, because it was to a large extent education (much of it indeed missionary education) that fuelled the movement for independence, and there was nothing strange in a leader in the struggle for independence either quoting (Banda) or translating (Nyerere) Shakespeare.

"They simply destroyed African culture"

Another accusation against "the missionaries" is that they were as destructive against African culture as the colonialists, or even more so.[47] Then they would not be just soulmates, but supersoulmates, even attacking the beautiful social institution of polygamy. There is no doubt that missionaries vehemently opposed some customs which they felt to be blatantly opposed to the gospel, one of the most prominent of these in early Malawi being the *mwavi* poison ordeal to identify witches.[48] On the other hand it must also be observed that missionaries in general worked hard to learn the language of their hosts, and that some did exceedingly well.[49]

---

[47] For the sake of historical correctness it must not be overlooked that even colonialism was not always destructive to African culture, as the concept of "Indirect Rule" can show. Sometimes colonialism seems to have even stabilized aspects of African culture that were already losing its grip on the people, like the Ngoni dominance in Central and Northern Malawi. Without the British support (to quite some extent negotiated by the Livingstonia missionaries) the Chewa might have long conquered the Ngoni chieftainships completely "by their women", a cultural process that has already gone far.

[48] In spite of their vehement opposition, witchhunts survived into more recent times, though forms seem to have changed somewhat.

[49] David Clement Scott's dictionary of the Njanya language has not yet been surpassed, in spite of Chewa having been the national language of Malawi for many years under the supervision of the Chewa Board; D.C. Scott, *A Cyclopaedic Dictionary of the Mang'anja Language Spoken in British Central Africa,* Edinburgh: Church of Scotland, 1892.

Much has been made of the missionaries' opposition to polygamy, perhaps too much since they all in different ways found some means of accommodation,[50] but it should also be emphasized that all of them strongly supported the family, which to me seems to be at the very heart of African culture (or any culture for that matter). They tried to hinder the breaking up of families through colonial interests like migrant labour. Does this already make them antagonists of the colonial system? I do not think so, but does it make them soulmates? I do not think so, either.

"He knew our language better then we did"

The British Church Missionary Society had started work among the Chagga on the slopes of Mt Kilimanjaro. When the Germans came in to rule and some Chagga resisted, the Germans accused the CMS of being on the wrong side. They withdrew under protest, and later handed over the nascent missionary work to the German Lutheran Leipzig Mission. That should qualify for missionary/colonialist collusion, shouldn't it? One of the early Leipzig missionaries was Bruno Gutmann.[51] That soon after his arrival he took a German settler to court for mistreating two Chagga, was a minor thing.[52] The above quote, not polite but realistic, reveals that he was deeply engaged with Chagga culture.[53] He was convinced that the Chagga social order, though not perfect, was much closer to the divine will than European

---

[50] Analyzed for Lutherans and Moravians in: Fiedler, *Christianity and African Culture*, pp. 56-63, 67f, 136, 183.

[51] He worked in Tanzania from 1902 till 1938, from 1910 in Old Moshi (Kidia). He was a great writer and became one of the leading German Protestant missiologists of the period between the two wars.

[52] "Bericht fiber den Prozell Mikaeli/Sauerbrunn vor dem Eingeborenengerichte Moschi und meine Beteiligung an ihm" (Moshi 12.2.1911). Gutmann failed to achieve justice.

[53] Reflected in his three volume study: *Die Stammeslehren der Dschagga* [The Tribal Teachings of the Chagga], Mittichen, 1932-1936 [most of the teachings were entrusted to him by Mlasany Njau, who wanted Gutmann to preserve them after his death] and in his: *Das Recht der Dschagga*, Munchen, 1926.

culture.⁵⁴ His attitude showed in close cooperation with the chief of Moshi (not a Christian), in his organization of his congregation along the lines of traditional neighbourhoods, in his (largely unwanted) endeavours to strengthen the clan structure, or in his (very successful) use of the traditional shield comradeships to inculturate Christian confirmation.⁵⁵

"They destroyed all of the African customs and culture", missionaries were and are being accused. If that is true - usually not much proof is attached to the accusation - definitely neither Bruno Gutmann nor his Leipzig collegues fit into that pattern. Take the example of circumcision, male and female. Gutmann did not go as far as Bishop Vincent Lucas of Tunduru (UMCA), who actually Christianized the rites,⁵⁶ but he never opposed the custom.⁵⁷

Among the Chagga it was not the missionaries who tried to abolish circumcision, but in 1924 the Chagga Lutheran church leaders (duly elected and not representing those who elected them).⁵⁸ Gutmann was away in Germany then,⁵⁹ and when he came back there was the seemingly strange spectre of a missionary defending clitoridectomy and male circumcision against the African leadership of the church. But was the spectre really so strange? Gutmann just defended the

---

⁵⁴ In his only English article he called European civilization "a blatant blasphemy" ("The African Standpoint", *Journal of the International Institute of African Languages and Cultures,* Vol. VIII/1, (January 1935), pp. 1-17).

⁵⁵ For an overview in English see: Ernst Jaeschke, *Bruno Gutmann: His Life, His Thoughts, and His Work. An Early Attempt at a Theology in an African Context,* Arusha: Malcumira Publications, 1985.

⁵⁶ Robin Lambum, "The Yao of Tunduru", in Noel Q. King and Klaus Fiedler (eds.), *Robin Lam burn - From a Missionary's Notebook: The Yao of Tunduru and Other Essays,* Saarbriicken/Fort Lauderdale: Breitenbach, 1991.

⁵⁷ As a Lutheran, he considered circumcision *as an adiaphoron,* something in between, being neither good nor bad in itself.

⁵⁸ Fiedler, *Christianity and African Culture,* pp. 75-84.

⁵⁹ The Versailles Treaty banned all German citizens from Tanzania from 1920 until 1925.

people's right to make their own cultural decisions.⁶⁰ A very democratic notion, which to further he even employed paternalistic methods. (Was he not a child of his times?) Whose soulmate was Gutmann? Of colonialism? Hardly so. Of European civilization? He would have been horrified! If he was anyone's soulmate, he was the Chagga's.⁶¹

A question of methodology

In spite of some sarcasm, what I have tried to do here is to write history. And the results of the writing of history depend to quite some extent on the methodology employed and on the premises assumed. Much of what I have discussed reflects two different, though not necessarily opposing methods of writing history: The methods of generalization and the method of differentiation. Both have their merits and demerits. Walter Rodney, though he is aware of many details,⁶² chose the generalizing approach, which is so common in Marxist conceptions of history. History follows certain immutable laws, and every detail of history can be related to these laws of historical development (and if that is difficult, it is always possible to bend a few interpretations or facts). In the generalizing method, aberrations from the proper picture are not overlooked, but they- can not change the overall assessment.

Much of the assessment in the generalizing method may be based on parallelism. In Germany over the last decade the population of storks declined by 50%, and so did the human birth rate. Both are facts, but which is to blame for which? Therefore it can be argued that much

---

[60] Clitoridectomy *is* bad, a fact that started to be recognized by Chagga Lutheran women in or close to 1972 (Communication Rev. Daniel Lyatoo, 1972). When I visited ICidia first in 1971, there was no visible opposition yet.

[61] The story goes that one day in Mombasa a thief stole a piece of his luggage. But as he shouted the word "thief" in Chagga and not in Swahili, nobody came to his help.

[62] In this he differs strongly from Konzelmann.

similarity between colonialism and the missionary enterprise is coextension, not the sign of any intrinsic relationship.

The generalizing method has its value for the study of large areas, periods or cultural movements. But I must admit that I prefer the method of differentiation. Yes, colonialists and missionaries had much in common, sometimes too much. But then this is to be expected. After all they were contemporaries, came from the same geographical region and directed their efforts to the same people. I therefore argue that their similarities are not that important, but that their differences should interest the historian foremost.

If I apply the method of generalization to my topic, the missionaries easily turn into soulmates of colonialism. And using different assumptions, the same method of generalization could be employed to make the same missionaries to be all antagonists of the colonial system.

Myths so easy, yet they must die ...

Whatever method one uses in writing history, assessments should be solidly based on facts, and therefore myths must die, beautiful (and useful) though they may be.[63] One such myth is that "the missionaries [can anyone be more precise, please)] were part and parcel of colonialism and implacably hostile to African life and culture". Such a myth is useful: if the past is so depraved, then the present can only be brighter, and since the missionaries got it all wrong, we are much better now! But nice as this myth may be, the facts do not match it. It is high time that the scholarly community put to rest such notions as that the missionaries were all alike and uniformly supported colonialism.

The missionaries were children of their times ...

Questions which offer two options for an answer are tricky, they tend to create the illusion that one of the two options might be the right

---

[63] I just heard a new one: The missionaries are to be blamed for the AIDS crisis in Malawi (10-20% of the population are HIV +). Why? "Because they never understood African sexuality."

answer. Such a tricky question was put to me for this essay: Soulmates or antagonists? Neither nor! For soulmates the missionaries were too often the colonialists' best nuisance, for antagonists, the missionaries were too cooperative.

When I had just begun my studies at Makerere University, my professor, Noel Q. King, a man as wise as his beard was long, told me: "Klaus, never forget, the missionaries were children of their times, just as much as we are of ours." This is part of the answer I want to give: The missionaries were children of their times. They shared many of the assumptions of the colonialists. Though they were often wiser, that was by degrees. Though they had no *chikoti* ready for instant use, they were not necessarily free of *all* feelings of racial superiority. Yes, they were children of their times. This can help us to understand them, and also to understand a few things which today we either do not approve or do not understand.

But to call the missionaries "children of their time" would be too simple. They were children of their time, but they had an agenda of their own. That agenda was older than colonialism, had strong otherworldly roots, made them willing to face hardship and to risk (and sometimes lose) their lives. This agenda was the agenda of the kingdom of Christ, a kingdom not of this world, but with quite some effects on it. This agenda often allowed for cooperation, often it demanded some kind of resistance. The interpretations of this agenda varied among missionaries, and the application of this interpretation to the historical situation varied, too. But another agenda there was.

... as we are of ours

If we admit that missionaries were children of their time, we also have to admit that we are children of our time. No history can be written without the writer interpreting the facts, and interpreting them as a child of his time. Admitted. But if the "child of his time" shows too clearly through the pages of the historian's interpretation, then I become suspicious, and I start to read the book not as a book about the subject indicated on the cover, but as a book about the author.

The Faith and Knowledge Seminars 1990-1997[1]

1. Moira Chimombo, "Christ - The Perfect Humanistic Language Teacher"
2. Patrick O'Malley, "The Bible as Literature, Poetry and Prayer"
3. Kenneth R. Ross, "Faith in Jesus and Historical Criticism"
4. Patrick A. Whittle, "The Physical Concept of Energy in Relation to Christian Belief and Experience"
5. Alistair K. Ager, "Psychology and the Troubled Soul"
6. Kings M. Phiri, "A Christian Appraisal of some 'Dark' Events in the History of Black People"
7. Rodney S. Hunter, "Classics and the Bible in Human Life"
8. John M. Dubbey, "Creativity in Mathematics"
9. John M. Dubbey, "A New Approach to Religious Education"
10. Kenneth R. Ross, "Scientific Revolutions: A Model for Christian Conversion in the Modern World?"
11. Richard C. Day, "The Family in Crisis"
12. Patrick A. Whittle, "The Physical Concept of Time and the Christian Concept of Eternity"
13. Alistair K. Ager and Stewart Carr, "How to Convert People: A Psychological Guide"
14. Msaiwale Chigawa, "The Theological Genesis of Human Rights"
15. Jonathan Q. Newell, "There were Arguments in Favour of Our Taking Up Arms': Bishop Mackenzie and the War Against the Yao in 1861"
16. John Rajbansee, "Liberation Theology and Third World Development: Some Alternative Perspectives"
17. Alistair K. Ager, "On Culture, Social Constructionism and Common Humanity"
18. Kenneth R. Ross, "You Did Not Dance: Christianity and Recreation in the African Context"
19. William H. King, "Faith and Knowledge in Physical Science"
20. Garton S. Kamchedzera, "Christianity, Law and Development"
21. John J. Moore, "The New Commandment and the Selfish Gene"

---

[1] All the papers are available for consultation at the Department of Theology and Religious Studies, Chancellor College, University of Malawi.

22. Klaus Fiedler, "Christianity and the Fall of Communism in Eastern Europe"
23. David H. Mundy, "Logic and Absurdity: The Use of Computers in the University of Malawi"
24. James Lawrie, "Ethical Problems in Modern Medicine"
25. Kenneth R. Ross, "Presbyterian Theology and Participatory Democracy"
26. Rodney S. Hunter, "The Case for Religious Establishment"
27. Stephen Carr, "Stewardship of the Environment and the Pressures of the Modern World: is there a Christian response?"
28. Isabel A. Phiri, "Christianity and Women: Liberation or Oppression?"
29. Rendell Day, "A Case for the Separation of Church and State"
30. Kings M. Phiri, "Reconciliation and Violence in a Pre-colonial Society: the Case of the Maravi"
31. Kenneth R. Ross, "Social Liberation in Malawi: a Theological Interpretation"
32. John J. Moore, "Ecology: a Christian Approach"
33. Kenneth R. Ross, "Christian Faith and National Identity: the Malawi Experience"
34. Klaus Fiedler, "Christian Missions and Western Colonialism: Soulmates or Antagonists?"
35. Lewis B. Dzimbiri, "Social and Natural Science Rationality and the Bible: a Disturbing Dilemma for a Born-Again in the Making"
36. Isabel A. Phiri, "Ecofeminism: a Malawi Case Study"
37. Moira Chimombo, "Back to the Future: Recovering Traditional Values to Tackle the AIDS Epidemic through Education"
38. Odreck J. Kathamalo, "Knowledge of and Sympathy for Others"
39. J.C. Chakanza, "The Mchape Affair at Liwonde: a Reappraisal"
40. Emmanuel N. Dzama, "Missionaries, Colonial Administrators, Contemporary Science Education and the Concept of the African World View"
41. Kenneth R. Ross, "Where were the Prophets and Martyrs in Banda's Malawi? Four Presbyterian Ministers"
42. Odreck J. Kathamulo, "Does Male Dominance Rest on Age-Old Prejudice?"
43. Klaus Fiedler, "National Sovereignty: An Outdated Concept?"
44. Francis Moto, "Religion in Malawian Literature"
45. Emmanuel N. Dzama, "Free Primary Education: Do we have a Dream for it?"

46. Kenneth R. Ross, "Does Malawi (still) Need a Truth Commission?"

47. Hermes F. Chidammodzi, "Feminism as Critical Theory in African Societies: the Malawian Experience"

48. C. Ellerton Chimbwete, "The Role of the Church in Demographic Data Collection"

49. Klaus Fiedler, "In the Beginning God Created them equal: Gender Equality in Genesis 1 and 2"

50. Andrew C. Ross, "19th Century Race Theory: its Impact on the Church in Africa"

51. Patrick A. Kalilombe, "My Life, my Faith and my Country" (Interview)

52. Klaus Fiedler, "Joseph Booth in Melbourne: A Search for Roots"

53. Watson Msosa, "From Aten to Mphambe: Images of the Divine in Ecological Anthropology"

54. Fulata L. Moyo, "Until Zabweka and the Chirunga Intelligentia Learn that 'Prevention is more Possible than Cure', AIDS is going to Wipe us out: A Theological Perspective"

55. James Tengatenga, "Singing, Dancing and Believing: Civic Education in Malawi Idiom"

56. Hester F. Ross, "Pass the buck, blame the rat: Guilt and Responsibility in some Recent Malawian Literature"

57. Garton S. Kamchedzera, "The Rights of the Child in the Christian Context"

Notes on Contributors

Stephen Carr was raised on a cattle ranch in South America and studied agriculture at London University. Coming to Africa in 1952 he spent twenty years in villages in Southern Sudan and Uganda learning from and working with local farmers. He subsequently held senior government positions in the Sudan and Tanzania and worked for eleven years with the World Bank in which he was principal agriculturalist in the Africa Department. Now living in TA Mlumbi's area near Zomba he does consultancy work for the World Bank, IFAD and the Rockefeller Foundation. He is a lay reader in the Anglican Church.

John M. Dubbey was Vice Chancellor of the University of Malawi from January 1987 - 1991. He was previously Education Officer in the Royal Air Force, 19551957, Lecturer and Head of Mathematics Division at Thames Polytechnic, London, 1957-1972, Head of Mathematics Department, Dean of Engineering and Assistant Director of South Bank Polytechnic, London, 1972-1986, Consultant Assistant Director, North London Polytechnic, 1985-1986, and Visiting Lecturer in History and Philosophy of Science, University College London, 1965-1970. He is the author of *Development of Modern Mathematics* (London, 1970) and *The Mathematical Work of Charles Baggage* (Cambridge, 1978). From 1991-1994 he was Principal of Botswana Polytechnic.

Klaus Fiedler is Associate Professor in the Department of Theology and Religious Studies of the University of Malawi, teaching missiology and church history. He studied at Hamburg Baptist Seminary and Makerere University, Kampala and received his PhD from Dar es Salaam University. From 1969-1976 he worked as a missionary in Southern Tanzania (Ruvuma region). His main research interest is in the history of churches originating in the more recent branches (from 1865) of the modern missionary movement.

Garton Kamchedzera is Senior Lecturer in Law at the University of Malawi and also Head of Social Policy; Advocacy and Communications at UNICEF-Malawi. He holds a Ph.D. (Cambridge University), an LL.M. (Warwick University) and an LL.B. (Hons) (Mlw). He has researched and published on topics such as human rights, gender and development, property law, law and development, intra-and-inter generational equity, environmental law, and labour law. He is also a poet and playwright and some of his plays have been broadcast on the BBC World Service. He is a Christian, married with one daughter.

Fulata Lusungu Moyo (nee Mbano) is currently a Lecturer in Systematic Theology and Church History in the Department of Theology and Religious Studies, Chancellor College, University of Malawi. She is also a part-time PhD student with the University of Malawi, working on Contextual Pneumatology: a survey and evaluation of how Christian Malawians conceive the Holy Spirit. After her Bachelor's Degree in Education from the University of Malawi, she obtained her Honours Degree and MA in Religious Studies from the University of Zimbabwe. She is involved in world-wide theological debate through the World Council of Churches, World Alliance of Reformed Churches and the Circle of Concerned African Women Theologians. She is married with three sons.

John Moore joined the Jesuit Order in Ireland in 1945. He studied science at University College Dublin (UCD), specializing in Botany, and after finishing his ecclesiastical studies (Philosophy and Theology) he became lecturer in Botany at UCD. His main research was in vegetation ecology. In 1978 he was awarded the European Prize for work in ecology and conservation in Ireland. In 1983 he retired from being Professor of Botany in Dublin and joined the Department of Biology at the University of Zambia in Lusaka where he participated in a survey of the Zambezi Valley threatened with flooding for a hydroelectric project. On his retirement in 1991 he joined the staff of St Peter's Major Seminary in Zomba where he teaches New Testament and sacramental theology.

David Mundy is currently on the academic staff of the Institute for Development Policy and Management at the University of Manchester where he specializes in information systems for development. He has been on the staff of a number of universities, including the University of Malawi. He holds a BSc in Computer Science from the University of London and a PhD from the University of Newcastle upon Tyne. He has published articles in the area of information systems for development, including human resource development, and is currently working with colleagues at the University of Malawi on research into factors enabling and constraining information management. Recent overseas assignments include provision of assistance to the Presidential Review Commission of the Government of South Africa and running a participatory training workshop in Tanzania

Jonathan Newell was educated at Nottingham University and King's College London in the Department of War Studies, where he received his PhD. From October 1989 until July 1992 he taught as a lecturer in the History Department at Chancellor College, Zomba. In November 1992 he took up a post to teach in the History Department of the University of Zimbabwe. He is an evangelical believer from a Christian Brethren background with a continuing interest in the history of colonial military institutions in Africa. He now lives and works in England with his wife and son.

Martin Ott, Dipl. Theol., M.A., PhD, has worked at the Catholic University of Eichstaett, for Missio Munich and with the German Commission for Justice and Peace. Since 1997 he has lectured in Systematic Theology and Religious Studies at the Department of Theology and Religious Studies, Chancellor College. His special interest is in the encounter between Christianity and African Traditional Religion with particular emphasis on African Christian art. He is a member of the German Society for Mission Studies, the Medical Mission Institute Wurzburg and the Academia Scientiarum et Artium Europaea, Salzburg.

Kings M. Phiri is a graduate of the University of Malawi and holder of MA and PhD degrees from the University of Wisconsin in the USA. Dr Phiri is currently Associate Professor of African and Black History at Chancellor College, University of Malawi, where he has taught since 1975. He has also taught and done research in Britain and the USA. He is co-author of *Twenty-Five Years of Independence in Malawi, 1964 - 1989* (Blantyre: Dzuka, 1989), and author of several works including those which have appeared in *Global Dimensions of the African Diaspora* edited by J.E. Harris (Washington: Howard University Press,

1982); and *General History of Africa,* Vol. V, edited by B.A. Ogot (Oxford).

Isabel Apawo Phiri has been and continues to be an important figure in promoting the study of Religion and Theology among (African) women. After completing her MA in Religious Education at the University of Lancaster, England in 1983, Dr Phiri returned to Malawi where she lectured at Chancellor College in New Testament Studies, Current Trends in Third World Theologies and African Traditional Religion. Dr Phiri received her Doctorate from the University of Cape Town and is currently Director of the Institute of Contextual Theology of the University of Durban-Westville in South Africa. She is the author of *Women, Presbyterianism and Patriarchy: Religious Experience of Chewa Women in Central Malawi,* (Blantyre: CLAIM, 1997).

Kenneth R. Ross, a minister of the Church of Scotland, is Professor of Theology at Chancellor College, University of Malawi where he has taught since 1988. He also serves as parish minister in the rural Presbyterian congregation of Nkanda, near Zomba. Among his works on church and society in Malawi are, *Gospel Ferment in Malawi* (Gweru: Mambo, 1995) and *Here Comes Your King!* (Blantyre: CLAIM, 1998). Since 1990 he has coordinated the Faith and Knowledge Seminar, on which this book is based.

James Tengatenga is Anglican Bishop of Southern Malawi and is currently studying part-time for a PhD in Theology with the University of Malawi where he formerly lectured in Systematic Theology and Church history. His interests are in Ecclesiology and Church - State relations. He also has a Diploma in community work from Birmingham University (UK). After getting his M. Div. Degree from the Episcopal Theological Seminary of the Southwest (Texas) in 1985 he worked as a parish priest in Lilongwe for eight years from where he went on to teach Theology, Homiletics and Pastoral counselling from 1993-1997 at Zomba Theological College.

Patrick A. Whittle, B.Sc(So'ton), PGCE(Brist.), M.Phil.(Lond.), M.Inst.P., has spent twenty-five years teaching and lecturing in physics and science education in Africa, including Lesotho, Malawi, Nigeria, and Uganda. His major research was conducted on science teacher education programmes in Anglophone Africa. After leaving Malawi, Professor Whittle became well known for his publication of *Innovative Ideas and Techniques for Science Educators in Africa,* and has recently been elected to the Executive of the International Council of Associations for Science Education. For the last three years Patrick Whittle has been in Nepal leading a DFID Secondary Education Project.

www.ingramcontent.com/pod-product-compliance
Lightning Source LLC
Chambersburg PA
CBHW021351300426
44114CB00012B/1169